Forced
to Be
Family

Also by Cheryl Dellasega

Surviving Ophelia: Mothers Share Their Wisdom
of the Tumultuous Teen Years

Girl Wars: Twelve Strategies That Will End
Female Bullying

The Starving Family: Caregiving Mothers and Fathers
Share Their Eating Disorder Wisdom

Mean Girls Grown Up: Adult Women Who Are Still
Queen Bees, Middle Bees, and Afraid-to-Bees

Forced
to Be
Family

A Guide for Living with
Sinister Sisters,
Drama Mamas, and
Infuriating In-Laws

CHERYL DELLASEGA, PH.D.

BICENTENNIAL
1807
WILEY
2007
BICENTENNIAL

John Wiley & Sons, Inc.

Published by John Wiley & Sons, Inc., Hoboken, New Jersey
Published simultaneously in Canada

Wiley Bicentennial Logo: Richard J. Pacifico

Design and composition by Navta Associates, Inc.

For general information about our other products and services, please contact our Customer Care Department within the United States at (800) 762-2974, outside the United States at (317) 572-3993 or fax (317) 572-4002.

Wiley also publishes its books in a variety of electronic formats. Some content that appears in print may not be available in electronic books. For more information about Wiley products, visit our web site at www.wiley.com.

Library of Congress Cataloging-in-Publication Data:

Dellasega, Cheryl.
   Forced to be family : a guide for living with sinister sisters, drama mamas, and infuriating in-laws/Cheryl Dellasega.
      p. cm.
   Includes bibliographical references and index.
   ISBN 978-0-470-04999-0 (cloth)
   1. Women—Family relationships. 2. Family. I. Title.
   HQ1233.D44 2007
   646.7'8082—dc22
                                                                    20077029071

Printed in the United States of America

10 9 8 7 6 5 4 3 2 1

*To the females in my family
and my husband, Paul*

Contents

Acknowledgments

Thanks to the One who created families, my agent, Joy Tutela, and Lisa Burstiner and the fabulous Wiley team.

Introduction

Women—families—conflict. It's not headline news or a novel concept, but in this era of fascination with female aggression, the idea of viewing female family feuds through the lens of relational aggression (RA, or female-type bullying) is unique. Although conflict among mothers, sisters, and other relatives is usually considered abnormal and even pathological, after studying female relationships for several years, I've reached a different conclusion.

Most, if not all, books about women's issues with their mothers, daughters, sisters, and in-laws have tended to focus on what, rather than why, which makes how-to-cope efforts more mysterious and difficult. Although insight into motivation isn't a cure-all, it is the important first step to conflict resolution and reconciliation that I use in all my programs. Often, an "aha" moment jump-starts the process of realizing that while women (young or adult) can act in mean ways, they aren't inherently mean.

Therefore, I believe "word wars" and bullying between relatives are the same kinds of behaviors women use to tussle in other arenas. Although they are an expression of underlying tension, they also tend to be a female brand of aggression seen at work and play as well as home. Weapons of mass destruction are often gender-specific: bombs, guns, and physical fights are for guys, and gossip, undermining, and exclusion are for girls. It's not surprising, then, that these behaviors might be especially pronounced among the women we are closest to.

As I worked on this book, I was struck by how many of the interactions among mothers, sisters, and in-laws parallel the topics in the many talks I give on RA to middle schoolers: intimidation, betrayal, belittling, the silent treatment, exclusion, jealousy, rivalry, and a host of other relationship-focused weapons that girls of all ages use to hurt one another. The blows among women may not be physical, but they strike deeply and inflict damage that may be all the more serious for their significance—especially within the family, where things are *supposed* to be different: mothers and sisters should be supportive, not scheming. In-laws may need to earn their way into the family fold, but while they are doing so, we expect them to follow the same standards as other relatives.

Yet "Relative RA" has happened to me, and I'm sure the women in my family would tell you I've caused it to happen to them. Most likely, you've picked up this book because it has happened to you, and you wonder, "Why?" (with the subtext being, "Am I so unlovable even my sister/mother/aunt/mother-in-law can't have a healthy relationship with me?").

That's the purpose of this book, which began to gel in my mind when I received many e-mails and submissions about female family feuds as I wrote *Mean Girls Grown Up*. Stories of sinister sisters, malicious mothers-in-law, and other relatives who used RA interactions prompted me to take a deeper look at the way women in families relate to and aggress against one another. That exploration led me to six conclusions that form the framework of this book.

First, women's relationships with their family are different from men's. Connected to their deepest sense of self and the natural inclination for kin-keeping, women have an emotional bond to their female relatives that is intense and complex. Men care, but not in the same way: most women bond to belong; men play sports.

Second, RA is more intense and qualitatively different in families. We expect more from our female relatives, but we also overlook some transgressions from them we would never tolerate from female friends. (And, in the same way, we can become more irate over certain infractions.)

Third, while Relative RA is abusive, it is different from physical and emotional abuse. It takes on a special meaning within the one-to-one relationship we have with our families and may hold significance only because of this. Friends are optional in life, a delightful add-on to the rotating and replaceable relationships we form at work, in school, and in other settings. Most often, female family members are a permanent fixture in our lives, with a special power to wound because they share a special lifelong intimacy with us. We have a history with our female relatives, many of whom have known us through different ages and stages of our lives. They know our likes and dislikes as well as our vulnerabilities. Perhaps most significantly, they are privy to information that can be used against us in unique ways. Childhood insecurities, romantic or professional failures, and long forgotten transgressions can all be used as emotional weapons in a female family feud.

Fourth, in-laws and blended families are an interesting subset of people who serve as kin, but are not. There's a different dynamic when you feel pressure to be kind to someone who is essentially a stranger.

All of this leads women to experience a different kind of hurt when the offender is a female family member and gives rise to feelings of rejection on the part of the victim as well as a sense of desperation on the part of the aggressor. Your belittling sister-in-law with the child prodigy nieces and nephews may not see any negative connection between her free-flowing commentary on your parenting deficiencies and her affection for you—after all, you're her family!

Which brings me to my fifth point: relational aggression can coexist with relational affection. Understanding that this is an interaction pattern women tend to use and not necessarily an indicator of true emotions frees you from feeling that you are inherently flawed and unlovable.

This insight also opens the door to change, which is explained in the conclusion of this book. There is always hope for learning new ways to cope with and even improve a relationship that may seem impossibly negative.

Forced to Be Family is not intended to be an academic research project that offers right and wrong answers, or a personal attempt to address an agenda with my own family. Rather, I write as a guide who learns a bit more each day about the mystery of female relationships. More than ever, I am persuaded that the biological basis of behavior is a key determinant of our day-to-day interactions: women and men have basic, unchangeable differences that will—and should—make a gender-neutral society impossible. (That doesn't mean women or men should be subjected to expectations or rules that dictate absolutes based on gender.)

I have tried to refrain from using words like *better*, *worse*, or any others that imply value judgments when referring to gender-specific behaviors. We are what we are as men and women, and the differences between us should be used to benefit one another, our families, and society as a whole.

I also offer another disclaimer. In both my beginning and graduate research classes, I teach that the certainty of statistics is this: there is never a 100 percent certainty of any conclusion. Therefore, it should be a given that there are no absolutes in this book or in any of my others. Obviously, there are men who gravitate to the nurturing role and express aggression in more social ways, just as women can be more overt and physical in their interactions. We will never be able to pigeonhole every personality we encounter; if we could, the world would be a different and duller place.

The material for this book came from a number of sources. First and foremost are the stories women shared in both written and spoken form. Each is presented in a way that is respectful to the author/teller and the woman or women they refer to. Specific identifying details are, in some cases, omitted or altered. I also include in this category of data hundreds of discussions with journalists, friends, and colleagues about what it means to be a woman within a family. Second, a mix of both scholarly and commercial books and articles enriched my understanding of "RA the family way," and provided information relevant to this work. Third, interviews with experts filled in the blanks, identified new issues, and prompted further explorations. I thank those who allowed me to pick their brains on this topic, specifically Drs. Susan McHale and Mala Chinoy, both of Pennsylvania State University. Fourth, a casual survey with thirty women and a focus group with several others provided me with factual information I felt would enhance the text. Both would never fall within the realm of academic research; I considered them "fact checks" in the same manner that occurs in other print media.

Finally, the Internet offers many message boards and Web sites where women feel free to candidly discuss their feelings (and in some cases, online RA is rampant, offering virtual insight into real-time family interactions).

As I write this, the phone rings. It is my sister, checking in from a "getaway" day with her husband. She knows it's been a rough week for me, so in the midst of having fun, she thinks to call and cheer me up. It's a comfort few others can offer. I know from experience that tomorrow there could be a different kind of phone call and a conversation that is hurtful only because we are sisters and sensitive to each other in a way my friends and I are not. Our conflicts are rare now: perhaps because we have matured or come to realize that underneath the words we say to each other is a love that unlike many others, won't change. Maybe, having gone through all kinds of friendships and work relationships, we appreciate, cherish, and respect the specialness of the bond we share.

PART ONE

Females in the Family Way

1

A Tale of Two Sisters

Trina is middle-aged, white, twice divorced, and one of seven sisters. She works as an administrative assistant and has a son and a daughter as well as a brand-new granddaughter. Renae is a decade younger, black, and still married to the father of her son. A high-level executive, she is the older of two sisters. Trina and Renae have never met, yet they share a deeply personal connection: both are in conflicted female family relationships, a situation that many of us share.

Trina

Trina, a petite blonde with a slow smile and thoughtful brown eyes, describes herself as the family outcast, a role she thinks her children have inherited. She has six sisters, in birth order: Lydia (who died traumatically at age twenty-one), Lisa, Annie, twins Marie and Carrie, and Nan. Trina is now the second oldest, with the siblings all separated in age by only a year or two.

Trina recognized early on that she was the odd sister out. She explains:

> It's funny, when you look at pictures you can see how Mom dressed us in groups, and I was always dressed differently, even early on. Lydia was a rebel who dropped out of school and was always in trouble with drugs and boys. I looked up to her because she had guts and was bold, her own person. After she died, I kind of took her place, going off to the military and leaving the family, then getting divorced, and so on.

Lisa was first in everything—she was my competition, but we got along really well when we got older and lived near each other, but then had a falling out because she's an alcoholic. My parents wanted us girls to patch things up—they even asked me to give her a car, something they wouldn't do themselves.

I stopped speaking to her, and to this day we are estranged. I go places knowing she'll be there, but we don't talk. It really bugs me that she deceives our parents about her alcohol problem and pretends to be so good. She's the "needy" one, but one of Mom's favorites. She'll do anything for Lisa.

Annie is the sister I feel closest to. Even though she is my next-youngest sibling, she is the one who took care of me. When I got my period, it was Annie who found out what I should do. Our relationship has gone through many cycles. She moved away and we were distant; then I found her a job where I worked, and I convinced her to move back north. For seven years we worked together and went to lunch every day. Then she up and quit to work somewhere else.

The twins are loud and boisterous. They have a love-hate relationship with each other and have even gotten into physical fights. Nan, the baby, lives close by my mom and spends all her days off with her. We're close, but that might be because there's a competition between Nan and Annie, so Nan sides with me on issues and supports me in my conflicts with Annie.

Trina's parents have had a complicated marital history. Her parents were separated for a period of time, during which her mom had a relationship with another man and became pregnant with the twins. They were raised by Trina's dad and accepted as his own. Her parents separated again and finally divorced when Trina was in ninth grade.

She recalls that when her mom left she went alone, but then came back and took Nan with her. Trina intuitively understood that it would be a natural choice to take the youngest child, but it still bothered her that only one daughter got to go. Eventually all the girls were reunited with their mother (with the exception of one twin, who stayed with their dad).

Trina's dad remarried, but neither Trina nor her sisters get along with their stepmom, whom Trina refers to as "my dad's wife." She has nothing to do with her stepsisters ("my dad's wife's daughters") and admits she is jealous of them.

She says, "She [her stepmom] took a part of our life away." This was apparent to her one time when Trina's father invited Trina and her sisters to a Christmas dinner but then ignored them in favor of his new family.

"I never really felt my parents were there for me—I still don't. They speak to me directly only when there's a reason; when I want or need information, I get it from Annie. Everyone talks to her." Trina looks sad and angry when she shares this.

There's been ongoing competition among the sisters, with Trina feeling like one of her sisters always bested her, either by needing something more than she did, or by getting more attention from their parents. Her main rival was Lisa, who even beat her to having the first grandchild. As Trina says, "I called my mom, all excited, only to be told that [unmarried] Lisa was already two months pregnant."

Although Trina's first marriage fell apart before she got to know her husband's family, she was able to establish a good relationship with her second mother-in-law.

"Things were very open and honest," she says. "But my sisters-in-law couldn't stand me. I was really hurt when my kids weren't mentioned in their grandmother's obituary because they weren't 'full-blooded' family. My daughter had gotten pretty close to my mother-in-law."

Annie is still the woman Trina calls her best friend—in fact, she doesn't feel close to any other women. Annie's kids were Trina's favorites and vice versa—Trina's daughter was more attached to Annie than to her grandmother. Trina explains her strong bond to Annie without hesitation: "I know Annie will always be there for me. My other sisters would, to a degree, but it's Annie that's the certainty."

Still, she admits that there has always been a subtler, more aggressive side to Annie, who has tried to sabotage Trina's relationships with men, set her up for problems with their mother, and criticized Trina's parenting style. That rivalry, to a lesser degree, extends to other sisters as well.

"Annie always wants what everyone else has, and she battles with Nan to this day for our mom's attention. She'll always try to be doing things with her and calling her to make sure she's more involved than Nan."

The close relationship between Trina and Annie changed this past spring.

"Annie called as usual and invited me for our traditional Easter dinner, but she refused to include Mark, the man I've been dating for over two years. I introduced the idea of Mark into my family very carefully, because at first, the thought of my dating a black man was very upsetting to some of my sisters and Mom, who made it all about her. Everyone eventually came around, but Annie has held out, which I don't understand. I can't believe she's that prejudiced."

After the revelation about Mark, Annie sent Trina a series of guilt-provoking e-mails and said she never wanted to see her again. With a sad shake of her head, Trina says if a friend had treated her that way, she would have cut off contact with her.

"I saw in Annie a person who was not very nice. I considered ending the relationship, because if I ever married Mark, he would never be invited over and she wouldn't even talk about him with me."

Although Trina's relationship with Mark continues, she avoids mentioning him to Annie, still hopeful that she can change her sister's mind.

"I should hate this woman," Trina says, reflecting on her sister's refusal to change her mind about Mark. "Twice she has set me up for problems at work, once which led to me getting fired, and now this."

Trina has met Mark's ex-wife and teenage daughter, as well as his sisters. They have all been welcoming and don't mind that Trina is white. In fact, Trina thinks she could have good relationships with all of them—but it's the friendship with Annie that matters most to her. It's clear as we speak that she still wants to find some way—any way—to resolve the conflict between them.

Trina will always carry a hurt inside her because of her past relationships with her sisters, particularly Annie. Those wounds are being played out in everyday ways as Trina sees her children slighted, herself excluded, and the rivalries ongoing among her siblings.

Renae

Although Renae comes from a small nuclear family, the pain she feels as a consequence of her female relationships is just as significant as Trina's is. Renae grew up with her mom, Pat, and an extensive network of women who are like family to her—but it's her only sister, Casee, that she's closest to.

"My mom, who is an only child, instilled in us that we must be very loyal to each other. We might have conflicts inside the house because, for example, I was light-skinned and had long hair and she was darker with short hair, but outside it was different—we stuck up for each other. Casee liked to fight, so she protected me many times."

Although their parents were careful not to label either of them, certain expectations were conveyed nonetheless. Every night Renae sat down on the sofa to watch the news and read the paper—she still has a mental image of herself surrounded by her dad's college textbooks. Meanwhile, Casee was free to play or do something else.

"Casee was the rebel, but her critical thinking skills are not sharp, so she would always get in trouble. For example, if I wanted to go out and meet a boy behind my parents' back, I would just say I was going out to meet a girlfriend. Casee, on the other hand, would do something dumb like not come home on time or sneak out of the house. Of course, she got caught—sometimes I think she wanted to."

Both girls were closer to their dad, which Renae attributes to her mother's fussiness. "With her, there was never enough," she explains.

Although Renae now appreciates that her mother's strict budgeting and discipline kept their family intact, when Renae was growing up, she viewed her dad as the good guy. That added further tension to a relationship that was already conflicted.

"Dad was a professional and made a lot of money, but he thought nothing of blowing his entire paycheck on presents, which meant we had many lean years and lived in the 'projects' early on. Mom resented that I never recognized this was my father's fault," she says, clearly ambivalent. "She was the responsible one, but then she expected us to turn against our father because of his behavior."

At age fifteen, Casee got pregnant. She wanted to marry the father and have the child, but she was forced by her parents to have an abortion, which led to serious depression and ongoing substance abuse. Before Casee graduated from high school, she got pregnant again but kept the baby, a girl named Shanay. Her third child, a son, was born right before Renae's wedding, although Casee wouldn't even admit she was pregnant.

"Sure enough, three days after she delivered, she walked down the aisle," Renae says, laughing.

After her parents divorced, Renae's dad remarried, so she also has a half brother. Clearly, though, relationships with other women are at the heart of her family: both those she grew up with and those who came into her life later.

Despite Renae and Casee's closeness, Renae's relationship with her sister has turned out to be a disappointment for both of them. "We've talked about it," says Renae. "Casee says I don't understand how difficult life is for her. She's tried so many programs through welfare but ends up with the same pattern of finding men who are abusive, which leads to a relapse with her addiction. She sees me as having an easy life with a husband and a son and a good job. She doesn't realize that while she was out partying, I was at home reading books to my kid, and while she was finding one problem man after another, I was in college."

Both of Casee's children have struggled. Shanay, now a teenager, lived with Renae for a time to try and change her life, while her brother, Bill, has been in constant trouble with the law. The sisters realize that in some way their children's lives mirror their own: Renae's son is on track to attend college while Casee's children face an uncertain future.

Still, Casee and Renae have managed to stay closer to each other than they have to their mother.

"Our mom created this situation," Renae notes. "After her own mom died, she wanted an excessively close bond with us, but we could never give her enough. So now we have this tight bond with each other, exclusive of her, sort of an alliance against our mom because we don't want to deal with her. We call her 'your mom' to each other."

Renae says her mom is a "people collector," a practice Renae has emulated in a different way, building a network of fictive kin that includes her godmother and various aunts.

"My godmom is another woman I'm close to. We're like spirits—I'm more her daughter than I am my mom's. When all three of us are together at a family gathering it can get strained, because both she and my mom want all my attention, and I get caught in the middle."

Renae clearly wishes her relationship with her mother were different, but their concern for Casee is the only area where they see eye to eye.

"My mom is always giving advice, always telling me to do such and such when she doesn't do it herself, and she's envious of my life, so she'll give me lots of suggestions about that. If my husband and I have a fight, she takes his side! That really gets to me, but I have been praying for our relationship to change."

Alice, her father's aunt, is another woman Renae is close to, but her mother tries to horn in on that relationship, which doesn't work: she doesn't understand that Renae and Alice love to shop and that they have their own special system for the excursions they take. "She gets upset when she's sitting waiting and is the outsider and doesn't understand why we don't enjoy having her along," Renae says.

Although Renae's relationship with her husband's sister got off to a rocky start, Renae has a better relationship with the woman who married her husband's only brother. "We both understand what it means to be married into the family," she explains. Her relationship with her mother-in-law couldn't be better.

"I love her," Renae says. "She gets that she's not there to criticize but to encourage, and that the relationship isn't about me and her. Some of the best advice I've gotten has come from my mother-in-law—very practical advice that prepared me well for marriage. She told me, 'Some years you will hate him,' so when the years came and I hated my husband, I was ready for that."

Renae talked about differences she sees between herself and white women when it comes to family: "The woman takes over the race issue. Many of the values, issues, and behaviors are the same, but ethnicity makes things play out differently."

She notes that because black women have had to head

households, there was often a need to create a powerful sisterhood that bonded them together. "I feel an automatic connection with other women who are black—we walk through life in the same way and have a common lens we use to view the world," she says. "I've lived in the projects and lived in a nice house, so I know both sides. But there's a poverty mentality, so that instead of understanding and being happy for me, the question is, 'How come that didn't happen to me?'"

Sister or Sinister?

Biological or social sisterhood can be intensely supportive or devastatingly destructive, as Trina and Renae discovered. While the type of bond may vary, the behaviors are strikingly similar: exclusion, ridicule, gossip, and a host of other relationally aggressive behaviors that fan the flames of "kitchen wars." These emotional battles among female relatives are larger in magnitude and impact than the offenses of even our dearest friends.

More love, more difficulty, more anguish, and more of everything are the hallmarks of both distant and close female relationships within families. Although the vow "for better or worse" is voluntary in marriage, we don't have a choice about the women we grow up with or those who enter our families and our lives for decades when we're adults.

The Kitchen Wars: Relational Aggression between Female Relatives

At any stage of life, women are more likely than men to express negative emotions through relational aggression (RA), that is, using words and behaviors rather than physical blows to hurt. From the car pool to the swimming pool, "word wars" are a dynamic that women of all ages can get caught up in during times of tension. Women express negative emotions in a variety of ways: by circulating rumors with ill intent, by shutting one woman out of a group or turning others against her, by controlling the behavior of others so that they join in on the abuse, by giving someone the silent treatment, and by threatening, teasing, or harassing. Men, on the other hand, are more likely to express aggression physically. The good news is that these behaviors are not personality traits that can't be changed—in fact, they may be easier to transform than many other problematic patterns of interpersonal dynamics.

The RA Roles

The initiator of RA is a fearful woman underneath, relying on her aggressive behaviors to intimidate others so they won't glimpse her insecurity. In the same way, the receiver of the abuse, the victim, is too unsure of herself to deflect mean behavior from others. Women in the middle often keep the conflict going by fanning the flames of the bully's seething anger or by trying to pit one woman against the other.

These roles may sound like those played by women who dislike each other, but even at young ages, girls use RA *within* their friendship circles. They may cycle through cliques on a weekly basis, start smear campaigns against a former pal who is now a targeted outcast, or fire off vicious e-mails to the same girls who attended a sleepover at their houses the previous weekend. Fast-forward to adulthood, and these behaviors persist, pitting one woman against another in pursuit of a job, a man, or a title.

Thank goodness there are places where we can relax in the company of women who care about us and our well-being: mothers, sisters, in-laws, and other relatives. We're safe because they are family—right?

Not always. Over the last few years, my work suggests that RA can be worse within a family than outside it. Consider these women:

- Domineering mother-in-law Diana regularly humiliates her youngest daughter-in-law, Franny, at family gatherings and holidays. Although Franny is a successful pediatrician, Diana takes every opportunity to put down anything her daughter-in-law says, usually arching her eyebrows and exclaiming, "Is that the kind of thing they teach you in medical school?"

- Bystander/encourager Tracy, also a daughter-in-law (married to the oldest son), wants to curry favor with the aggressor, Diana, but is uncomfortable with the humiliation she sees dished out to Franny. Sometimes she goes along with the bullying behaviors, but at other times she watches in uncomfortable silence. After all, she could be next if she intervenes.

- Victim Franny doesn't defend herself against Diana's putdowns for fear of upsetting her husband and his family. At work, Franny wouldn't hesitate to express her genuine feelings; around her in-laws she is tense and anxious. Her father-in-law and brothers-in-law are actually quite supportive and jokingly ask her, "What's up, Doc?" each time they see her.

Maybe there isn't a female physician in your family, but the dynamics of this situation can occur anywhere. Ironically, it doesn't necessarily mean one woman hates the other or that there's no affection in the relationship. As Marsha describes in the following story, animosity and affection can coexist between two female family members. Marsha, now in her fifties, doesn't question the love she and her sister feel for each other, although the relationship never feels completely safe.

Linda is ten years older than me, so I think she was entrenched with being an only child and I messed things up for her. I idolized her when I was little because she was gorgeous, like Marilyn Monroe, but she didn't have too much to do with me then because she had her own life and was into boys already.

Whenever she had to babysit me, her feelings came out because she resented having to do it. I remember spending an entire day when I was home sick, sewing an outfit for a little doll I cherished. I don't know why, but Linda got mad at me for some reason and ripped it to shreds.

As adults we drifted apart, but I still felt she resented me, maybe because she got divorced and I had a husband and two kids. I was living on the West Coast when she and her daughter had to move back home with my parents after she got divorced, which must have been horrible.

Linda is very critical of my children. If I ever say something about one of their accomplishments, she immediately says something mean about them to bring me down from the high I'm on. It isn't my fault I have two good children and a husband who is nice to me, so I feel like there is nothing I can do about it.

She once hurt my feelings so much she brought me to tears, and all over a gift I had bought her, innocently thinking she would be touched by how special it was. She blew up at me, and I just ran upstairs and wouldn't come down. I didn't have any way to respond. I didn't know what I was supposed to apologize for—giving her a present?

She did call me a week later to apologize, but then proceeded to tell me everything that was wrong with me, my husband, and my children. She said some incredibly cruel things, and if the gift incident stunned me, this was even worse. After a while, I just put the phone down and sat there. The worst part was I couldn't tell anybody. Why would I want to inflict the hurt on my family that she inflicted on me?

She eventually apologized again, but not really for the things that she said. I have forgiven her because she is my sister, but I have never forgotten, and I don't see how I ever will. I don't know how someone could be so miserable and unhappy she would strike out at the one person who loves her unconditionally and would do anything for her. Our parents are dead, so she is my only family, and there is no way I could just never see her again.

Marsha ended our discussion by labeling her relationship with her sister "weird." Her final words summarized emotions I heard over and over again as I gathered material for this book: "She's got a very mean streak, I think. If she wasn't my sister, I couldn't tolerate it. But she is, and so we are very close and love each other very much."

The RA Way of Relatives

Still not sure how RA might play out in your family? Review the following list of behaviors and determine which ones, if any, you or a relative might use to excess.

- Gossip. Humans by nature are storytellers, and women in particular tend to discuss relationships when they're together. A line is crossed, however, when the information shared is twisted to reflect badly on another person, blatantly distorted to cause trouble, or generated for destructive purposes. RA is evident when this is the predominant form of communication a woman uses.

- Exclusion. Naturally, you and every other female relative will have varying levels of comfort with your kin. A sister you grew up with might be more familiar and "safe" than a new mother-in-law you have yet to bond with. It's one thing to gently avoid cantankerous Aunt Lulu (not RA) and another to purposefully shut out your new sister-in-law from kitchen talk, especially when the exclusion is obvious and persistent (definitely RA).

- ▌ Manipulation. Using motives like guilt and anger to subtly coerce a relative into doing something she doesn't want to do falls under this rubric. Occasionally reminding someone of their obligations to the family may be part of the baggage of motherhood or sisterdom, but using this style of interaction to the point of excess or the discomfort of another is inappropriate.

▌ Withholding approval or showing preferential treatment. Naturally we feel closer to some family members than to others. Picking favorites among your children, adult female relatives, or their children and making sure others know about it, or maneuvering yourself into the middle of a battle for affections is relationally aggressive behavior.

▌ Humiliation. While good-natured teasing can be a part of family interaction, sometimes a woman becomes the object of repeated ridicule, or potentially embarrassing information is deliberately revealed by those closest to her. There's never an excuse for public or private put-downs that are meant to belittle another woman.

▌ Betrayal of confidences. Secrets are meant to be kept between you and the person who told them to you. Disclosing sensitive information to others in the family or circulating it through the rumor mill is first-degree RA, even if it's disguised as concern.

▌ Shifting loyalties. Pretending to be best buddies with a relative one day and not the next makes you suspect to others. If you're always in the midst of drama you created by pitting one woman against another, this category fits.

▌ Jealousy and envy. Admiration is one thing, but coveting the material assets or emotional resources of a relative to the point of passive-aggressive spitefulness, caustic competition, or out-of-control lust is negative and wrong. (Remember Annie in Trina's story.)

- ▌ The silent treatment. A variation of withholding approval, this behavior is one most women know well—deliberately refusing to acknowledge another woman. It can be either a temporary or a chronic pattern of behavior; within families it can be devastating.

- Cliques. These are subgroups of women who band together within the family, shutting out all others. They may be related by blood or marriage, and their purpose is to maintain a tight bond with one another and no one else. Drop in on any family gathering and these gals will be off by themselves, roaring with laughter at a private joke they don't care to share or huddling close together to whisper or exchange secrets.

While RA is a form of abuse, it differs from physical or emotional abuse, which would be hurtful to anyone in any situation. A father, a boss, or a husband who regularly berates you for being stupid is different from the sister-in-law who starts a rumor about your sex life. A mother, an aunt, or a grandmother who beats a child with a broomstick is blatantly abusive; the cousin who refuses to speak to you because you used to date the man she married might use much subtler tactics.

How can you differentiate the RA roles and behaviors just described from normal emotional ups and downs faced by most families? Ask yourself the following questions about yourself or your female relatives who may fit some of the descriptions above:

1. Are the hurtful behaviors nonphysical, that is, no slapping, punching, and so forth?

2. Do relationships with this woman *always* result in someone being hurt emotionally, even if it's not you?

3. Is one person the only target of a bullying woman, or does she use the same behaviors with all women? (In other words, is she an equal-opportunity aggressor?)

4. Has the RA behavior been lifelong, or is this a relatively new dynamic?

5. Would someone describe you, or the other woman, as difficult, dramatic, or hard to get along with?

6. Are you, or is the other woman, quiet and withdrawn at family get-togethers, feeling afraid to speak up?

7. Is it hard to express your true feelings at family functions for fear of being publicly humiliated by female family members?

8. Has the destructive behavior been so persistent that it has led you, or others, to seek professional help?

9. Do you, or does the other woman, find that other female relatives seem to get along well with each other, but not with you?

• 10. Is the behavior in question not the kind that is openly recognized by others as abusive?

The more questions you answered yes, the more likely it is that you or another female family member could be caught up in a "Relative RA drama." Although RA causes short- and long-term wounds, it can be difficult to determine whether the behavior in question is an occasional aberration or a pattern deeply ingrained in the woman's personality.

What She Sees Is Not What You See

The filter of perception is all-important and unique. Your memories and feelings about events may not be universally shared. For example, some women in your family may consider the time you poured champagne on your newly engaged sister insulting rather than congratulatory. Consider:

▎ Twenty-four-year-old Debbie refuses to attend a family function because her sister-in-law "jokingly" called her a bitch.

▎ Thirty-six-year-old Greta is so offended by her sister's forgetting her birthday that she cuts off contact for months.

▎ Fifty-year-old Sandra writes an irate e-mail to her mother-in-law, who failed to send Sandra's child (but not her other grandchildren) a graduation present.

Each of these incidents can provoke a little, or a lot, of hurt, depending on the circumstances surrounding the situation and what each woman thinks of them. If Debbie's sister-in-law is a conservative person who never uses offensive language, her comment will be received differently than if she were heavily tattooed and fond of using ripe words in every conversation. Greta's sister may never have forgotten her birthday before, making her "absent-mindedness" more likely to be received hurtfully on the single occasion when it occurs. The same is true with Sandra's mother-in-law, who may or may not have been generous in the past.

I'm also willing to bet that if any of these scenarios took place between friends instead of family, the emotional impact would be different. Family members are *expected* to feel affection for one another, and in particular, women hold their female kin to a higher standard than they might their friends or male relatives, expecting more loyalty, greater understanding, and unlimited forgiveness. In return, our willingness to forgive transgressions by a female family member can be hard to predict: in some situations (like Trina's), family members are given a wide berth. In others (like Renae's), offense is taken more quickly.

The Hierarchy of Hurt

RA behaviors can range from occasional mistreatment to consistent "mean" episodes, and even to prolonged serious abuse. For example, imagine that it's Thanksgiving and your adorable toddler has just smeared sweet potatoes all over your mother-in-law's heirloom white tablecloth. Shortly after you've cleaned up that mess, your six-year-old thinks it would be funny to break the tension by lobbing a spoonful of cranberry sauce at his father. Your mother-in-law might glare at you and respond in a number of relationally aggressive ways:

Mild	Moderate	Severe
"Why don't you teach your children some manners, anyway?"	"It's about time you start punishing your children for their bad behavior!"	"What's wrong with you? Your kids are spoiled brats!"

Add some eye rolling and heavy sighs to each of these statements, and the hurt factor increases accordingly. I've discovered that it also matters *who* is delivering the verbal punch: mothers usually wield the most power.

The Definitive Twists

Not long ago, I was part of a crowd of women having dinner at a restaurant. My friend Abby was expecting her entire family to visit that weekend, and she was already fuming because she'd had four calls from her sister-in-law Shauna.

"I've had to change the menu every time," Abby said. "No doctor has ever diagnosed her son Simon with any kind of problem, but Shauna is convinced he has a 'sensitive stomach' and all kinds of food allergies. Whenever we're together, every meal is based on what Shauna thinks Simon can and can't eat. Once she even had me read all the ingredients on the labels of the cans of food I was going to be using so she could make sure it was okay. My mom can't understand why I get upset, but I swear, I've seen this kid stuff the worst kind of candy and junk food in his mouth as soon as his mother's back is turned, and he's just fine. So much for yellow food dye number five!"

As we continued to talk, other examples of the preferential treatment Simon received emerged, and it became clear that what Abby was really upset about was the special attention he, the oldest grandchild, got from relatives while her own children went virtually unnoticed. That resentment will continue until Abby and women like her realize the situation is based not on her or her children's deficits, but on a complex mix of expectations, cultural conditioning, and history.

From Decade to Decade

A destructive pattern of interaction between mother and daughter can be inadvertently passed from one generation to the next, as happened in the following example of intergenerational RA.

Mama Drama That Ruined Relationships
Miriya Kilmore

"She hated her from birth," my father confessed not long before he died. "I never knew why."

He was referring to me, and I never knew why, either. My mother took that secret to her grave. I have no memories of her arms comforting me or her voice proud in praise, only an abundance of pain. Her resentment was even in my baby book: "She was named Miriya, as her dad always has his own way."

That phrase made my joy evaporate eight years later when Gene Autry became my first boss. This happened because my dad's ponies were often used in movies, and when Autry created the television series *Buffalo Bill Jr.*, they needed a girl to play Buffalo Bill's little sister.

Within a day of being chosen, I was seated before Autry's huge desk, surrounded by silver saddles, wooden Indians, and movie posters. Soon I was in full costume riding down Main Street at Melody Ranch, a western movie town in Newhall, California. For years, I'd begged for long braids like my friends wore, but my mother said no. That changed as the movie hairdressers braided black strips of hair into my curly blond locks, then sprayed my hair black. I loved them, but unable to deny the needs of the job, Mom yanked on them whenever I got near.

"You always get your own way, don't you?"

Mom said I was eventually fired because I did a lousy job. I can still hear her raging, "You're nothing but a failure."

She worked hard to erase the memory of that wonderful time: my photos and souvenirs disappeared, and I wasn't allowed to talk about my adventure. Before she died, she gave the last mementos to my siblings, leaving none for me, but she missed my original work permit. It showed that I had worked every day listed until the job ended. I wasn't fired, nor was I a failure.

My first husband was violent and dangerous; during our divorce he stalked me and tried to kill me more than once. I obtained a restraining order and moved often, but he always found me—until I realized my mother was passing on each new address to him. When I confronted her, she smiled and sneered.

"He has rights. You can't just walk away." She even objected to my resumption of my maiden name: "You have no right to it. You're a married woman."

Raising two daughters alone, I graduated from college in my early thirties with a 4.0 GPA in both accounting and journalism. As the editor-in-chief of the school newspaper, I'd garnered several awards in newspaper design, editing, and writing, as well as commendations from the chancellor, the president, and the dean of instruction. The plaques hanging on my wall were a source of pride. However, I'd learned not to share my successes with my mother for fear of her anger.

That's why her phone call caught me by surprise: "Do you always have to embarrass me?" I wasn't sure what she was talking about.

"How could I embarrass you? I haven't seen you in six months."

It turned out a customer at the post office where she worked knew about my accomplishments and had commented, "You must be very proud of your daughter's awards."

She didn't know about them, of course, and thus her rage.

The following year, she died from breast cancer. Her final calls to me were angry and full of ridiculous arguments. On my last visit, she asked me to tell my brother she was wrong for the horrible things she'd said about him.

As I stared out of her bedroom window, I couldn't help but hope we could lay the past to rest. I asked, "What about me?"

"I was never wrong about you."

Her harsh voice is still clear today, a quarter of a century later.

Sorting through her papers after she died, I found letters from her mother. They contained phrases I'd heard my entire life: "You're too fat," "You're stupid," and "No one will ever love you." My grandmother was a distant figure in my life, but her vindictive rhetoric taught me a lot about my mother. Although I felt sorrow for all my mother suffered, I didn't go to her funeral, as I couldn't bear to hear the laudatory eulogies. The woman they honored wasn't the mother I knew, but she never knew me, either. She only knew the hate she chose to pass along as a maternal inheritance.

Much of what Miriya describes now sounds like obvious emotional abuse. At the time these events took place, however, the subtle RA behaviors of preferential treatment, manipulation, and clever humiliation could have easily been overlooked. And, as is almost always the case, the negativity of Miriya's mother had little to do with any flaw in Miriya—rather, they were manifestations of an inner conflict that began when this unfortunate mother was a child and a victim to her own bullying parent.

RA Gone Amok

Every woman is capable of expressing irritation and conflict in socially aggressive ways—in fact, I would argue we are inclined to. I've yet to meet a woman who can't recall a time when she acted too aggressively too or passively with her family (yours truly included), or one who didn't sit in silence when another relative was verbally trashed.

However, not every woman becomes so entrenched in these dynamics that she can't act any other way, and fails to recognize the damage done to her and others. Consider movies like *Monster-in-Law*, where Viola, played by Jane Fonda, waged a war against her daughter-in-law-to-be, Charlie, played by Jennifer Lopez, that cost her dearly. The movie *In Her Shoes* features older sister Rose, played by Toni Collette, as a perpetual victim to the manipulation of her only sibling, a grifter sister, Maggie, played by Cameron Diaz. Although each bully had unique personality problems, their aggression was expressed through a variety of relationally aggressive behaviors.

All too often, women who are aggressive have difficulty recognizing their behavior for what it is. They may believe their actions are assertive, or that they are just outspoken. At other times, there's a perception that certain women somehow deserve to be put down. Finally, bullying women may just be giving vent to their own unhappiness or perceived lack of control over their lives. Their self-esteem may be so low that tearing down others becomes a way of building themselves up.

After they read this book I expect to hear from women who have loving, supportive relationships with their female relatives, and from others who claim it's the men who stir things up in their families. My point isn't that women are the *only* ones who feud, or that *all* women are bullies or victims with their kin: clearly, female family members can offer one another significant support and help. My goal for those of you nodding your heads in recognition as you turn these pages is to learn how to overcome the destructive dynamic of RA and discover the positive power of female relationships.

3

The Female Family Clique

F amilies exist and persist for many reasons, most of which are beneficial to the human race. Yet what family means and what constitutes a "normal" family (a question I was recently asked by a journalist) is not defined easily now, if it ever was. One thing is certain: conflict is part of the life of most families.

Dr. Leonard Felder, a psychologist and the author of *When Difficult Relatives Happen to Good People*, says, "One of the great ironies of life is that most people say hurtful things to their loved ones that they would never say to a stranger or even to an enemy." Curious to know more about how families function, he conducted a random telephone survey of over a thousand adults. Some norms he discovered:

▮ 75 percent had regular family get-togethers.

▮ 32 percent found the get-togethers enjoyable.

▮ 41 percent found them sometimes enjoyable, sometimes difficult.

▮ 27 percent said they were rarely enjoyable but were considered an obligation.

Digging deeper, Felder found:

▮ 77 percent said there was a family member who "gets on their nerves."

▌ 58 percent dreaded a family event because of a relative.

I'm willing to bet most of the respondents were women.

Once Upon a Time

Our concept of family starts in childhood, when we read popular nursery rhymes and fairy tales to our children. Most of these fictional characters would qualify for the label "dysfunctional family" today: the girl abandoned by her father in "Rumpelstiltskin," the negligent father in "Beauty and the Beast," and the demanding mother of "Jack and the Beanstalk." Perhaps more telling are the themes about female family relationships:

▌ Snow White's evil stepmother attempts to kill her because she is potential competition.

▌ Cinderella's mean stepsisters and stepmother humiliate and mistreat her.

▌ Sleeping Beauty's mother agrees to send her away from her home to protect her from a curse.

While stepmothers take the brunt of blame for distressing circumstances, it wasn't until television offered the image of the Good Mother that women were portrayed positively. Donna Stone, June Cleaver, and Ruth Martin were TV moms who wore spotless, neatly pressed dresses, never raised their voices (unless Timmy and Lassie were lost), and always had a pleasant smile, perfect makeup, and a neatly coiffed hairdo. Even zany Lucy Ricardo qualified for model motherhood because she was so cute and ditzy when she violated the Good Mother rules that we knew she wasn't really serious.

In a different but just as compelling way, the Cruel Mother draws our attention. The opposite of TV fantasy moms, these women defy many of the cultural expectations that go along with childbearing. Consider these tell-alls:

▌ Jennifer Aniston stopped speaking to her mother, Nancy, for several years after an interview in which Nancy made disparaging comments about her famous daughter's weight struggles. The talk show tell-all was followed by Nancy's book *From Mother and Daughter to Friends: A Memoir* in 1999, which further elaborated on Nancy's view of her daughter's flaws.

▎ Drew Barrymore's mother tried to auction off childhood memorabilia on e-Bay that other mothers might hold dear and treasure.

▎ At the time of her death, the mother of Dr. Laura Schlessinger, the famous talk show host, was not on speaking terms with her daughter.

▎ Meg Ryan and Kim Basinger have been estranged from their mothers.

▎ Brooke Shields and her mother severed their relationship for a time but managed to reconcile after a painful separation.

▎ Demi Moore and her mother were estranged, but they reconnected. Demi was at her mother's bedside when she died of a terminal illness.

There are far fewer reports of men who are alienated from their fathers. Why? Perhaps it's because the betrayal and disloyalty shown by Jennifer's and Drew's mothers go against the grain of model motherhood and hint at underlying aggression. Brooke Shields was controlled by a manipulative mom who appeared more interested in her own success than in her daughter's. Meg Ryan and Dr. Laura were both betrayed by mothers who committed the ultimate crime of abandoning their families both physically and emotionally.

Extreme Relational Aggression

More classic and riveting than tales of estrangement are those of maternal abuse that are RA in the raw. Christina Crawford was the first to break the "loyal daughter" taboo by penning a memoir portraying her mother, the actress Joan Crawford, as incredibly cruel. Humiliation, manipulation, intimidation, exclusion, and many other covert behaviors were used so subtly that they had meaning only for mother and daughter. Many who observed their nonphysical interactions failed to consider them abuse.

In one classic example, Joan deliberately wired her daughter a telegram every birthday after adolescent Christina sent one to her, believing it would be viewed as special rather than a last-minute gift. (It wasn't.) Passive put-downs that were rendered even more hurtful because of the meaning they held were Joan's forte, according to Christina. Some have suggested that the diva's movie roles as evil and scheming women like the one she played in *Queen Bee* (1956) may not have involved much acting.

B. D. Hyman's memoir of her mother, the actress Bette Davis, is another example of rampant RA. Bette Davis's oldest and only "natural" child was her mother's caregiver throughout life, taking on the role of nurturer even when her mother was truly hateful: manipulating, controlling, and belittling. Davis's RA extended to B. D.'s children and husband, and included faked suicides and temper tantrums.

Although this abuse wasn't physical, it left deep wounds in B. D., whose book was considered "Joan Crawford lite." She and Christina Crawford paid dearly for writing their books: both were disinherited. Others in and outside both families criticized these women for daring to suggest that their mothers fell short of the kind and loving maternal stereotype.

We Are Family

Despite the hurts inflicted by both male and female kin, we hang on. Our tenacious ties to family are best explained by David Barash, a professor of psychology and zoology at the University of Washington and the author of *Revolutionary Biology: The New, Gene-Centered View of Life*. Taking a historical view, he explains that survival initially meant not only staying alive, but also passing along your genes to continue the family line. Sons and daughters were the preferred way to pass on genes, but in a pinch, nieces, nephews, and cousins also counted. According to Barash, the closer the genetic connection, the more likely you are to go out of your way for the relative, a process called kin selection. Simply stated, when a building is burning and you dash inside to save someone, you are more likely to rescue a family member than a friend.

For women, the bonds with family go deeper than biology. To explore how you might feel about your connections to your female relatives, see how much you agree or disagree with each of the following questions:

1. Conflict with a coworker, a gym partner, or a PTA mom is less distressing than conflict with family members.

2. I am more vulnerable to criticism about my appearance, my children, or my spouse from female family members than from women in other settings.

3. In an RA situation, I can assert myself more readily to a coworker than I can to a female family member.

4. A basic trust is broken when a woman in my family is cruel to me.

5. Even if I have no other friend in the world, I expect to have the support of my sisters, my mother, and my in-laws.

6. Home is a shelter from RA for most women.

7. I am less likely to feel jealous of my sister than of my friend.

8. Male relatives get along better than female relatives.

9. My relatives should love my children because they love me.

10. Women tend to continue living out their childhood roles with their family into adulthood.

Since the answers to these questions are a matter of opinion, they don't have an absolute true or false value, but here is how women in general might respond:

1. While women in families (especially in-laws) may feel like strangers, in reality, they are part of a circle of intimates who can know the deepest secrets of your past: the childhood • fears that paralyzed you, the romances or marriages that didn't work out, the foibles of your children and husband; in short, the most personal details of your life. Therefore, many women agree that family hurts are worse than friend hurts.

2. Connections to family can give negative behaviors an extra nuance. Many, but not all, women agree that striving for the stamp of approval from members of their immediate family can be as important as a major promotion or a significant

romance. Therefore, criticism in the particular areas mentioned seems to have a special sting.

3. Your willingness to confront a bully boss, to mobilize against a malicious woman-in-the-middle, or to try to free yourself from the victim role is often dependent on the setting. It's much riskier to attempt this with a female relative—you, and your entire family, may suffer indefinitely if the relationship ends up being fractured completely. You can always find a new job; you can't replace a family member.

4. Our culture holds family relationships sacrosanct; women are not permitted to attach labels such as "bully" to their immediate or extended female family members, or to think of their mothers, daughters, and sisters as cruel or relationally aggressive. On the other hand, men are allowed and even expected to ridicule their mothers-in-law for bossy behavior.

5. When a woman discovers that this stereotype of unquestioning support does not hold true, her self-esteem can be shattered and the sense of betrayal intense. Most women agree that family members are expected to love and support you, no matter what.

6. When you go home for a family gathering, most women expect it to be an escape from the kind of sniping and back-biting that goes on in the workplace. One reason holidays are so stressful is that family tensions get layered on top of preexisting Relative RA, resulting in a full-scale kitchen war that ruins everyone's chance for a retreat from the stress of day-to-day life.

7. Jealousy seems to take on a particular flavor with female siblings, and it often relates to the need for approval and attention from parents—even in adulthood. Many times rivalry with a sister (or sister-in-law) is spurred by a sense that she is somehow more valued or accomplished than you, whereas competition with a friend is usually more about the relationship between you and her, rather than the approval of a third party.

8. Male relatives view family so differently that they may seem to get along better. Loyalty issues often prevent an open airing of complaints, as does the male tendency to avoid discussing emotions. Men also have different expectations and feel less of a need to invest time and energy in maintaining relationships. When a crisis occurs, however, you can count on them to be there, ready to try to solve the problems at hand.

9. Relatives are expected to love children who are part of their family, but you can't assume that their feelings for you will automatically transfer to your children. Some of the harshest parenting criticism comes from women within the family, which can make you feel that both you and your children are unloved.

10. Countless women have shared stories with me that suggest they learned a particular role within the family early on and then carried it with them throughout life: the smart one, the nurturer, the black sheep, and so on. Sometimes these roles even extend to life outside the family.

This quick survey illustrates the complex, caring, and sometimes cruel ways in which female family relationships get carried out. For women, the psychology of connection begins at birth. We enter and leave this world oriented toward the "tend and befriend" attitude that the UCLA researcher Shelley Taylor documented in 2002. That means women are more likely to turn to friends and to gather family close during times of stress, whereas men are prone to fight or flight.

Bonding to Belong

The therapist Janet Surrey identifies the three critical aspects of the healthy mother-daughter relationship as connection, mutual empathy, and mutual empowerment. One might argue that these same traits hold true for any female family relationship, but her belief is that when early bonding fails to take place, the emotional impact can be devastating. I thought of her writings when I heard the following story.

Jacqui, a young mother, had an angry expression on her face as she talked about her childhood: "My mom isn't normal. By that I mean she never spent time with me, never seemed interested in how I was doing, and never truly cared about me. If I did try to share something with her, she'd automatically turn it around on me and say, 'Oh, you shouldn't have done that!' or 'What a silly thing to say!' She resented any attention my father would pay to me and would go out of her way to make me look dumb in front of him."

Now thirty-six, Jacqui admits she has little patience for her "Queen Bee" mother, whom she believes continues to stir up trouble: "After she and my dad divorced, she decided she wanted me and her to be close, but there's no way that will ever happen. I don't trust her, and I don't feel safe around her. She's still manipulating and bossing me around like I'm five years old."

I told Jacqui it made me sad to hear about the loss of two relationships: the actual one she had with her mother while growing up and the potential one she was passing up as an adult. Although she agreed with me, I could tell by her determined expression that what happened in childhood had poisoned her feelings for a lifetime. What she didn't seem to appreciate was the amount of energy she had invested in maintaining her anger and resentment, or the unconscious message she was passing along to her own daughter about female family relationships.

Another woman shares an experience similar to Jacqui's:

A Lifetime of RA
Gail Fonda

When you are a very shy, introverted female and grow up in a dysfunctional and loveless family, there's a good chance you are going to be bullied by other women who are family members. The lack of self-esteem and the inability to stick up for yourself make matters even worse.

My mother described me as "someone only a mother could love," and never complimented or encouraged me. When I graduated from high school she didn't want to attend my graduation because she "already did that with Marvin [my brother]."

When I needed some spending money during college, she said, "I used up all the money on Marvin. There's nothing left for you."

My father was so proud of me when my story made the front page of the *Daily Kent Stater* in college. He took the article to a relative's house to boast, but my mother said absolutely nothing. I continued to publish articles, but my mother never made one comment about them. My guess is that she was jealous.

I should have expected what happened when I graduated from college.

Her words? "I didn't think you could do it." No gift, no congratulations, no party.

Gail's relationship with her mother influenced her throughout life. She says, "To this day, I have always had closer relationships with men than with women because to me, women play more games and enjoy hurting each other." Whenever I encounter women who have a similar perspective due to their past experiences, I feel sorry for the many opportunities they have missed for friendships both in and outside of their families.

Long-Term Effects

When RA takes over a relationship, it can feel as if there is no love between the women involved. Often, a pattern of negative interaction gets turned back on the aggressor, who is blamed for everything that has gone wrong in the victim's life. At other times, a victim's failure to defend herself can escalate a bully's anger, increasing the frequency and intensity of her attacks.

Sometimes transference can occur when a woman acts out or projects feelings she has about people in the past (such as a relationally aggressive mother) onto people in her present life. Dr. Debra Mandel, a psychologist and the author of *Your Boss Is Not Your Mother*, has worked with hundreds of clients who live with unhealed childhood hurts that play out again and again, causing problems at work. She says, "At every level of society, millions of women and men suffer from unhealed emotional bruises that get played out in unnecessary drama and conflict in their adult relationships. These old sore spots don't have to be traced to major violations like child abuse, neglect, or abandonment, nor need they have been intentionally inflicted. Most often, the emotional bruising we suffer developed through relationships with loving caregivers." The next time you encounter a bully, ask about her past, and you may find that she was the long-ago victim of a mean mother.

No one can say for sure what the long-term effects of bullying are, but many adult women claim they are still reeling from adolescent RA. In the same way, I've wondered whether difficult formative relationships with family females might affect peer interactions later on. The things I've been told suggest this is true: "I don't trust women," "All my friends are men," and "I just keep to myself."

These comments are similar to Gail's and come from women who were traumatized by female family aggression during childhood. Feedback from some women suggests that the absence of satisfying relationships with their female family members led them to seek to fill that void with multiple female friends.

Reactions to Relative RA are never simple or uniform, but something that happened to me after a workshop I led on adolescent girls and school bullying is typical. At the conclusion of my talk, one woman lingered behind the others who had gathered to speak with me. After the rest cleared away, she approached hesitantly and said, "What you just talked about is exactly what I went through with my sister—and I couldn't get away from it. My growing-up years were torment because she constantly manipulated me, but now it's gotten worse without my parents around to mediate. She is a classic bully. Have you ever heard of relational aggression taking place in families?"

I shared with her that I had and that it seemed to me that it could cause even greater hurt than other types of RA because we expect to be immune to bullying by members of our own family. She nodded her head in agreement, then sighed.

"She's my sister. Anyone else would think of her as a bitchy woman, but she's *my* sister," she said with a sad smile.

Malicious mothers, sinister sisters, and devious daughters-in-law aren't women we invite into our lives, but rather, they are thrust upon us with little option for continuing or ending the relationship as we might with a friend. However, these same women are also, ironically, the ones we are most likely to turn to for help in times of trouble, just as our great-great-great-grandmothers did.

Hardwired to Care:
The Kin-Keepers

Have you noticed that in your family, news about one person is often relayed to others through an invisible female walkie-talkie system? As the news bearers and the grief sharers, women within families own, and sometimes even vie for, the role of chief kin-keeper, which is a vital part of the connection process. Someone has to be in charge of remembering the family stories, keeping track of new births and deaths, and maintaining contact among members, even including those related only distantly by blood—like a great-aunt's second cousin twice removed.

Woman Care and Keeping of Families

From our mothers and grandmothers, we learn how to tend to families: not just cooking, cleaning, and caring for children and a husband, but also how to perpetuate the attributes unique to our clan. Our foremothers are our earliest role models, and whether we emulate or consciously reject the lessons they have shared, we, too, maintain family traditions and solidarity by passing these same practices along to the next generation.

Kin-keeping, or the care and maintenance of family relationships across generations and geography, is a role that has fallen almost exclusively to women since the beginning of group living.

The family Bible may display lengthy records of lineage, but it's the women who could probably tell you which ancestors were good-for-nothings who neglected their children and which ones made positive contributions to the clan. Attempts to kin-keep can bind women closely or pit them against one another as they are forced into ongoing intimate relationships with other women, some of whom might be enemies had marriage not made them relatives.

Dr. Linda Burton, formerly the director of the Center for Human Development and Family Research in Diverse Contacts at Pennsylvania State University, is one of this country's experts on the generational aspects of family life. She has summarized the kin-keeping roles of women as:

1. Keeping track of and continuing the family history

2. Encouraging a family ethos

3. Working to achieve and maintain family unity

4. Cooperating with the "work" of the family

I would suggest a fifth function: serving as the emotional lightning rod of the family. No one is the recipient of more relational aggression than a mother—I've been told this happens because mothers are safe targets of our frustrations and hurt and will offer unconditional love regardless of how they are treated. I wonder if fathers would be regarded in the same way or if the roles would be acceptable if they were reversed; for example, if mother Jane picked a fight with daughter Wendy because Jane is having marital troubles.

When I read *I Am My Mother's Daughter* by the journalist Iris Krasnow, this "lightning rod" theory of motherhood manifested itself throughout. The author asked adult women to describe their relationships with their mothers, and in story after story both ambivalence and anger were expressed toward mothers, who probably deserved it. (Should my daughter write about me, I would expect much the same.) What was surprising, though, was the almost unilateral view of mothers as responsible for the "universe" of family life. By this, I mean that even when fathers were abusive to daughters and mothers were not, mothers got blamed. (The reverse was not true, as shown in the exposés of Joan Crawford and

Bette Davis, in which men who might have intervened to help were not blamed for failing to do so.)

The Myth of Mean

This willingness to take responsibility for the emotional life of a family seems to be a universal one, with girls shaped early on to be kin-keepers. As Carol Gilligan proposed in 1982, girls form their identity through relationships, often as early as age three. While boys play team games oriented toward goal achievement and don't stop when a quarrel breaks out, girls are more likely to engage in activities that require turn taking and cooperation. They *do* stop when disagreements occur.

Females are not by nature cruel, but they can act in very cruel ways, both in and outside of families. Again, David Barash's fascinating historical overview offers some reasons for this. The fiercest feuds as well as the most lasting loyalties occur between women in family or kin groups, he believes, dating back many millennia to the time when clans were forced to live together in close spaces. In that setting, men tended to adjust their behavior and collaborate toward achieving common goals such as hunting for food and ensuring safety for the community despite the personal cost. They were the risk takers and meat gatherers, while women literally kept the home fires burning as they waited for the men to return.

Such an arrangement would logically lead to intense competition, since pregnancy and child rearing rendered women dependent on men for meat and on one another for emotional and material support. (Yes, there were female warriors who were hunters and gatherers, but they were rare or the exception.)

Imagine yourself living in those days, hardwired to form connections that could be both life sustaining and life draining. You would need a man to provide high-quality nutrition (protein) and physical protection, but your gal pals were equally valuable, especially if they were kin. Having sisters meant that if you got sick, there was someone else to step in and keep your kids alive until you were back on your feet. The downside, of course, was that these same women were competing with you for the services of a limited number of men.

The Drive to Survive

In the cave days, almost all of the women in your life would be related to you in some way: sisters or sisters-in-law, so to speak. There might be an occasional cousin, aunt, or grandmother thrown in, but for the most part your friends were also your kin. They were both your confidants and your competitors.

Could there be a more extreme situation of being "forced to be family"? An uneasy alliance had to exist, because while the bigger, stronger, nonchildbearing men were out working together to get food, women had to band together, caring for children and looking to one another for support. Given the high mortality rates during pregnancy and childbirth, the lives of your children could literally be saved by your "sisters," the only other source of milk and nurturing, should you die or become incapacitated.

For modern women, it's hard to imagine living in such circumstances. Clearly, we can and do take care of ourselves and our children quite nicely, thanks to infant formula, day care, and a number of modern services. Yet can we completely escape the legacy our ancestors passed on?

The drive to survive by connecting with a man for material resources and with women for nurturing remains one of the most basic instincts we have, explaining the persistence of so many social institutions that encourage group cohesiveness. While salary gaps still make most men the breadwinners, immediate female family members are usually the preferred substitutes for mothers when the need arises.

Since a majority of women continue to live close to family (Ha and Carr, 2005), it's natural that their feelings for one another will exist on an uneasy continuum ranging from intense rivalry to close companionship. Consider one of the oldest stories we know of relational aggression—straight from the Bible. Sarah and her slave Hagar most likely shared the intimate details of each other's lives, as they are the primary female characters in the story. From day to day, they probably spent more time with each other than either did with Abraham. Had things gone differently, they might have ended up as elderly companions, comforting each other in old age.

Instead, Sarah manipulated Hagar into bearing her husband Abraham's child, and Hagar retaliated with ridicule and condescending behaviors that led to her ejection from the camp. There is no mention of whether other women in the group escalated the conflict, but you can bet they were involved in one way or another—if only to watch and listen as Hagar boasted about her fertility and Sarah retaliated with cruelty.

Ironically, Sarah accused her husband of ruining her relationship with Hagar: "Then Sarai said to Abram, 'It's your fault that Hagar despises me.'" (Genesis 16:5). In a way, Sarah was right. Vying for the affections of the same man created an environment ripe for RA, which splintered the connection between the two women—a scenario to be repeated later with sisters Leah and Rachel, both married to Jacob. (For an interesting contrast on how men handled rivalry, read about Cain and Abel or Jacob and Esau.)

Sarah's hostility and the withdrawal of Abraham's protection nearly caused Hagar and her child to lose their family and their lives. Things haven't changed all that dramatically in one way: the ability to bear children is still a source of competition and rivalry among women.

The Family Name

Surprisingly, a woman's inability to conceive can still prompt thinly disguised aggression from other female relatives, who might be expected to help her weather such a challenge. Denise, a thirty-something who is in the midst of problems with infertility, has become an open target for meanness that is most likely unintended.

"So when are *you* going to make me a grandma?" asks her mother-in-law, who has many grandsons and granddaughters from her other children.

"You put your career first for so long—no wonder you can't get pregnant!" Denise's sister-in-law comments.

No one pesters Sam, Denise's husband, about the situation, nor has he mentioned it to his friends. Meanwhile, Denise assumed that her mother and sisters (and in-laws) would be her strongest allies as she and Sam tried one infertility treatment after another. Instead, hidden resentments or envy have led to relationally aggressive remarks.

Issues with infertility are a good example of inherent male-female differences in feelings about family: the motivation to have children is stronger among women than among men, and the failure to do so is more distressing. Most often, women are the ones to initiate fertility interventions, according to the counselors Linda Hammer Burns and Sharon Covington. Perhaps that relates to the kin-keeping role: children further cement a woman's place in the family legacy, leaving those who can't, or won't, get pregnant subject to scrutiny.

"My sister-in-law remarked that she wasn't surprised I couldn't get pregnant because I was 'too old,'" one friend in her early forties told me. "She pointed out that even if I did conceive, there were likely to be problems because I was past the prime childbearing age." I was astonished by the comment, but I have to believe it wasn't meant to be cruel.

Even adoption can be seen as a not-quite-acceptable second choice to producing your own child, and a woman who chooses to remain childless in or out of marriage can be outright threatening. She's challenging the premise that a woman's primal role is as a mother and raising questions about her commitment to continuing the family heritage.

Polygamy is another rare but modern-day equivalent that evokes some of the same issues in Sarah and Hagar's story. Although a "plural wife" on the Mormon Web site www.principlevoices.org says, "My sister-wife and I are best friends. We share a bond with each other that could not be there if we were not sister-wives," other accounts suggest that this arrangement is much less harmonious, especially when it comes to the bearing of children. (More on this later.)

Why We (May) Do the Things We Do

Switching back to present-day life, picture how this kind of scene might play out in your family. Everyone has gathered at the beach for a vacation. Your new sister-in-law is young and stunning—her never-pregnant body looks incredible in a bikini and the heart tattoo between her generous breasts seems to attract every man's eyes—if they weren't there already. Furthermore, she's married to your only brother, who was your closest sibling and the baby of the family before *she* came along. As you waddle after your toddler on the beach, every pound of postbaby weight seems to flap in the breeze, even as you wear a new "conceal-all" bathing suit.

Would you be jealous of such a sister-in-law? Who wouldn't at least admire (or envy) that kind of physical perfection? It would be natural for any woman to at least feel wistful, but maybe those feelings hearken back to the days when a woman like your new in-law was truly a threat to your ability to obtain vital resources (food and protection) that would help you and your child survive. Her ability to challenge you is obvious: she has already claimed the attention of every male who might act in the role of protector.

It's not surprising, then, that when you find your nine-months-pregnant sister in her beach chair next to the water, the first words out of your mouth are a bitter diatribe against your sexy sister-in-law. You might even find yourself more vigilant than usual, watching her every move for the rest of your time together to see if there's any indication that she's going to steal your husband (and add to her supply of protectors) at the first opportunity.

Does this scenario sound silly? A bit—but biology and evolutionary psychology explain female behaviors that are sometimes considered negative: the instant sizing up women give each other when they first meet, for example. Admit it—whether you want to or not, your first impulse on being introduced to a new woman is to look her over. Could it be that unconsciously you're doing what generations of your female forerunners have done: judging whether she will be friend, foe, or something in between?

Gossip might be another ingrained behavior. As storytellers and communicators, women like to talk with one another for extended periods and discuss emotionally laden topics that men shy away from. This may have evolved from the need to keep everyone in a clan informed of the status quo, but it's easy to see how such conversations could cross over into gossip. Studies have shown that the willingness to self-disclose (especially negatively, as in, "What do you think of so and so? I can't stand her!") is a mechanism that can promote closeness between generations of women.

According to Deborah Tannen, the author of *I Can't Believe You Said That*, women have historically looked for similarities between themselves and others as a way of connecting: we feel instantly closer to those who are wives, mothers, career women, and so forth, if we ourselves fit that role (and perhaps instantly hostile to beach-babe sisters-in-law with provocative tattoos). This natural tendency explains another common relationally aggressive behavior: exclusion.

Keeping It All Together

To create an album for my parents' fiftieth wedding anniversary, I interviewed them separately about the many years they had spent together. My father talked about career milestones and accomplishments; my mother described family relationships. For the first time, I appreciated how hard she had worked to keep our family connected, even if her compulsive planning for reunions and her insistence on our being together for the holidays defied my understanding at the time. The traditions that I found tedious as a child suddenly seemed touching in the context of decades held together by her energy. It was a shock to recognize many of her values and behaviors in myself, including the sometimes inaccurate news bulletins that get passed from mother to other adult children. By the end of our talk, her ability to put together different pieces and patterns of material to make her trademark quilts took on new significance: she had kept our family emotionally "sewn" together for decades. I was reminded of the time my daughter gave me a copy of Alanis Morisette's touching song to her own mother, aptly titled "Heart of the Home," because, she said, it reminded her of me.

Being forced to be family often involves a delicate dance, with women most often the lead choreographers. It takes a special partnership and a lot of practice to move together so smoothly that you intuitively anticipate and understand one another's next move. While you may never get to the point of always going with the flow of your family, you can create a situation where you make the choice to move with the music of others or feel comfortable dancing to your own.

5

Men Are Like Bricks, Women Are Like Mortar

When I married my first husband, I quickly discovered I had also married his family. For better or worse, we were going to be seeing a lot of one another, because most of them resided within a ten-mile radius of our small apartment. Since my parents had never lived near their extended family, the idea of being this close to my somewhat foreboding mother-in-law initially made me a bit panicky. In time, however, I grew to enjoy, and even look forward to, get-togethers with my crowd of new in-laws, who ranged in age from newborn to elderly. Two relationships I especially cherished were with Peg, the wife of my husband's older and only brother, and Aunt Jean, my husband's great-aunt.

Peg was like the older sister I never had. Although she and her husband lived in Texas, they came home to Pennsylvania frequently. They invited my husband and me to visit them in "Hewston," and treated us royally while we were there. In between get-togethers, Peg and I, but not my husband and his brother, spoke frequently—and at length—on the phone, but our husbands rarely, if ever, did. Perhaps they knew that Peg and I were exchanging all the news fit to report and that we would share things on a need-to-know basis with them. Soon after I told Peg I was pregnant, a huge box of gently used maternity clothes arrived—most of them exactly what I would have picked out for myself. Peg became the big sister I never had, guiding me through pregnancy and childbirth and making it clear she cared about me as a person as well as a sister-in-law.

Aunt Jean was a different kind of role model. Single and close to retirement, she was an unusual woman: she had never married, and she pursued an active career during an era when both might raise eyebrows. I never saw her depressed or even sad, despite some very difficult life circumstances. One memorable summer I went to the beach with her and my mother-in-law, and although it rained continuously, we had a blast, playing cards, watching TV, and talking nonstop. Twenty-five years later, I still think of Jean fondly when I look at the dried-flower picture she made for me.

My impressions of my husband's relationships with my family were completely different. While he was polite and even friendly, he never suggested we trek north to visit them. I doubt that he would have described my family as his "friends" or even as people who were especially important to his life.

My ex-husband was not cold or unfeeling. Like most of the men I've known (including my second husband), the need to be connected to immediate or extended family doesn't manifest itself in men the same way as in women. That doesn't mean that family is any less important; in fact, studies have shown that men are more likely than women to consider their spouses their best friend and to feel a deep sense of responsibility for taking care of their immediate relatives. Women, however, view families as an integral part of who they are and how they fit into the world.

That's why it was doubly difficult when my first husband and I divorced. Although Peg and I gamely tried to stay in touch and even called each other a few times, it soon became apparent that our relationship was over. Aunt Jean sent me cards occasionally, and once, when we talked on the telephone she cheerfully assured me she still wanted to stay in touch. Nonetheless, we, too, have drifted apart.

I've moved on to another husband and a new set of relatives, but the loss of Peg and Aunt Jean, although understandable, saddens me, and I continue to ask about their well-being from time to time. As for my ex-husband? I know he hasn't stayed in touch with any of my family members, and on the rare occasion when we see each other, he, unlike me, doesn't ask for updates on how everyone is doing. I wonder if many men would—which is not to imply that my ex-husband and I are better or worse people because of our behavior.

The Boy Wars

Don't men have conflicts with their dads and brothers, too, and can't their behavior be every bit as hostile as women's? The answer is clearly yes. Men and women express their feelings for family and conflict in very different ways, however—not better or worse, but distinct. Consider these "female family facts" that may partially explain why men and women tend to feel differently about families:

▌ Even in high school, women spend far more time performing core household tasks than men and are therefore more central to the family and tied to its identity.

▌ Women are more likely to take on the role of the nurturer after they're married and have children—even their appearance becomes more feminine. This phenomenon was first identified by the sociologist David Guttmann as the "parental imperative."

▌ Motherhood (and creating a family) is a "normative" event for women but not for men. Girls are far more likely than boys to identify having children as a life goal.

▌ Women are more likely to believe men over women, creating an atmosphere of mistrust and competition among themselves. Maass says, "Daughters of beautiful mothers often feel as if they are living in the shadow of their mothers, whereas aging mothers may feel threatened by the fresh beauty of daughters" (2002, 241).

▌ While boys are encouraged to follow in their father's footsteps, girls rarely are encouraged to be like their mothers, and in some ways, women consider "turning into my mother" or "becoming my mother" a negative development.

It's All in the Brain

In his book *The Essential Difference*, Dr. Simon Baron-Cohen offers an explanation for these types of gender-specific behaviors. Dr. Baron-Cohen, an eminent psychologist, believes that women's brains are biologically inclined toward empathy, while men's brains specialize in systematizing. The evidence shows up early—one-day-old males already show a preference for looking at a mechanical mobile, while one-day-old girls prefer faces. (Even if you're not inclined toward science, check out this book—there's a fascinating test on reading faces that makes a great party game.)

Empathizing and systematizing are not behaviors with superior or inferior qualities—they are different brain processes that lead women to be more oriented toward language and men to excel at spatial abilities. I'll add my caution to Dr. Baron-Cohen's: this is not true for *all* men and *all* women, but, based on an impressive body of research, these observations generally hold true.

Of course, there are always those cases we call "outliers" in statistics, because they don't fit within the normal curve of group experience. The author Shari Thurer may have an explanation about those folks: at the time of conception, receptors for testosterone exist in both male and female brains; thus, at that moment we are unisex. Hence, men who receive less testosterone stimulation in utero may tend toward more traditionally feminine characteristics, and vice versa.

In general, boys compete in groups, while girls prefer one-on-one interactions and are more likely to self-disclose. Their dominance hierarchies break up more quickly, and the potential loss of friendship is more troubling. Boys, on the other hand, project a macho image and even relish it, rarely, if ever, speaking of their weaknesses. Their friendships are based on shared activities, especially if it's an activity they are good at, while girls bond around disclosure and connection. Even when children are studied as they tell stories, girls will talk about relationships while boys describe conflicts.

Dr. Baron-Cohen's book offers as support a study he did on children going to summer camp. Boys immediately began to establish their place on the social ladder by being tough, while girls bided their time, acting nice initially but then using indirect methods like exclusion, withdrawing affection, and other subtle behavior to establish a hierarchy of popularity.

Studies have shown that women unconsciously absorb an amazing amount of information about one another and form opinions before even a single word is spoken. (They also give men a once-over, but usually with an eye toward their potential as partners/providers.) Unfortunately, these first impressions often shape the interactions that follow for a long time, for better or worse. A concept called "hostile attribution" leads some women to almost automatically view another woman's behavior as negative (threatening), even when it's not. I've seen this in girls who *always* interpret a curious glance as "mean," an innocent comment as "a put-down," and imitation (especially with clothes) as an open challenge.

What does this have to do with family relationships? Everything. Sure, there are notorious brother-sister and father-son feuds that inflict incredible damage, but the nuances of these conflicts aren't the same for men, who see achieving a goal (family cohesiveness in order to promote the survival of offspring) as more important than connection and closeness.

One woman described it this way: "With my husband, his family is on automatic pilot. I'm responsible for making regular long-distance calls to both my parents and his, and I arrange our get-togethers. My husband assumes I'm keeping up with things and will let him know if his input is needed."

Too Close for Comfort?

Rebecca Douglas, a University of Illinois extension educator, says that family feuds are fueled when family members live together or even nearby one another. Her theory is that the struggle for control between generations motivates many fights, with clear gender differences. Women focus on trying to keep the family intact, so the *number* of conflicts bothers them, while men focus more on the issues underlying the conflict, especially as they relate to authority.

A final difference between male and female views of family relationships is that for females family ties are usually more like a spiderweb than a lifeline. All members are connected to one another by a blood tie or a legal vow, but for women, alienating your sadistic sister-in-law may mean alienating her interesting mother as well. If a full-fledged feud emerges, you might stand a chance to at least remain cordial with the men, who hesitate to express their true feelings out of loyalty or denial, but only if their wives side with you. Time after time, hostility and rivalry between two women spreads out to affect other female relatives.

Alice found this out when she defended her younger sister-in-law Mia, who was perceived as snobby by the women in her family. This was the subject of discussion during one female conclave at a recent holiday get-together: "When I called her to ask what dish she was bringing, she acted like she was too good to cook for everyone, and said she hadn't even thought about it," commented cousin Celia, queen of the kitchen clan. "She couldn't get off the phone fast enough."

"Oh, come on. Give her a break! You probably just caught her in a PMS moment," Alice joked. Her attempt to intervene was received with dead silence by the group of women who had murmured their agreement with Celia's sniping, as they usually did.

Within days, all contact between Celia, Celia's husband, and Celia's children, and Alice's family was severed. Alice's mother-in-law even got involved, choosing to side with Celia. This left Mia, who was enraged by the jibe, and Alice in a strong alliance against Celia and the rest of the clan, even though their husbands, the oldest and youngest brothers, hadn't been especially close and found the whole drama hard to understand.

"I just wish you all would get over the hissy fit and make up," Alice's husband, Ben, complained to her. Ben didn't understand that what was going on among his female relatives was deeper than a brief, petty conflict. Gossip, power struggles, manipulation, and betrayal were all outward manifestations of an underlying tension each woman intuitively felt in her relationship with the others.

Perhaps, being new to the family, the normally reserved Mia acted in a way that came across as arrogant. Having been a recent newcomer herself, Alice may have been quick to defend Mia because she understood her behavior, and they were of the same age and developmental phase of life. Celia, long accustomed to calling the shots among the women, might see it as her job to keep "intruders" who might threaten family stability, and her power, on her radar. Of course, Alice's mother-in-law would side with Celia:

although they were only distantly related, they had grown up together in a small town many years earlier.

None of these scenarios are attached to a set of value judgments; rather, they are descriptions of a dynamic that involves misguided Relative Relational Aggression. Key to the conflict is the instinct of most women to keep the family intact, no matter what. They decide who will host Thanksgiving dinner, compile guest lists for wedding invitations, and keep tabs on the minute details of a niece's or nephew's progress in school. (Although at a recent professional event, one woman took me aside and told me her husband did all the planning for Thanksgiving, and later his daughter informed me it was her dad who taught her to sew!)

The One-Track Act

With either gender it's not the occasional aggressor or intermittent victim who causes concern, it's individuals who are stuck in a particular pattern of behavior and literally can't be any other way: cousin Grace, always at the center of the gossip wheel, stretching the truth to reflect badly on those involved; Aunt Linda, who can never come to a family reunion without searching out and attacking her sister Sue, who is attractive and more accomplished; or chronic victim Barbara, who was bullied by her sister for decades and is now the target of her adult daughter, Nancy.

Most numerous, as always, are the bystanders, those who watch as the same script gets played out again and again with certain relatives in the lead roles and everyone else an unwilling audience who just wants the conflict to end. Unlike men, women usually don't end up in prison or at war for their aggressive behavior, but they will pay a price for it.

If You Don't Believe Me . . .

The notion that female family feuds are more distressing than macho male matches might sound far-fetched, but here's a reality check you might try: for one week, read the "Annie's Mailbox" and "Dear Abby" columns in your daily paper. Tally how many requests for help with Relative RA come from women versus men, and what the RA behaviors might be. In the span of three days, I found two. In the first, "Betrayed and Miserable" was bothered by her husband's cousin's wife, a woman who bad-mouthed not only the writer's family, but her friends. Soon after that, "Grateful We Moved Far Away" asked how far she had to go in tolerating weekly gossip fests at her mother-in-law's home. I'm still searching for an equivalent number of letters on these topics from men, although I'm sure there must be some.

6

Competition:
A Help or a Hurt?

Long before the word wars begin, differences in the ways that men and women compete fan the flames of relational aggression. When the August 21, 2006, issue of *Business Week* magazine polled twenty-five hundred business managers on who they felt was the world's most competitive businessperson, not a single woman made the list. This is not so surprising—a combination of biological inclination and cultural conditioning gives girls the message that it's somehow wrong to compete with one another.

Go for the Gold

I can well remember the furor surrounding the passage of Title IX, because I was in high school, a girl who loved to swim but with no school team to be part of. When word reached us that legislation had been created so that young women who could qualify must be included in boys' sports teams if there were none for girls available, my small community was shocked. Why would any girl want to be an athlete? (Keep in mind this was 1971.) When my best friend, Nancy, and I ended up swimming for a full season on the boys' team, most people were supportive. Even so, a few naysayers couldn't help wondering what was wrong with girls who would want to be on a sports team dominated by boys.

That was a year of intense learning, and fun, for me. I observed boys who were archrivals in the pool joking with each other on the deck before their event was announced. When a swimmer got knocked out of his position as number one, he was angry, but that anger was soon channeled into a passion to do better and regain his status.

I also discovered that I focused my sights on the few girls who were part of other teams, believing at 118 pounds dripping wet I could never defeat a boy. (In fact I did, but not as often as Nancy— her broad shoulders and compact body propelled her to several second-place finishes, causing the boys she bested to take a lot of grief for being "beat by a girl.")

The next year there was a girls' team, and the dynamics were completely different. Personalities came into play, such that my archrival in the freestyle was labeled a "jerk," and her many social faux pas were pointed out to me. We weren't a team—really, we were a group of girls who warily eyed one another as potential friends or foes, rather than as one-time competitors.

You might think, "That was then, this is now," but these inequities and the messages attached to them continue: over half of college and high school students are female, but female athletes get about one-third of all sports operating expenditures, 42 percent of all college athletic scholarship money, and 32 percent of all college athlete recruitment spending (see www.womenssports foundation.org).

Unequal funding for career-enhancing opportunities, which persists to this day, can create uncomfortable situations from girlhood on, when the chance to advance oneself academically or athletically requires a degree of what should be good-natured rivalry. Women fail to see the "good-natured" part of the equation, often believing that competition is a catfight with one winner who has managed to claw her way to the top. Where would these feelings manifest more intensely than in a family, the first arena where girls and boys learn how to compete and cooperate with each other?

Is Competition Our Curse?

As women, our biology programs us to view overt aggression as potentially severing an important person-to-person connection, something to be avoided at all costs. Irene P. Stiver, a therapist, finds that women rarely come to therapy for career issues, while men often do (Stiver, in Jordan et al., 1991). She believes that the only time competition is sanctioned for women is when they are vying for a man. In the professional arena we want to be liked by all as we climb to the top.

The sociologist Anne Campbell, an internationally recognized expert and academic and the author of *A Mind of Her Own: The Evolutionary Psychology of Women*, writes extensively about female violence. She says that early on, girls and boys learn a different set of behaviors, which leads to different kinds of aggression. For example, women rarely use weapons to hurt one another during disagreements or conflict. In the same way, if a woman wants to steal money, she is more likely to embezzle than to hold up a bank or a gas station. By nature or nurture, women are uncomfortable with overt conflict.

You Can't Be Competitive with Your Family, Can You?

As with so many other aspects of RA, women unconsciously believe that families will somehow follow different rules. Mothers are never competitive with daughters, and while siblings may squabble, once they reach adulthood, their rivalry must be sugarcoated and "made nice." I hadn't expected to find so many women who admitted that competition was *more* extreme among their female family members, and that yes, their mothers did envy them at times.

Does it matter if you are the oldest, the youngest, or the middle child? Frank Sulloway believes so. In his book *Born to Rebel: Birth Order, Family Dynamics, and Creative Lives*, a discourse about birth order, he suggests that parents unconsciously invest in their children differently. Based on her perceived potential, one daughter may receive more attention and approval than her sisters; these circumstances can create a breeding ground for deep-seated sibling rivalries.

Sulloway believes that children search for their own niche within the family in order to avoid having to compete against and risk failure with other siblings. Firstborn children are the luckiest: they get the most parental attention and the best opportunity to claim their niche. I thought of Sulloway's book when I was recently interviewed about pairs of celebrity sisters, where younger stars must compete in the same arena as their siblings. Think of Paris Hilton, Jessica Simpson, and Hilary Duff—hard acts to follow whether you're younger or older.

Bettering or Battering
Our Brothers and Sisters

Tension with our siblings can be intense, sometimes bordering on bullying. Kimberly Updegraff and colleagues found RA to be present in all constellations of the 197 families they studied: older sister–younger sister, older sister–younger brother, older brother–younger sister, older brother–younger brother. The frequency was fairly consistent and involved acts that were more subtle than a kick or a punch: being excluded, manipulated, and intimidated are just a few of the behaviors reported. Probing further, these researchers discovered that the aggression was:

- Tied to qualities of the sibling-parent relationship: siblings who felt less acceptance from their parents experienced more discord.

- An inhibitor of closeness and support for both girls and boys.

- Increased when fathers spent less time with their children.

Victor Cicirelli, the author of *Sibling Relationships across the Lifespan* and the Overly Professor of Developmental and Aging Psychology at Purdue University, is another expert on family and especially sibling relationships. His studies show that sisters tend to be closer to one another than brothers and more bothered when conflicts arise between them. He comments that rivalry between siblings declines as brothers and sisters reach adulthood and that there is generally less rivalry *across* sibling genders than *between* them. Nonetheless, his research suggests that 71 percent of adult siblings feel rivalry at some time and that 45 percent are still experiencing it in adulthood. Most typically, oldest siblings, with the exception of me, tend to be the aggressors and younger siblings the victims.

Still, there remains a moral imperative to support our siblings in ways we would not support friends or non-kin. Consider the public reaction to siblings who "betray" each other: the brother of the Oklahoma City bomber and the sister of Scott Peterson were both curiosities because they "betrayed" their siblings.

The Family Hellidays

Shortly after Christmas break one year, I happened to run into my friend Jess in line for coffee at work. She's a midcareer woman like me, and we often chat casually for a few minutes when we pass in the hallway or the bathroom. As we discussed the postholiday burnout that seems to be everyone's favorite topic in January, Jess told me that for her, "family time" is not always quality time. She spends summer vacations, children's birthdays, and extended holidays with all of her immediate and extended family: her parents, her two brothers and their wives and children, and her two sisters and their offspring. Often, a feud ignites during their time together—almost always among the women.

"With my sisters-in-law, my mother-in-law, and even my own sisters there is such a thing as too much togetherness. Anytime we're forced into close contact for too long, it's like this turf thing comes out and the competition starts. The guys go off and watch TV or throw a football, but we're all stressed beyond belief trying to get along with each other."

When asked to elaborate on sources of conflict, Jess explained that rivalry, jealousy, and aggression drive many of the women in her family to bicker about whose children are best behaved, whose home is the most expensive, and whose appearance is most appealing. Without a doubt, she believes that the women—whether born or sworn into the brood—have much more relationship conflict than the men.

"Men sit around and watch TV together—their biggest disagreements are over who might win the next football game," she observed.

Caring and Competing

The instinctive emotional drives that draw female family members together can also divide them deeply. You love your sister because you have a long history of shared experiences. You don't have to describe to her how Dad shuffles outside in his boxer shorts to get the newspaper every morning—she's seen him do it.

On the other hand, she is also your most intense rival, competing early on for the physical and emotional resources from the parents you share. (And not uncommonly, for a man that you are both interested in, as happened to Trina in chapter 1.)

Often, the relationship with your sister involves the most subtle of relationally aggressive behaviors: undermining, setups, sly gossip, public exclusion, and worse. Some have suggested that in this way sisters provide a testing ground where girls learn how to relate to women outside the family. Resolving conflicts, vying for attention, and forging connections are all invisible skills that are almost impossible to teach, yet for women, they are an important component of self-identity. "On-the-job" experience may be the best teacher.

The Mother-Daughter Contest

A broadcast of the BBC's *The Woman's Hour* radio show dealt specifically with rivalry between mothers and daughters, in anticipation of a start-up reality show called *Generation Sex*. The show was to feature mothers and daughters competing *against* each other, unlike beauty pageants where mother-daughter pairs compete *together*. The show's host and her guest, Suzy Orbach, a relationship expert, debated whether the onset of a daughter's puberty, which so often occurs in conjunction with a mother's menopause, might initiate or influence feelings of competition.

My investigation into the topic suggested that mothers do sometimes resent their younger daughters for their ability to attract men and bear children, as well as having a career.

"Am I jealous?" said one mother, Sara, laughing bitterly. "Well, let's see: she's beautiful and has a great job, an adorable daughter of her own, and a husband who dotes on her."

Sara has been divorced since the birth of her second daughter, often working three jobs to make ends meet. I was drawn to chat with her and ask whether she thought this question was an issue when a mutual acquaintance noted that Sara often dressed like her much younger daughter and competed with her for attention from any men in the immediate area. Sara even adopted a hairstyle nearly identical to her daughter's. (I didn't point that out to Sara, but it was a curious coincidence I hadn't noticed previously.)

Envy can go both ways, though, with daughters looking at their mothers as the embodiment of what they are meant to be. "My mom is so accomplished I'll never be able to achieve what she has," says Cassie, a midlife artist who regularly engages in word wars with her mother whenever she visits her childhood home. "I keep trying to explain why I'm so dedicated to my painting, and she just doesn't get it, so I end up making these awful passive-aggressive comments about her two 'marriages for money.' I know it's hurtful to her, because I'm the only daughter, but I can't help it. She really knows how to get to me, and vice versa."

In an informal survey of women, I asked about rivalry between mothers and daughters as well as other RA-provoking issues. The responses were all consistent with stories I had already heard in person. They involved:

- Favoring one daughter over the other and making sure the favoritism is clear—a form of exclusion
- Ridiculing a daughter by commenting on a specific aspect of her appearance but pretending it's just helpful feedback
- Talking about daughters negatively to others—a form of gossip
- Showing disloyalty by betraying secrets that the daughter would prefer to keep private

The following excerpt, from my friend and blog cohost, Demian, is taken from a fascinating story of relational aggression that existed on many levels. (The complete story can be found at www.miyasansdaughter.com.)

Unwanted
Demian Elaine 'Yumei

My mother was born in China in 1926, with two older brothers and a mother who never hugged her or held her close. She was sold around the age of two to a Japanese couple. She often told me the story of when her stepmother came to take her: the exchange of a gold coin and the strange streets she memorized as she left the familiar ones she and her brothers had played in.

Somehow she managed to get away. Running back to her mom, expecting to be embraced with obvious relief, she was greeted with a shocked expression and then these words to the woman who came to retrieve her: "This time close the door. She will follow."

She remembered the sound of the closing door.

Her new family took her back to their homeland. There, my mother suffered abuse from her stepfather. Her first stepmother provided a sort of buffer, but when she died, her stepfather remarried, and his wife encouraged her husband to beat my mother more severely and more frequently.

She stood on a balcony looking out into the sunset over the Yangtze River, waiting for her brothers to rescue her. They never came, and though she traveled thousands of miles from Japan to China and eventually to the United States, a part of her never left or stopped waiting to be rescued. A rescuer never appeared, not in her family or in any of the other men she turned to afterward.

I was an accident on my father's part. My mother wanted him more than anything: he was in the navy and was being transferred back to the United States. The last time they were together, she informed him she was pregnant and intended to get an abortion, because my father was Catholic and she wanted him to feel bad.

He married her.

My father seemed to adore me. I was the one who became "Daddy's girl"; as our family grew, he played my sister and brother and me off against one another. He was a pedophile, but no one spoke of things we couldn't even acknowledge. It wasn't until I was thirty-one and my sister twenty-seven that the two of us spoke of the truth. My sister was so overwhelmed by her memories that she chose to cut off all contact with her biological family for a number of years.

My very existence seemed to bring suffering to my mother. I knew how much she had given up to marry my father: her career as a model, the country she grew up in, the freedom to communicate in her native language, the ability to take care of herself, and another son. She never told me these things in an accusatory tone of voice. She would just list a litany of misfortune that happened ever since she married my father—which, presumably, was because of me, even though I now realize that was the excuse, not the reason. Somehow I needed to do something that would make me worth it, that would somehow justify the suffering, the loss, and the sacrifice.

So I took care of Mom, partly because of that and partly because I loved her and felt her vulnerability and need. But I also resented her, because she was a weight no child should ever have to carry.

I don't remember her being outwardly mean to me; she just chose my sister over me. She wasn't a monster, though at times she could act like one. What her favoritism meant and how deep it was rooted in resentment did not fully reveal itself until we started dealing with the incest.

One time, I remember telling my mom what was surfacing up for me: a memory concerning my uncle and my father. As I spoke, I got a sudden rush of nausea and went to the sink to throw up. As the realization of what happened to her daughters sunk in, my mother said, her voice full of emotion, "Oh, poor Vernice." (That was my sister.)

When she saw the look on my face, she said, "Oh, you too."

Another time, in speaking about the abuse, my mother responded, "Well, at least you had him."

I'm not making excuses for her—it's just that as I get older, I am becoming more understanding and more compassionate toward the great burden she carried within her soul, the stone she wore around her neck and with many fewer resources or opportunities to heal from them as we have today.

My mom died angry at me. I was pregnant with my third child, and I had let her down—again. I could tell she felt betrayed. She got "that look" on her face. Lying in bed in the nursing home, she turned her back to me before I left. I can still see the side of her face—that pained, upturned look that said she didn't want to speak to me.

She died that night.

I was angry with her for years, but since then I've been humbled by my own mistakes, by the things I have done that I now realize made my children feel unloved, neglected, perhaps unwanted at times, and I know—I know without a doubt how much I loved them, always, and how much they meant to me.

And I believe my mother loved me, too. This isn't wishful thinking. It's remembering all the things that she did lovingly that I was too angry to remember before. It's reclaiming what rightfully belongs to me now.

Everything was stacked against our ever being close, and in life, we never really were. Cultural wounds, family wounds, dynamics that arise out of abuse—sexual, emotional, and psychological—stood in the way, but some things are so strong that they persist in making themselves known, even when life passes. One of them is the bond between mother and daughter. I don't care that ours was imperfect or even downright warped at times. This bond, what we shared, not only as mother and daughter but as women, is mine, and by letting myself claim that, I am made stronger.

Demian's story captures the complex dynamics of RA: competition, manipulation, exclusion, and revenge. It also shares an important truth: love and caring can exist side by side with negative, and even ugly, emotions and behavior. Recognizing this does not negate the wounds of RA, but it does empower women to do what Demian has done and walk a path that can heal all women involved.

7

How True, and for Whom?

The more I listened and read, the more curious I became about female family feuds and the lack of information on the role of relational aggression in this dynamic. After surfing from Web site to Web site, I decided to do my own casual survey of thirty diverse women to learn more about how they experienced RA in their families (all of them did, to some degree). I also reviewed studies from other cultures to see if RA is a universal phenomenon and not just part of the American way of life.

The RA Results

Most of the women who responded to my questions considered relationships with female family members more difficult than those with men or between men. "Women are completely untrustworthy" said one. Several added that female aggression was far more intense within their families than with any outside acquaintances.

What caused conflict? Parenting styles, a woman's choice of partner, and the tendency of older women to try to control get-togethers were all behaviors that could ignite an outburst. M.M., aged sixty-four, noted that women argue about people, while men argue about sports or politics.

When women bickered, the chief fodder for fights related to child rearing, gossip, and rumors. Other sources of tension included religion, ethnicity, alcohol, and money. Feeling that your in-laws thought you were not "good enough" for them was another conflict-generator.

I asked, "Do you see cultural differences in female conflict?" Those women who had relevant experiences commented:

- "Some cultures are more oriented toward women being domestic."
- "White women think they're better than others."
- "Latinas keep to themselves."
- "Hispanics are closer and more emotional."
- "White American women are more materialistic."
- "African American women treat each other like true sisters."

"Is it normal for women to compete?" was my next question. Yes, the respondents said. "All women do" and "It's a drive in any society" were examples of their comments. "There is rivalry over attractiveness," noted M.M.

The RA role women most often saw played out in their families was that of another woman (usually older) as a bully taking advantage of a younger victim/target, but competition was most frequent between sisters. Sometimes the intensity of that rivalry made a peaceful relationship difficult.

"I can forgive my friends more easily than I can forgive my sister," several said.

"She's the one who's not supposed to hurt you," one woman explained.

A very telling comment from a twenty-two-year-old woman captured the ambivalence others felt: "My sister doesn't show anyone in our family compassion and love. She has always seemed to resent us. I still love her and want to back away from her in my life until she matures and apologizes. I will always forgive her, though."

In terms of sisters-in-law, women felt they would never be as close to their in-laws as they were to their blood relatives and that it took time for them to fit in with other family members because they weren't "real" family. One forty-four-year-old woman remarked that she got along better with her brothers' wives than with her husband's sister. Another woman appreciated her sisters-in-law because they provided strength in numbers to deal with their difficult mother-in-law. It is quite possible to hate one sister-in-law and love another, so the feelings go deeper than a label attached to a relationship or preconceived beliefs about blood ties. A forty-seven-year-old women considered her sister-in-law a bully because she interrupted any conversation her husband might be having with another woman, and would speak for him. "I can tell it frustrates my brother," she added.

Women were divided on whether they felt competitive with their own mothers: about half said they thought it was normal to be envious. Others felt a constant pressure for one-upmanship over the life choices they made: needing a more accomplished career, a satisfying marriage, obedient and caring children, and a higher income than their mothers. Only one participant noted that her mother was clearly envious of her and the life she led.

Sometimes feelings about family spilled over into relationships with other women. "My mom is very aggressive," said B.R., aged twenty-five. "That's made me less accepting of other women." R.D., aged fifty-seven, commented, "My mother was never a nurturer—I look for that in my relationships with other women."

From the feedback these women gave, my theory of a "hierarchy of hurt" was supported: aggression from those born, rather than sworn, into a family hurt more. At the top, the aggression and rejection of real or surrogate mothers wounds deepest because of what it represents. Sisters, daughters, and other blood relatives who know us well and with whom we share a history are next on the pyramid of pain: the closer the relationship, the more serious the sting.

In-laws seem to provoke a more overtly angry response than blood relatives. While expectations and beliefs about relationships with the women in our immediate family are inherently high, interactions with in-laws may be guarded from the beginning and these "newcomers" viewed as a potential threat to the well-being of the family.

Around the World

In some cultures, aggression and hostility between relatives are not only tolerated but expected: Neema Coughran, an academic and a contributor to my previous book *Mean Girls Grown Up* (Wiley, 2005), shared an article she wrote about a practice in South Asia. Food and other resources are given last to the youngest daughter-in-law, who is considered to have the lowest status and is relegated to a role similar to that of a servant. This dynamic of the bully mother-in-law and her fearful victim daughter-in-law is based on long-standing cultural mores that establish a power hierarchy among women in the same family. Most likely, the women who observe this treatment are both relieved that it isn't them and terrified that it could be should they attempt to intervene.

Other scholars describe the same tradition in other areas of India. Daughters-in-law are expected to submit to their mothers-in-law, and a hierarchy from oldest to youngest dictates how the wives will be treated: in some situations, the youngest is little more than a slave. The mother-in-law breaks down her daughter-in-law's confidence through ridicule, rebukes, physical exhaustion, and even beatings. However, these practices are changing in urbanized areas where education and economic status are improving, but they have nonetheless reinforced a stereotype of cruel women, often seen in movies where mothers-in-law are portrayed taking out their frustrations on their daughters-in-law.

To explore further what I learned from my reading and casual conversations, I conducted a small focus group with five women from various parts of India. They began by drawing me a picture of their country and explaining that each state within the country has its own unique culture: foods, language, dress, and so on. This immediately presents a potential challenge, since families whose members are not from the same geographic region may be confronted with a completely different set of traditions and expectations.

The women had various life situations: married, unmarried, with children and without, but all were in professional positions, so they acknowledged that they represented a more elite group. We began by talking about families in general, and one woman remarked on how open American society is about discussing issues that would be considered very private in India: "We don't even display pictures of our family, but here you go in someone's office and they're everywhere!"

After admitting that extreme forms of female family conflict could exist in rural areas, the consensus was that for the most part this practice was atypical. We moved on to discuss sibling rivalry, a concept understood by all. Interestingly, these women viewed it as a good dynamic, because the oldest daughter sets the standard for her younger sisters. Each subsequent sister is expected to surpass that standard, but there was no resentment because of this; if anything, competition was considered a helpful motivation.

"It's a good thing for me to do better than her," one woman explained, in reference to her older sister.

In each of the different subcultures represented, once a woman married, her "family" changed. "Our society is oriented toward preservation of the family and respect for elders," said one. This means when an oldest brother marries, he and his wife move in with his parents to provide care and support. They also take on responsibility for the well-being of other siblings.

Sometimes the blending of families goes well for the newlyweds, but if it doesn't, the goal of every family member is to work together to help resolve the difficulties. A large group of people may get involved in mediating a marital conflict: first family, then friends, then whoever else might be helpful in the situation. No matter how serious the problem, divorce is not an option, because it carries such a stigma. Therapy for marriage or any other kind of counseling is unheard of, because it is the family's responsibility to take care of its own.

One woman spoke of an incident that happened after her father died. "I was grieving, and it was very obvious I was sad. Someone asked if I had considered therapy, and I responded, 'What do you mean, therapy? I've lost my father, not my mind!'"

"Fitting in" with a new family means that the existing daughters are "replaced" to a degree, because the oldest sister-in-law becomes most important. This can cause problems for the women born into the family, but sometimes more problems arise for the new wife sworn into the family. In one case, a woman's sister, who enjoyed wearing casual, American-type clothing, was expected to wear a sari once she was married. "It was very difficult, because she didn't want to do it," the storyteller explained, "and maybe it would have created big problems for the marriage, but her husband was very wise. He told her to just do it for a short time, and then after that, they could begin to try and change his mother's views." Thankfully, this strategy worked, preventing turmoil within the entire family.

It is assumed that the females in the family will provide child care for one another. The women I spoke with agreed that it was automatic for mothers or mothers-in-law to babysit while the parents worked. In this way, there were always plenty of women available, but I was curious as to what happened when opinions about child rearing clashed.

One woman explained, "If you don't like something they do with your kids, you just tell them. You say, 'Listen, I don't want this,' and they will go along with it."

When I asked if it was difficult to entrust the care of your child to another woman, especially if you didn't approve of her, they admitted this could be a problem. Still, the benefits of such a child-rearing practice far outweighed the drawbacks.

The following interview with a young woman from India further elaborated on many of the focus group's statements:

I am twenty-eight, and once every two years I go back to India, where all my relatives still live. Only my husband is here; we've been married a year. His family doesn't live here, either.

I have a sister-in-law, but my interactions with her and my other in-laws have been very limited. I was at their place for only two weeks. In India, we do have problems with in-laws and things like that. My sister and I are very close, but I have problems with my mother, conflicts basically, but we can forgive each other and go back to the way we were.

A lot of it will be natural when you're living together, but a daughter and daughter-in-law are similar but not the same. The same is true for sister and sister-in-law: I could forgive my sister more easily than my sister-in-law. When I look at my family, my mother and her relations with her sisters, she has pretty good relations with one, but she has quite a bit of trouble with another one. Not that they're rude to her, but you see a lack of warmth. That woman had a lot of problems, I think, personally.

For example, my cousin came to stay with us for a while because we were nearer to her school. Her mother had "concerns" about how her daughter was being raised in our household. She was being raised the same as my sister and I were raised: she wasn't given any bad treatment and neither was she given any special treatment. That's maybe what my aunt wanted. It was a one-person thing; overall, everyone has fights but also gets along.

One difference I see between India and here is that I might have a problem with my mother or sister but I don't complain about them or discuss my parents with my friends or my colleagues. Here, I have seen my colleagues discuss mothers, boyfriends, mothers-in-law, parents, sisters, etc.; they discuss that they did something that was not right. I might agree with that, but I may not discuss it with my colleagues.

That is something I initially found very difficult. People talk about mothers-in-law in India but not mothers or sisters. Maybe I don't want people I work with to know anything negative about my family. I feel stronger toward my mother than my mother-in-law, since I don't know my mother-in-law. Maybe that's why I don't have as many qualms about talking about her. With very close friends, yes, you do discuss this happened and that happened, but not at work for anyone to hear.

Living in the midst of a culture different from one's own and interacting daily with women whose views of female family relationships are dramatically different can give rise to another type of RA style conflict. Intermarriages bring women from culturally conditioned backgrounds into close contact. During a time of tension or discomfort, a woman who has been socialized to openly discuss family strife may appear aggressive or hostile. At the same time, women from cultures where dialogue or airing grievances is not the norm may find diatribes about a challenging mother-in-law shocking and even grounds for disapproval.

Different Perspectives

Other cultures are bound to traditions that unintentionally provide a breeding ground for friction between female relatives, but research is sparse and focused on certain geographic areas. Perhaps the "Good Mother" and the "Loyal Daughter" traditions are a universal phenomenon. The following are summaries of a few interesting studies that illustrate Relative RA around the world.

In Taiwan, it is customary for the adult son to remain in his parents' house and to bring his new wife there, a process called "marrying in." In a study of sixteen mothers-in-law and sixteen daughters-in-law, Sandel (2004) found that the younger women complained about dual child rearing and discipline and the expectation that elders are automatically to be respected. Mothers-in-law complained about the same issues: grandchildren and the lack of respect they received from their daughters-in-law. Since grandmothers are expected to be the primary caregivers of children while mothers work full-time, the major disagreements involved the parenting philosophies of the women, with men uninvolved.

In another study of Asian culture, Keith and Choi-Lee (1995) interviewed thirty-two couples about their relationships with in-laws. Wives were more likely than husbands to report difficulties with in-laws and to experience distress over it.

A report from Israel by Linn and Breslerman (1996) begins by describing an informal survey conducted decades ago in the United States when a radio station asked for postcards from listeners identifying the most problematic person in their families. Over five thousand were sent in, with nine out of ten women complaining about their mothers-in-law. Jewish mothers topped the list (Duvall 1954). The second-most-problematic person was the husband's sister. The top three problem behaviors were meddling, possessiveness, and nagging.

Linn and Breslerman went on to study fifty-four Israeli women, who interested them because they were from a unique population in a small geographical area, with a rich tradition and subject to security threats that created a culture of support for men and the military. In their study, mothers-in-law rated their relationships with their daughters-in-law more positively if there was more than one son. Most of the daughters-in-law (75 percent) *weren't* satisfied with their relationship with their mother-in-law, while 88 percent of mothers-in-laws *were* satisfied.

In Egypt, single mothers (but not fathers) are likely to live with their daughters later in life, which suggests a reciprocity of caregiving: the mother provided care during her daughter's childhood; in exchange, the child will care for her as an elderly adult. Yount (2005) argues that elderly women in this situation are vulnerable to mistreatment, because they are more likely to be widowed, poor, and disabled. On the other hand, residing with sons is more common when the father is still alive, and in this situation mothers will be the ones with authority over daughters-in-law.

The following story from Ruth, a young woman from Kenya, is a good example of variations in expectations of women:

> I am twenty-seven years old and come from Kenya, where the firstborn child has a position of great responsibility, whether that child is male or female. As firstborn, I was conscious of needing to be a good role model for my younger siblings (two brothers and a sister), which influenced our relationships. My job was to set a good example, and my parents urged the younger ones to look to me as a guide for their behavior. I imagine that if I was my younger sister, it would be hard to be told constantly to "be like your older sister." In her place, I think it would have made me jealous, but we have never talked about this.
>
> In the future, if I marry, I will become a part of my husband's family and will leave my family, so to speak. My place will be with his parents, and I will be expected to take care of them, just as my brothers' wives will in my family. I think I will get along well with my in-laws because it is a good thing for someone to marry a woman who is educated in the U.S., as I am.
>
> My sister will always be my closest friend, because she is the one I can trust, without doubt. Even though we don't see each other often, we e-mail, and when I did confide a big secret to her, she did not tell anyone until I gave permission. It is hard to find this kind of relationship with another woman, but it may be part of my culture and the fact that I am now living in the U.S., where I am constantly aware of being from a different country.

When women are raised abroad and come to the United States, they may face problems with acculturation to female relationships, as pointed out by Ruth. Here is another story from a slightly older woman, also from Kenya:

I am forty-two and am from Nairobi, Kenya. I have been in the United States ten years, where I live with my husband and children. I also have a sister-in-law, a brother, a brother-in-law, and some cousins in this country. I have only been back to Kenya once because I have children, and when I travel, I need to take them along. My sisters, parents, mother-in-law, and also my brothers and sisters-in-law still live there, along with tons of cousins.

In Kenya, sisters are generally very good to each other, but for women married into the family, like my brothers-in-law's wives, there is a little competition because they get into tension on how things are to run within the family. And sometimes, depending on an issue that comes up, they may not be very friendly.

It also depends on the environment you are living in, the rural area or the city. In the city you are part of the family, and you can be nice to each other because you live in your own home and just visit with each other, so your interactions are very little. But in the rural area, you share the same parcel of land, so your homes are adjacent to each other. If you farm, your animals will be in the same farm area, and there will be more tension. Having families and children in a close environment increases tension.

I have seen conflicts with my brothers-in-law's wives, because they were sharing the resources and living on the same land. There seem to be issues about the children: sometimes you simply don't like how they are doing things as parents or there are conflicts between the kids. One set of kids may be doing better in school than another.

The financial aspect can be a problem if someone is financially more stable than you. There is hostility because they are not at the same levels. It's expected that you respect the elder ones, which can cause problems.

In the United States, we are more like friends, which is like in the city back home. We interact at a distance, we go out together, or if they come to my house, we have a good time. City living in Kenya and America is the same—it's the rural areas where things are more different, because people are living together more closely and so they have more conflicts.

Her comments are underscored by the findings from a study of coresident women in sub-Saharan Africa conducted by Madhavan (2001), where many different constellations of women can live together with one man, including sisters, in-laws, and co-wives. There is always a husband in residence, but the number of women and their relationship to the husband varies. In many ways, the arrangements described in this article are very similar to my earlier discussion of group living in times gone by.

Many factors can influence the level of cooperation among women; for example, whether she enjoys her mother-in-law's favor, or a woman's ability to bear children. In a dynamic not so different from that in developed countries, some women become so obsessed with elevating their status that they can relate to other women only in competitive ways. However, there are incentives to cooperate, such as each woman's need for support in assimilating into the household and in dealing with their shared husband.

As in historical times, women must both compete and cooperate to ensure the survival of their children, who face many health risks before age five. Ironically, Madhaven points out that stronger cooperation and reduced competition could provide more leverage to get resources from the husband, but this realization eluded the women. As it does to their "sisters" around the world, RA alienates rather than unites the family (or families), much as it did in the days of the cave.

Friend versus Female Family Feuds

While relationally aggressive behaviors within a family can mimic those in the outside world, the similarity ends there. Relative RA has a special power to hurt because of what family means to most women. Your best friend might comment on the cut of the new skirt you're wearing and you take it as a conversation starter. The same remarks from a sister feel like a full frontal attack. It's a simple truth that we expect more from our women kin, and consequently, we are hurt more by their transgressions.

Family versus Friends

Every woman usually has a least one female relative to deal with (her mother), but that's about the only truism that applies across the range of possible female family connections (or disconnections). Some families involve a cast of hundreds, distantly related, while others are distilled down to only immediate members. It's natural that conflict will play out differently in each situation, but whether a woman is bred or wed into a family, the ties she forms with her female relatives are unique. As my friend Andi put it, "That's the one place where you should be safe from the kinds of nasty things women do to each other."

Yet nasty things seem to happen quite often in most families. (Including homicides, where family members are always the prime suspects.) Troubles may bubble up on holidays, when stress is greater and contact is more intense, but conflict can still simmer when relationships are long-distance. Ironically, this doesn't mean affection can't exist side by side with aggression, but unlike friendships, we can't just walk away from a hurtful relationship—nor can we deflect the impact as easily.

"If my own mother treats me so shabbily," reasons victim Laura, "there must be something truly unlovable about me." The connection she has with her mother is not a satisfying one, but unlike friendships, which change with each new job or living arrangement, Laura's mother is there for a lifetime. Her influence on the past, present, and future of this bright and likable young woman may outweigh all the positive ones.

Artificial You?

A combination of complex roles and relationships, history, and expectations prevents most of us from presenting our authentic self to our families, as we might with friends. Like me, you may hesitate to have a beer or two in your mother's company because you know she disapproves. Conversations are censored, clothing changed, and your own family members warned to be on their best behavior prior to a family gathering (I'm guilty of this one, too). All this occurs because we want to maintain our image as mother, daughter, sister, aunt, wife, or in-law, along with all the expectations attached. However, the pressure to be on best behavior 24/7 when around your family can be tension-producing in and of itself; worrying about whether those associated with you (for example, husband and kids) will also perform well heightens anxiety further.

Jen, an outspoken attorney, discovered this firsthand. Her best strategies for assertiveness in the courtroom did little to rein in her bullying mother-in-law at Christmas celebrations. Rather than push further to defend herself, Jen retreated into silence. "I didn't want to risk creating hostility that might endure for a lifetime," said the crisp professional woman, who is known to trade barbs with opposing counsel without hesitation.

A few other factors may explain why Relative RA is more complicated to address than "regular" RA with non-kin:

▍ It's much harder (and sometimes impossible) to sever ties with a bullying female family member, because even if you do, she will still be part of your family and, therefore, connected to you in one way or another. You may only have to see her once a year—but that contact can have fallout that extends well beyond the few days or hours that you're together. Even if you don't see her, she is an invisible presence you will be reminded of whenever you're with other family members.

▍ Friction with one woman can affect many others, especially when relationships are close. Tension between sisters-in-law can spill over to include hostility from a mother-in-law or other sisters-in-law and their respective relatives. Soon, the family that used to be a haven from the rest of the world is engaged off-hours in a full-fledged feud that exhausts everyone.

▍ We believe ties with immediate and extended families are *supposed* to be close ones, so women in particular are more reluctant to end, or even challenge, them. Many would rather endure the put-downs of a clannish kitchen clique than risk severing the connection, possibly forever.

▍ Women are kin-keepers, intuitively driven to hold families together and to preserve the family "story," even if it's complete fiction. They will do almost anything to smooth over the rough edges of family life and keep the unit intact.

▍ RA within families is a unique situation, in that men can become intimately involved and emotionally affected. Although they may not be caught up in the actual word war, they can be torn by conflicting loyalties to different women they care about deeply. This is different from the romantic competition that often spurs RA in the world outside of families, although loyalty issues are paramount.

▍ RA may be more prevalent between women in families than with coworkers, acquaintances, or friends. Both immediate and extended female family members may play the role of bully, victim, or bystander (or all three), because their relationship is not one of choice. Adult women who won't tolerate relational aggressive friends accept similar behaviors from family because they feel they have no alternatives.

▌ Difficulties in relationships between female relatives are often multifaceted, originating in feelings that range from territoriality to outright jealousy, often manifested in varying types of RA behaviors. With friends, acquaintances, or coworkers, tensions are usually more narrowly focused.

▌ Much of the RA drama within families arises from a history or "script" that has been playing out for generations. Daughters who watch their mothers being a bully or a victim can learn early on that this is the expected and tolerated dynamic within their families.

▌ RA within families is a taboo subject. While many television shows, movies, and books glamorize the mean behavior of female friends or coworkers, the same behaviors within families are considered inappropriate, unless they involve a mother-in-law.

▌ The rivalry that can occur between mother and daughter, sister and sister, or any other combination of women has a history and a context that is usually not present with coworkers, acquaintances, or friends.

What Lies Beneath

Driving the RA dynamic and its power to hurt is the degree of perceived threat to yourself (or your immediate family), feelings of rivalry, and whether you are the target or the perpetrator. A remark about your husband's failure to carry his plate to the kitchen after a meal is less likely to offend than the same comment about your child. (Put-downs about your husband may actually relieve your concerns about another woman's interest in him. Criticism of your children, on the other hand, can feel like a potential injury to your "cubs.")

Contrast the motivation for each of these Relative RA scenarios with a non-kin situation:

▌ Gail is an only child who married into a family of six siblings—half of whom are women. While she constantly struggles to get along with her new "sisters," it's hard for her to understand the family "rules" each of them knows so well.

Since her husband's two brothers haven't married yet, Gail is the sole outsider. All too often, the sisters gather together in the kitchen and don't include her—deliberately?

▌ Abby, a divorced mother, maintains a cordial relationship with her daughter's paternal grandmother, the only real relative her child has been close to. Her former sister-in-law (who is childless) resents this contact and goes out of her way to let both of them know it. She spreads rumors about Abby to the rest of the family, "forgets" to give her mother Abby's telephone messages, and refuses to attend her niece's birthday parties.

▌ Tess and Wendy, two cousins-in-law who grew up in the same small town, now stay in regular contact although they live far apart and can meet only on holidays. Often their e-mails turn hostile as they compare the accomplishments of their children, the successes of their husbands, and the relative superiority of their lives. When the correspondence gets too acerbic, one will give the other the "silent treatment" via the Internet, refusing to respond to e-mails.

▌ Rival mothers-in-law Meg and Kathy are engaged in an emotional tug-of-war over the affections and attention of their son and daughter. Kathy attempted to be "friends," but quickly gave up when Meg's RA attack escalated during the planning of their children's wedding. Whenever they are forced to be in one another's company no one would guess the depth of their animosity, but as soon as they part, Meg invariably goes to her daughter with a new and exaggerated complaint about Kathy.

Intergenerational RA

As mentioned previously, RA isn't confined to two women and one generation. Sometimes a female family feud extends across time to relatives who have never met one another. This was the case for Marilyn, whose family of origin consisted of three sisters and two brothers. When Marilyn's mother died, the siblings discovered that Lucy and Grace, the twin "babies" of the family, had convinced their mother to leave most of her fortune to them. Surprisingly, it was Marilyn who took this news the hardest. She maintained contact with her brothers but refused to discuss Lucy, Grace, or her mother with anyone, or to respond to her sisters' later overtures to reconcile. Marilyn's children were forbidden to have any contact with their aunts, even though Marilyn's husband disagreed and thought "bygones should be bygones." Marilyn prevailed, both a victim and a perpetuator of relational aggression.

The following story is another example of the power of RA and how this dynamic can replay from generation to generation, passed on from grandmother to mother, from mother to daughter, or, as for this woman, from aunt to niece.

A Legacy of RA
Lane Bennett

I grew up in a black family where skin color was the major focus for most of my life. My mother was the oldest of nine children and very light-skinned, with freckles. She told me that she passed for white a couple of times, something she would never share with anyone else in the family. I think it gave her a sense of power, but she would not want her siblings to think she was ashamed of being black.

Mom had two younger sisters—both with darker skin. My aunt Bess had beautiful, flawless black skin. Aunt Libby was never happy with her medium-brown skin, always using bleaching creams to lighten it. My grandmother said Libby was not "quite right" emotionally—I gather from my uncles that Aunt Libby was always very selfish and mean-spirited.

When my grandfather left my grandmother, my mom was forced to quit school and stay home to raise the other eight kids. Mom ran away from home at seventeen, met my father, who was also very light-skinned and could easily pass for white, and got married. She traveled around the country with my dad, my older sister, and me. Aunt Libby was at home helping to raise the three younger brothers. She wrote to Mom every week, begging her to come home, because it was not fair that Mom got to be married and have a life away from the family. Eventually, Mom was so flooded with guilt, she told my father she was homesick and tired of moving every two years, and she went home to help her sister raise the younger brothers.

The change in our lives was dreadful. We left a nice two-story farmhouse to live in a shack with an outside toilet. My sister,

Mary, and I struggled to make the adjustment. Mary was in first grade and developed a stammering problem; I had lactose intolerance and asthma and remember feeling sick a lot. Nevertheless, my mother stayed to do her family duty.

When my mom and my grandmother reconciled before her death, her last request was for Mom to take care of Aunt Libby. My mother was always a caretaker. She immediately became the maid, housekeeper, and subservient person in Aunt Libby's household. Aunt Libby threw temper tantrums whenever she did not get her way.

Aunt Libby would fight with Mom because she thought Mom wanted her husband, or she would say Mom stole her watch (which Libby had misplaced). She was very jealous of Mom, who truly enjoyed helping others. She took every opportunity to put Mom down about her lack of education, her "sickly yellow skin," her freckles, etc. My mother never retaliated, calling her black or the "n" word. Mom always cautioned me about retaliating; she said I should never use that word or refer to anyone's skin color. Mom said my life would be difficult enough because I was a light-skinned, pretty girl who would have a hard time making friends anyway because of my looks.

As children we would also have to cater to Aunt Libby, which meant anticipating how we could please her. Mary did Aunt Libby's hair every morning at 5:30, I made all her clothes and cleaned her shoes, and our younger brother Jack took care of her car. On Mother's Day, we could not give a bigger acknowledgment to our mother; it had to be the same for Aunt Libby.

At one point, Aunt Libby wanted Mom to allow her to adopt me because she wanted a little girl and only had a son. Almost every Sunday, Mom would dress me up and force me to go visiting with Aunt Libby and her husband, much to the displeasure of my sister, who never got to go and grew to resent me because I was favored for my light skin.

Eventually, Mom became depressed and stopped taking care of herself completely. She gained weight and did not take care of her hair, which provided more fuel for Aunt Libby to put her down. She lived under Aunt Libby's control, making all the meals, doing the laundry, and cleaning the house, while hearing nothing but criticism from Aunt Libby.

My older sister, Mary, could not wait to leave home. She

hated the life that Mom chose for us, and she went off to college, where she got pregnant. Aunt Libby was furious, partly because Mary left home and never asked her opinion. She ostracized my sister from the family, and Mom went along with the whole thing. Mary had her child alone without any family to support her. I used to go over on weekends to visit her and help out, which really got me into hot water with Aunt Libby, but I was ashamed of how our family treated Mary, and I prayed I would never be shunned like that.

My second year in nursing school, Mom had finally saved enough money to buy a townhouse. She was thrilled because she always wanted to own a home after moving so many times with my dad. There was a big confrontation when Mom tried to move away from Aunt Libby (after fifteen years!). Eventually Aunt Libby moved in with Mom, and we continued in the same pattern of bully and victim. When I graduated from nursing school, Aunt Libby chose not to attend.

I wanted to come home to live after nursing school, but Mom said no, because living with Aunt Libby would be more difficult as she witnessed my success in nursing. I was very hurt but had to spend about two months there while I looked for an apartment, and it was like living in hell. Aunt Libby would attack me verbally and physically with no provocation and accuse me of thinking I knew everything because I was an RN. When I would try to talk Mom into kicking Aunt Libby out, she would point out that Aunt Libby had no one. Of course not—she had driven everyone out of her life! But my mom had promised her mother she would look after her.

Eventually, Mom, Aunt Libby, and Libby's son, Joe, were the only ones at home. Mom had developed chronic pulmonary problems, but I was confident Joe would look out for her since they were close. Even after she had to go on oxygen, she never faltered in taking care of Aunt Libby. It was difficult for me to watch this, because Mom clearly needed someone to take care of her. Before she died, Mom tried to get me to promise to take care of Aunt Libby. I could not make that promise, and sometimes I feel guilty about it.

Now Aunt Libby lives alone with Joe, trying to manipulate his life. She is estranged from most of the family, only seeing my brother and sister when they come home at Christmastime.

It's remarkable to compare the behaviors used by Aunt Libby with the ones that are reported to me by adolescent girls: manipulation, intimidation, harassment, gossip, and exclusion abound in both situations, to the detriment of all involved. This story underscores the importance of intervention before it is too late to change the situation for the better.

It can be difficult, if not impossible, to differentiate the behaviors of the "Queen of Mean" in middle school and the "Drama Mama" in your kitchen, just as the furious spats of adult caregivers can resemble kindergartners arguing over a toy on the playground. There is a major difference between the two, however. Being family may cause Relative RA to occur more often and render it more hurtful. When it comes to conflict, there really is no place like home, which is why repairing Relative RA is so important.

PART TWO

Mothers, Sisters, and Daughters

9

Motherhood Revisited

While sad stories about physically and emotionally abused children are reported all too regularly, a relationship mired in relational aggression may not be easily recognized as such. This isn't the mother who occasionally, or even frequently, says things she wishes she hadn't, or uses manipulation to get her way.

Women who are stuck in the RA way use *only* this style to interact with others and are unable to connect in a healthy or normal way—even briefly. This behavior can fracture a child's self-esteem and instill a lifetime of limitations, both for the daughter who is always waiting to be targeted and the mother who is constantly on the attack, bullying in ways that may pass under the radar. This happens for a couple of reasons:

- Unlike physical and emotional abuse, RA is an interaction style that would be hard to report to authorities. For example, no one will be arrested for giving another person the silent treatment, yet this behavior can cause the same degree of hurt as more overt forms of emotional abuse (consistently berating a child, screaming, threatening, or the like).

- The context of RA is essential to its ability to hurt. The mom who slaps her daughter across the face is using physical aggression, no matter what the circumstance. In the same way, a mother who repeatedly tells her daughter she is stupid, fat, ugly, or whatever, is emotionally abusive. The RA dynamic has a particular meaning for the parties involved, and it exists because of that and the relationship they share; "setting up" a daughter with her father by interpreting comments or actions in a negative way, using guilt to manipulate a desired behavior, and giving one daughter preferential treatment over the another are examples of subtle RA behaviors that may not register with those outside the family.

Many RA behaviors have been almost "trademarked" as female—think of the last time you heard men discuss giving someone the silent treatment or excluding him from a men-only event, yet almost every woman understands what this is—and the hurt that goes with it.

The Mom Dynamic

Another of my colleagues, Dr. Karen Fingerman, an associate professor of developmental and family studies at Purdue University, has studied adult mother-daughter dyads extensively. She found that mothers tend to feel more positive about their relationships with their daughters than vice versa. Another study by Wilson, Shurey, and Elder (2003) found that the greatest levels of ambivalence in family relationships were among women. In particular, daughters-in-law and mothers-in-law had the strongest feelings of ambivalence toward one another.

The linguist and author Deborah Tannen says this about relationships between mothers and daughters: "Each yearns to be seen and accepted for who she is while seeing the other as who she wants her to be—or as someone falling short of who she should be." This, Tannen argues, makes relationships between mothers and daughters especially intense, and therefore, I would argue, more prone to RA as a way to express negative feelings. When the "relationship equilibrium" is fragile, feelings expressed in more covert and subtle ways can tip the balance toward hostility, as Brenda Nixon discovered.

Girl on the Outs
Brenda Nixon

Growing up, I'd look at my older sister, whom I was often compared to, and my younger brother, and wonder where my place was.

Many times, I went to my room as directed, confused—not knowing what I'd said or done that made my mom so frustrated. Silence followed. Mom could hold out and not speak to me all day. When she did, it'd be a sharp, cutting remark in a tone that I recognized as restrained anger.

In fifth grade, Mom and I had a squabble to which she finally screamed, "You just get yourself up for school. I'm not going to wake you in the morning."

I stayed awake all night for fear of oversleeping and being late. The rule in our home was if you're tardy you're spanked.

As I grew, I gravitated toward Dad because he seemed more emotionally predictable. However, Mom was competitive and jealous of our relationship, especially when she'd hold in her frustration until Dad came home from work, and then tell him how I mouthed off so he'd be annoyed and scold me.

There were happy holidays, consistent routines, plenty of food and friends, and times of affection, but my spirit felt neglected. "Brenda's too sensitive" or "Stop feeling sorry for yourself" was the response Mom gave when I shared an emotionally hurtful experience.

As a teenager, I began to see what might lie behind Mom's comments and behaviors. I learned about her traumatic childhood that thwarted her maturity and made her unpredictable.

The physical and emotional space college afforded provided an opportunity to observe my family from a distance. I signed up to see the campus psychologist and gained some insights. No family is perfect. We all have some dysfunction. I was aching to be connected with and accepted by my mother, although she made it impossible.

The psychologist helped me see strengths in myself, and communication with Mom became easier, partly because I was maturing and partly, I'm convinced, because I no longer saw her as a daily challenge.

Then graduate school brought a liberating epiphany, when one of my professors said, "It's not bad to be sensitive." He explained, "You'll be able to connect with and help people because of it."

A few years after I married, my husband and I learned I was pregnant. We excitedly shared our news with family, but my sister said, "Mom's mad at you."

"Why?" I asked bewildered.

"Because when you told her you were pregnant, she said 'my grandbaby,' but you corrected her by saying 'It's my baby.' That hurt her feelings."

Again, I had failed.

When my child was nearly a year old, I wanted to ensure healthy parenting patterns, so I saw a counselor. A gentle, fatherly type, he always found something good to say about me. During one of our sessions, after I shared my sense of family isolation, he looked me in the eye and challenged, "Do you know what your mistake is?"

"My mistake! What do you mean?" I asked.

"Do you know the real reason your mother cannot accept you?"

"No."

"You have no penis."

"What do you mean?"

"Your mom wanted a boy."

"It's not my fault," I sighed, realizing there was nothing I could've done—or ever do—to deeply please her. Since then, I've been able to accept myself and her limitations.

Brenda's story portrays a mom stuck in an RA rut, much to her and her daughter's detriment. Sadly enough, the dynamic is one that was learned from a drama mama grandmother, who seems to have mistreated Brenda's mother in a similar fashion, which is the enduring tragedy of RA.

Under the Radar

While some mothers are simply emotionally incapable of bonding with their daughters, others display overtly aggressive behaviors that are reminders of the worst Queen Bee tactics. Subtle put-downs, ongoing manipulation, and overt intimidation can all victimize a targeted daughter. The sabotage can continue for years without detection, much as teachers often fail to pick up on covert forms of aggression in their classrooms. This leaves a daughter feeling confused and inadequate. Iris Krasnow, the author of *I Am My Mother's Daughter*, suggests that this kind of subtle subterfuge many even be at the root of eating disorders in women.

While no mother is perfect or can claim to have never spoken harshly to her daughter, we're talking about women who are mired in meanness: the only way they know how to interact with their daughters is in a relationally aggressive style. Over a lifetime, given a daughter's natural inclination and desire to believe in and trust her mother, these hurtful comments and behaviors are interpreted as an indication of some defect on the daughter's part: "Why hasn't anyone else come up with the same perceptions about me? Surely, they must be true."

Talking about Taboos

The author-journalist Victoria Secunda discusses the "Bad Mother taboo" in her book *When You and Your Mother Can't Be Friends* (1991). She believes that our society is so rooted in stereotypes about motherhood that any deviations or difficulties are assumed to be the daughter's fault. On the Amazon.com Web page for Secunda's book, readers indicate they agree, describing destructive dynamics with their mothers that include many relationally aggressive behaviors (excessive criticism, overcontrolling, guilt provoking, and manipulation). Woven through their online feedback is the desire for a close and loving relationship with their parent, tempered by the acknowledgment that this would most likely be impossible because:

- Those whose mothers are "normal" find it hard to believe anyone else's mother could be so hurtful.

- Daughters deny that their mothers' behaviors are abusive.

- Daughters blame themselves for problems in the relationship.

- The "Good Mother" myth suggests that all mothers are nurturing and incapable of harming their children.

- Daughters often assume the impossible burden of trying to make the relationship with a challenging mother "right."

- While some so-called experts suggest that it's possible to simply coexist with an abusive mother, many of those in the trenches know it's not.

Had the authorities been called in by any of these daughters or their family members, it's not likely any action would be taken; RA is in some ways a form of legalized child abuse. Nonetheless, the scars that remain are as deep as those from more overt physical and mental abuse, as shown in the following narrative.

Lesson Plans
Donna Riddlebarger

Explaining the relationship I had with my mother and understanding the nature of the conflict has taken many years. We had the ups and downs of the ordinary mother-daughter relationship and many hidden undercurrents that unconsciously predisposed me to endure an abusive marriage. The problems stemmed from the competition for my father's love and attention, and my attempt to prove I loved both parents the same. With both folks deceased, I've had time to process what progress we made.

My parents married in 1947. At thirty-three, my mother was older than most first-time brides and seven years older than my dad. That age gap seemed to be the beginning of Mom's insecurity about their relationship. After having her first baby at age thirty-seven via C-section and developing a breast abscess, she was advised not to have more children. I sometimes wonder if she was grateful for the reprieve from childbearing, but it compounded the difficulties by making our family a triangle.

When I was younger, my mom and I were buddies, but as I got older and became my father's best pal, the competition became more overt. I distinctly recall excursions with my father to get the Sunday morning bakery goodies and the newspaper, fishing trips, and running errands with him, as well as my mother's emotional distance when we'd return. She seemed to wonder what we were up to, no matter how innocently we were actually spending our time.

The worst problems occurred when I was fifteen and got involved in a love relationship with an older boy. As I look back now, I realize the relationship was overly encouraged, not to discourage me from pursuing a college education, but even to the extent where the young sailor was allowed to spend weekends sleeping on a sofa at our house so he wouldn't have to find a ride back to base. I would never do that for my fifteen-year-old daughter, but on reflection, I think my mother hoped my boyfriend would be my ticket out of her house, leaving Dad more available to her.

Two years later, I was pregnant, and the sailor and I were married, news that was met with stony silence from my mother. Her mixed messages, although unspoken, were bizarre. I was damned if I did and damned if I didn't. Mom wanted Dad's complete attention, but I was scorned for my actions in making that possible. I felt more emotionally abandoned than ever before.

By staying in my unstable and abusive marriage, I was trying to prove to my mother that I loved her enough to keep out of her way in her marriage. I moved six hundred miles away and forged the way to recovery and love. By having no friend in my mother, I had to become my *own* best friend, which took decades, but life has odd ways of forcing us to resolve what we can if we're willing. When my parents divorced after I moved away, I realized my mother had made me and my dad into her adversaries because of her own self-doubt, fear, and jealousy. Still, I thank her because she taught me to become my own advocate and good friend.

Underlying Donna's recollections of her childhood is a sense of bewilderment many can relate to. Why would her mother turn on her, when the relationship had been loving at one time? How could the woman who is supposed to protect her actually place her in harm's way by manipulating her into a marriage that turned abusive? It would be interesting to hear her mother's side of the story, which could possibly answer these questions in a way that opens the door to reconciliation.

The Ammunition

The tactics moms can use to belittle and berate are often subtle. Consider these examples:

- Nancy's mother criticizes her for her weight in front of the entire family during Thanksgiving dinner and suggests maybe she shouldn't be helping herself to seconds, especially the mashed potatoes. "They'll go right to your hips, dear," she says with a sweet smile.

■ Laura's mom refuses to send Laura to college, but dips into a savings account so Laura's sister, Lucy, can go halfway across the country to the school of her choice. She explains, "You're just not as bright as your sister, Laura. I might as well shovel my money into the garbage disposal as send you to an expensive school."

■ Diane's mom makes daily comments about Diane's "buck teeth": "No wonder you can't find a boyfriend! Who would want to kiss a mouth like yours?"

■ Iris, the mother of Joan and Tim, treats Tim with obvious partiality, priming him to be the family success and constantly putting Joan in second place. She tells her husband that Joan is a "difficult girl" who needs to be disciplined, and suggests they send her away to boarding school.

Clearly, there may be a legitimate concern underlying each of these bitter blitzes, but the point is that RA behaviors are an unhealthy way to express whatever emotions a mother may be feeling, especially when there's no off switch to temper her behavior. If friends or even other relatives treated us so shabbily, we would walk away. It's much harder to dismiss a mother from your life, because the desire for her love and approval normally remains with us throughout our lives.

The Excluding Mother

Mothers can wound by showing preferential treatment to one child and excluding another. Remember Trina's story in chapter 1? Many years later, she still recalls the hurt of her mother choosing to take only one daughter with her when she left the family.

Another woman experienced a more extreme form of abandonment, a wound she has carried into adulthood.

Left Behind
Leigh Perham

A friend told me that any mother who claimed to love all her children equally was a liar. She said that although she loved her daughters, she accepted the fact that she simply loved her son more.

I don't remember how old I was when I realized my mother loved my sister more. Maybe it was just a fact I always knew, even though I remained puzzled by her choice. My sister gathered teachers who loved her and bestowed valedictorian grades and academic honors upon her from elementary school to the completion of her Ph.D. She made my mother proud. Still, temperamentally, I was more my mother's kindred spirit. We both delighted in art and theater, literature and music, mysteries and poetry. My sister achieved success as was expected, but she never responded to the things my mother loved.

When I was nine and my sister was seven, my mother, twisted up in some unknown adult angst, took my sister and fled to Canada, leaving my father at a loss to explain to me where they had gone or what had even happened. One evening in spring, my mother simply did not come home from the college where she taught graduate students. My sister had been suddenly pulled from her second-grade classroom in the middle of a spelling test and was contending with a distraught parent, as well as losing a parent and a sister.

All my father could tell me was that my mother had removed my sister from school that morning and both of them had simply disappeared. He bought me a tuna sub at Gregory's Pizza that night. While I sat at the plastic table crunching potato chips and smushing them into my sub roll, my father plunged his straw repeatedly though the ice cubes in his Coke and tried to explain the note he had found on the desk after his afternoon class.

"I think your mother just needs some time to sort out her life. She's a complicated woman, you know."

"She is supposed to behave like an adult," I objected.

"Yes," my father agreed. "She is supposed to do that. Do you want some more chips for your sandwich?"

Reaching over to a metal rack and pulling off another bag of potato chips, he spilled them onto the table. On a normal night I would never get two bags of potato chips.

Apparently, my sister cried for seven days before my mother turned around and brought her home. Neither my father nor my mother ever spoke about the incident again, but my sister slept curled up beside me holding on to her Laurie doll for over two years.

I wonder if this explains the difficult spiritual pilgrimage that would shape my sister's life—and my willingness to keep her secrets from that point on?

Leigh's story is another example of how childhood experiences can shape the trajectory of future relationships—a trajectory that can, fortunately, be modified. As many of the women who shared stories for this book discovered, naming and claiming the hurts of their past was the first, and perhaps most powerful, step toward transformation.

10

Distressing Daughters

Can the door swing both ways? I have heard far fewer stories from mothers who openly admit to feelings of hostility toward their daughters. If anything, writing my first book, *Surviving Ophelia* convinced me that even when daughters act in overtly abusive or hurtful ways, the strongest emotion mothers report is love.

Dr. Charney Herst, a psychotherapist, offers an apt summary of what daughters want: they have grand expectations, naive assumptions, and long memories when it comes to their mothers. Mom is expected to be perfect, she's not supposed to care how she's treated, and she has never been forgiven for the one time she was late picking you up from school in first grade.

In her book *For Mothers of Difficult Daughters* (written with Lynette Padwa, 1999), Dr. Herst describes some of the more hurtful behaviors daughters regularly use to bully their mothers: brush-offs, cruel comments, manipulation by guilt, and disrespectful treatment. As a counselor and therapist, her training took place during an era when mothers were blamed for every problem their children experienced, which she believes caused women to hesitate to criticize their daughters for their behavior.

Dr. Herst and I must have been reading the same textbooks—I got the same indoctrination in my doctoral program, and I have continued to be amazed at the parenting double standard (especially in the area of eating disorders, a situation described as "mother bashing" in my book *The Starving Family*). A mother who called her daughter a bitch and accused her of loving her father more than she loved her mother would be considered abusive, yet the same kind of message from a daughter is tolerated.

Herst writes about the time she took a chance and spoke up about difficulties she was having with her daughters, only to be roundly chastised by her colleagues and classmates. This was the motivation for her book, which reveals the downside of mothering daughters, who have the capacity to be aggressive and bullying throughout their lives, just like mothers.

I've received plenty of e-mails about such daughters, but I have yet to read a "Daughter Dearest" equivalent of the Joan Crawford book. Is this because "mother abuse" is considered a normal part of the parenting relationship, while child abuse is not? Mothers are often the first person daughters turn to in times of distress, but their intense emotions may lead to an attack instead of a request for help.

The Lightning Rod

"My daughter is always in a state of crisis," Elaine told me at a party. "If it isn't one thing, it's another, but who does she always get mad at? Me. She'll say the meanest things she can think of to me, and then, ten minutes later, ask me to babysit!"

Elaine isn't the first mother to complain that her daughter (rather than her son) becomes nasty to her when personal difficulties occur. Another discouraged mother told me:

> My twenty-six-year-old daughter has turned our house into a living nightmare. Part of it is due to her eating disorder, which causes her to lash out at me when she's angry or malnourished. Another part of it is that I am the classic "victim"—willing to do almost anything to make her well. If she tells me to go to the store and buy a certain food, I do it. Oddly enough, I am much the same at work. If there's extra work to be done, I'm there finishing it long after everyone else has gone home to their families and a nice dinner. My daughter makes fun of me for that too and calls me a wimp. She says I have no spine. Some days I am simply exhausted from trying to keep up with her insults and put-downs—yes, I feel like that eighth-grader everyone threw

spitballs at because she was such a loser, but I have no idea how to break out of this pattern.

This woman has clearly failed to achieve what the author Deborah Tannen believes is our deepest wish: "to be understood and approved of by our mothers and our daughters."

Dear but Difficult Daughters

Deborah Spungen, the mother of Nancy Spungen (who was murdered in her early twenties by the punk rocker Sid Vicious of the popular British music group the Sex Pistols) describes her tortured journey with a daughter doctors insisted was normal. In her bittersweet memoir, *And I Don't Want to Live This Life*, Deborah says her daughter began life with a difficult birth that seemed to set the tone for the rest of her days. Deborah faced challenge after challenge with her daughter, resorting to many institutionalizations and ongoing therapy for Nancy in the hope that something would help a loved child who was clearly in distress, despite medical opinions to the contrary.

Constantly on the attack, Nancy intimidated her mother, her sister, her brother, her father, babysitters, and her grandmother, threatening to kill them for no apparent reason, in addition to launching more subtle verbal assaults in between her violent outbursts. She accused her mother of not loving her (a daughter's most powerful weapon), made fun of and taunted her sister, and manipulated situations to her advantage.

Deborah does not offer a single complaint about her daughter—if anything, she continues to see the good person she believed was inside Nancy, dismissing the outward behavior as a consequence of substance abuse or another unknown problem. After one disturbing incident, she says, "What I really wanted to do was shake her and scream: 'Look what you've become! You're not my Nancy! Where's my Nancy? I want my Nancy back!' There was no point in saying anything to her. I couldn't reach her. She was lost to me. My arms ached to hold the baby Nancy, ached for a fresh start."

In *Hold Me Close, Let Me Go* by the journalist Adair Lara, and *Augusta, Gone* by the writer Martha Tod Dudman, more loving stories of daughters who went through a challenging adolescence are shared. In both books, mothers are targeted for the worst types of relationally aggressive behaviors, as if the daughters understood instinctively that their words had tremendous power to wound.

Single mother Dudman, whose daughter became involved with drugs, recalls a moment where she thought, "Just talking with her is like sticking your hand in a garbage disposal." Desperate for help, she sent her daughter Augusta to a therapeutic school where regular meetings with parents were required. One session involved Augusta reading her a list of ten deeply personal complaints that summarized Martha's failures as a mother: not listening, not acting like she loved Augusta, not being there when Augusta needed her, and so on. After the session was over, Dudman says, "I am stunned by everything Augusta has said. She's right, I think dumbly." Nonetheless, still in a state of shock, she returned to the school the next day to take her daughter out for a special lunch, pretending none of the hurtful things had been said. (Dudman was never asked to share a list of her complaints about her daughter.)

In her book, Lara recalls an incident when her daughter Morgan was openly defiant, telling her to "suck dick" when she didn't get her way. The insult was rendered more hurtful when Morgan accused her mother of always having to have things her own way. Lara writes, "I walked out of the room, so shocked that I felt as if the room were tilting. I remember only a few months ago, bragging to somebody about how close she and I had stayed, how she never called me names, and never said she hated me." Despite the nastiness she received from her daughter, Lara continued to support her and to try to find a way to make things better, always responding to insults and put-downs with attempts to help Morgan.

When mothers are cruel to daughters, it causes lifelong scars. When daughters are cruel to mothers, the offenses are forgotten in a wash of love and guilt. My friend Julie has a daughter, Tia, who was particularly hurtful during adolescence, tormenting her mother with words and behaviors that might sound silly in retrospect, but that broke Julie's heart. The repertoire included making fun of her mother by mimicking her in front of others, ruining clothes that she "borrowed" without permission, sulking when she didn't get her way, and even reporting her mother to school authorities for abuse after Julie lost her cool and screamed at Tia to stop being so difficult. Now Tia is grown, and her relationship with Julie is much improved, perhaps because she has a child of her own. Nonetheless, Julie tells me, "I still never let my guard down around her. I have forgiven all the things that were said and done, but I will never forget that she has the capacity to show absolute hatred toward me."

Another midlife mother expresses similar feelings in the following story.

Bruised Heart
Anonymous

Last week I saw the engagement announcement of one of my daughter's high school classmates in our local paper. I couldn't stop looking at the lovely image smiling back at me, and remembering the few times I'd spoken to the young woman who was now starting a new life with a handsome man and a promising career.

"She's one of the nice ones," my son had said years ago, when I asked if he knew the girl in the picture.

His sister was not—is not. I denied that for a long time, and even now I don't like to say it, but it's true. She's not nice. It's a topic I don't discuss, because who would believe a daughter could break her mother's heart and then say it was deserved?

She's graduating from college now, so I know her mommy meanness isn't just a passing phase. She would never treat anyone else the way she does me. Is it abuse when your daughter writes a two-word note that says only F—— You! Will there be a time when she doesn't plunge that verbal sword of hers into my heart, telling me I'm a horrible mother and that I never really loved her?

She was in therapy, and I asked the counselor if the things my daughter said were the signs of a tormented mind, rather than just her normal personality. The therapist evaded my question until I asked it right out: "Can she control this?"

"Yes. I think it's completely voluntary," she finally answered, avoiding my eyes.

"Completely voluntary" makes it even worse, because I'm the only one she targets with this behavior. I'm not a perfect mom, maybe not even a good one, but I'm not the total failure she makes me out to be . . . or so I tell myself.

It's sad and ironic that one of the closest relationships in a woman's life can also be the most devastating—it's a door that swings both ways. Regardless, mothers seem reluctant and even unable to give up on their connections to their daughters.

Breaking Through

Part of a mother's challenge is communicating with daughters in a way that establishes a connection and finding shared interests to bond around, whether for the sake of adult and child or siblings. My friend Marcia has a daughter in her late teens, and she often wonders if they have anything in common. "We couldn't be more different," Marcia told me, "and because of that I feel she doesn't really love me in the same way my son does—in fact she seems to go out of her way to do things that will offend me and emphasize how different we are, always in an 'in your face' way. She doesn't miss an opportunity to comment negatively on my weight, my hair, or my clothes—things that are off-limits in my conversation with her."

Marcia ended our conversation by saying, "It's true that I love her—but that's because she's my daughter. I can't say that I like her much at all."

The same goes for Beth, a mother of four, but most frustrated with her daughter, the oldest. "I can't believe she would expose her sisters to her behavior," she said, describing an incident in which her daughter "set her up" to appear physically abusive in front of her other children, insinuating that Beth had also mistreated the sisters. "She told me I play favorites, and that I had always liked her younger brother better. This went on over the course of a day, but it was all so subtle that I actually felt like the bitch she was making me out to be." Beth went on to describe her daughter's confrontational personality, which included making belittling comments about her mom when they were at large social gatherings. Then she confessed, "I can't say I'll be sorry when she's out of my life."

Clearly Beth was dismayed by her feelings, but her daughter may discover a wisdom Iris Krasnow points out in her book *I Am My*

Mother's Daughter: "What felt like a bad mother at age fifteen can feel like a good mother—or at least an okay mother—by age fifty." In the meantime, Beth tries to do the little things that might show her daughter how much she wants their relationship to be better: a pretty barrette for her hair, a book of poetry, a blouse the color of her eyes. It works—until the next time there's a problem and Beth is the convenient target.

Righting Relationships

An illness such as anorexia or other mental health problems can challenge the mother-daughter relationship on many levels, as can the normal ups and downs of adolescence. However, there are daughters who seem to get stuck in an RA persona for life. My years in geriatrics brought me in contact with the best and worst of grown daughters. There were many times when I walked out of a house or an exam room and was struck by the near sainthood of a caregiver, but just as often I exited shaking my head at the bullying interaction between an adult daughter and her frail mother.

A mother's concerns about RA aren't necessarily limited to one daughter, or to how daughters treat their mothers. Kin-keeping women long to have their children get along well with one another, and to show signs of a shared bond that will outlive their mother. The following story shows a different aspect of dealing with daughters, speaking to a mother's desire for healthy sibling relationships among her children.

Drawing Blood from Nonblood
Barbara Trainin Blank

Nothing in my own life had prepared me for the rivalry, hostility, even hatred between my daughters, a hatred mitigated only recently and then incompletely. There have been times I've literally had to pull them apart, as my physically stronger elder child would pummel her sister, and the younger, more verbal one would hurl insults. By the time she turned thirteen, my younger daughter had been pinched, squeezed, hit, aggressively tickled, and pounded. She in turn had screamed out such pleasantries as "stupid," "reject," and "pervert" and had accused me of not stopping the abuse she was suffering. My older daughter retorted with "Miss Perfect" and then blamed me for loving her sister more than her, if I loved her at all.

My brother and I are close, and although the degree of that closeness has varied during the different times of our lives, never had there been any cursing, screaming, or long-term feuding, let alone violence, between us. Perhaps the reason was that my brother and I are three years apart and of opposite genders. We didn't compete for friends or interests (in our youth, we happened to fall comfortably into the stereotypes of sports versus dolls). Or perhaps it was that both of us are biological siblings, although our starkly different appearances led many to conclude otherwise.

My children, in contrast, are twenty-one months apart. My older daughter is adopted, the younger, biological. I've tried to raise them with equal love and respect, but that isn't always easy, especially when they have such different temperaments. It is true my biological daughter looks and sounds more like me and has adopted more of my interests (or inherited them, for who knows how to sort out the nature-nurture conundrum?). I've often wished both my children had been adopted, so they could have started life on an equal footing. But then there probably isn't a combination of siblings on earth who can't foment rivalry.

Still, the intensity of their particular rivalry has been one of those long shadows over my life. Once I was so maddened when my older daughter intentionally caused her sister's nose to bleed that I scratched her face and drew blood. It never happened again, but it was one of those horrible moments that comes to you when you're feeling down about your parenting skills and despairing that the two of them will never get along, let alone be friends.

Of late, they haven't been fighting, but I can't say for sure if the thaw is real or long-lasting. Possibly it's only a truce brought about by distance, since the younger one is now attending boarding school out of town. We'll see what the summer brings. (During spring break, at least, there were few arguments or even teasing, and you'd think they were actually, well, sisters!) We keep telling the girls the usual clichés, that someday we won't be around and they'll have to be there for each other.

Speaking of clichés, I was offered plenty over the years from well-meaning people. Some refused to believe my older daughter could be so aggressive because, as they said, girls may be "catty," but they're never that "physical." Others said they "know" her, and can't believe this sweet, shy girl could possibly pummel her sister, let alone draw blood. So much for stereotypes and people who think they know children better than their parents do.

At other times, women regaled me with stories of how they used to fight with their sisters but now are "the best of friends." Others promised the problems would evaporate after some life-altering crisis. My fear is that this "crisis" will be my death, and I won't get to see the newfound peace and sisterly love between them except from a heavenly perch.

In the end, maybe a most-of-the-year school separation and sheer maturation will improve things more than any theories or inadequate attempts on my part. Maybe they'll marry men who like each other and who will propel a troubled relationship in a new, brighter direction. Maybe they'll have children who accuse them of favoritism, and they'll realize how stupid it is to expect perfection of parents any more than of themselves. Or maybe they'll have children who want to hang out together. I hope!

Ironically, as I was in the middle of writing this book, a distant cousin shared a similar, somewhat tragic story with me. Her husband's stepmother tried throughout her life to create a sense of closeness between her two biological children and her two stepchildren. It didn't happen—until, as Barbara feared, the mother died. Now those children have forgotten whatever it was that separated them in the first place and are closer than they ever were during her lifetime.

11

Sweetly Sinister Sisters

Okay, I admit it. From time to time, I coach my nieces and nephews to say, "Aunt Cheryl is my favorite aunt!" (It counts only if said with great sincerity and enthusiasm.) While I never suggest it, secretly I hope that sometime, at a large family gathering, one of them will spontaneously burst forth with this declaration, which will establish me once and for all as Number One Aunt. What can I say? I'm the oldest of three sisters and one brother—I'm expected to be the best at everything.

Of course, this is good-natured rivalry, but it is also part of the way my family relates, as it is with many others. And sometimes, teasing or good-natured competition can turn into tension. A friend I had lunch with recently shook her head and admitted with regret that she, too, is an oldest sibling. "I've always been jealous of my sister because she's prettier than me," she said, "but I suspect that's nothing compared to how she feels about *me* because of all the times my parents compared us."

Wanted: A Sister

There are no guidelines for being a sister. Susan Scarf Merrell (1995) describes siblings as living through "relationships without rules." Sisters can be nurturing and helpful toward each other, or they can be cruel and destructive. How does one differentiate between normal sibling rivalry and a truly sinister sister?

Consider sisters Libby and Marci, who "just don't get along." For the sake of their mother, they agree to attend family get-togethers, but while there, they maintain as much distance between them as possible. "Marci is, quite frankly, emotionally brain-damaged—she always has been," relates Libby. "She and my first husband used to make fun of me to my face, commenting on how fat and frumpy I was after I had my kids. One day I blew up at her and told my husband I didn't ever want to see her again. Granted, he was a jerk too, but she's my sister. She's supposed to feel *something* positive for me. You'd never know it if she does—ever since we were kids she's been just plain mean."

Margaret Mead has observed that "sisterhood is probably the most competitive relationship within the family." At the same time, the journalist Roxanne Brown points out that although the sister-sister relationship is more intense than the brother-sister relationship, sisters can often nurture and support one another in ways that are more profound than any other relationship. Her hypothesis is supported by Debra Ginsberg's memoir *About My Sisters.* Ginsberg is open in sharing both the ups and downs of her relationships with her siblings, but she conveys a strong message of special love and caring that seems unique to female siblings.

Some experts believe sisters can shape our gender identity and self-esteem in ways that are as significant as a mother's influence. In a society where two parents are not necessarily the norm, it is still likely that there will be a sibling, and Dr. Dennis E. Chestnut, the president of the Association of Black Psychologists, believes that when there is more than one child in a family, competition will be greatest between same-sex siblings, especially when they are close in age. The noted psychologist Vern Bengston further elaborates on the complexities of sibling relationships: there are both egalitarian and hierarchical aspects, so it isn't surprising for sisters to be both friends and bullies to one another at different times.

My Penn State colleague Dr. Susan McHale, a professor of human development, is a noted researcher on sibling relationships. Her studies show that girls who grow up without a sister but with a brother tend to seek out girlfriends more readily, and work with her team documented that sister-sister relationships were more intense, at least in adolescence.

The Long-Term Impact

Sisters: Devoted or Divided?, a book by the author and academic Susan Shapiro Barash, contains a telling quote by the psychologist Ronnie Burak: "Often the nature of the adult relationship is a reaction to the character of the childhood relationship." This means that women's adult friendships can be shaped, for better or worse, by the formative experiences they had with their sisters, perhaps in the very ways Dr. McHale has documented. In addition, the quality of the relationship may play a role: if it was rife with relational aggression, you and your sister may find yourselves replaying the roles of victim and bully, or bystander, with women you're not related to, perhaps for the rest of your life.

The researcher Aurora Sherman and her colleagues examined this issue further in a study of 102 young adults, concluding that adolescent relationships with siblings have a profound influence on relationships formed outside the family in adulthood. Among their findings:

- Same-gender friendships were less conflicted than sibling relationships.

- Women reported more conflict with siblings than men did.

- Siblings who scored highest on conflict in their relationships were also lonelier and had lower self-esteem.

- Having a satisfactory same-gender friendship could make up for having difficult sibling relationships.

- There may even be similarities between our sibling relationships and our friendships; that is, we seek out friends who are like our sisters.

Researchers question whether sibling relationships might improve when those involved are no longer living together and therefore not engaged in as much day-to-day conflict. Dr. McHale tells me many of her students energetically agree that this is true—being away at college offers a new appreciation and tolerance for siblings.

The Best of Friends

While sister RA is an issue for some, in other situations sisters can seem to fulfill all of a woman's needs for companionship. In Barash's book Dr. Ronald Cohen says this of sisterhood: "When it works, it really works, providing a sacred bond that few of us outside its realm can comprehend."

Offhand, I can immediately think of two friends that statement applies to. They are so close to their sisters it seems there couldn't possibly be reason or opportunity for RA in their relationships. They never argue, they understand each other intuitively, and they seem not to need any other women pals than each other. Who wouldn't envy that?

I do have somewhat of the same situation (if you delete the words "never argue" from the previous sentence) with my "baby" sister, Elizabeth, who was born in my senior year of high school. (Her children can't believe that I used to change their mom's diapers.) Our lives have paralleled one another's in interesting and unpredictable ways, and we now live only a few miles apart. She's at the top of my mental Rolodex of female pals to call on in times of trouble because, amazingly, she has an instant understanding of my feelings, and a shared perspective on life that's hard to duplicate in a nonrelative.

Expect More, Accept Less

Often, our relationships with our sisters come bound with expectations that are higher than those we might have of a female friend. One of my younger colleagues described it well: "If my sister says something hurtful, I just can't let go of it like I would with a friend." At the same time, sisters are often, but not always, granted a latitude we are less willing to give a gal pal.

Recently, my sister Elizabeth listened to ten minutes of complaining about book deadlines, work responsibilities, kid concerns, and life in general. After my long rant she was silent for a second, and then commented, "Gee, look who has a 'poor me' complex today." I laughed at her directness—but I wonder if a similar comment from a friend would have seemed quite so amusing.

When a sister hurts you, how far can or should loyalty go? Your bond with her can be as close as the mother-daughter one, with many of the same expectations, but with less of the same loyalty, unless you're like Renae in chapter 1. Depending on birth order, our sisters may have known us all our lives, so their support—or judgment—can be all-important.

After interviewing hundreds of women, the sociologist Marcia Mullman attributes some sister conflicts to the difference between an imagined sister and a real one. She describes the imagined sister as one we craft out of our dreams and needs. Too often, it is the imagined sister we relate to and are disappointed by.

A young woman I'll call Sarah understands this concept well. For a lifetime, she has longed for a relationship with her sister that was apparently not meant to be. In her twenties, the hurt was still audible in her voiced as she shared her story.

> I grew up with one sister and one brother (my parents adopted another sister after I moved out of the house to go to college, so I have two altogether). Anna was three years younger than me, so I naturally expected we would be close friends, especially as we got older. Instead, she ended up favoring our brother, Bill, who was two years younger than her. Sometimes her preference for him was almost embarrassing—she would leave me mid-conversation if he walked in the room and run to his side. As we got older and had kids, she extended that preference to the nieces and nephews, doing things for his kids she would never do for mine. They vacationed together, and at family get-togethers she would always be right next to him. Sometimes I wondered how his wife felt about "sharing" her husband with my sister!
>
> When I approached my sister about my desire for a closer relationship, she made it clear that it was too late for that to happen. I guess I had made a major mistake with her at some point in my life, but how can I correct it if I don't know what it was? Meanwhile, my younger adopted sister is my parents' obvious favorite—she came from a rough situation so they've spent years trying to compensate for that. Where does that leave me?

In a way, I can empathize with part of Sarah's story. My mom and her only sister have always been close—I know my aunt Nellie well, and I have always recognized that she was an important part of our family. With that role model, I assumed my next-youngest sister and I would share a similar relationship (my version of the imagined sister). What I failed to consider was that I graduated and left home during her high school years, while our brother, who is only eighteen months younger than her, was still there, sharing teachers, car rides, and acquaintances. Naturally, she grew closer to him. But when I read Debra Ginsberg's description of her sisters as "the keepers of one another's secrets and protectors of one another's childhood memories," I wished that my imagined sister could be real.

Tessa, a nurse at a large urban hospital, never felt safe around her older sister: "She used our childhood to humiliate me whenever she could." Tessa recalled her sister revealing incidents (always in public) that although long past, she would have preferred to keep private.

Like Sarah and Tessa, my friend Caryn never got along with her older sister, Lenore. While Caryn and her two younger brothers were able to work out the occasional conflicts they had, there was no end to her trouble with Lenore. "She always stole my things and went out of her way to make life miserable for me. Her biggest talent was 'guilting me' into doing something I didn't want to do. She'd say, 'Come on, you're my sister,' and I'd do it. At home, she and her friends treated me like their servant, but at least I was included. At school, when they saw me and I'd say 'hi,' they acted like I didn't exist." Caryn, the founder of a successful business, frowned as she shared further details with me.

Put-downs, humiliation, and manipulation are behaviors remarkably similar to the mean tactics I hear about from middle-school girls on a weekly basis when I meet with them through my programs. Caryn's wounds, which began in adolescence, are understandably deep. She left home the summer after her senior year and didn't bother to stay in touch with Lenore. Like Tessa, Libby, and myself, she still can't leave her imagined sister behind.

Ten years later, the only news Caryn has of Lenore are tidbits of information passed along by their mother, who constantly voices her wish for the girls to be closer. Caryn refuses, recalling the last time she was with her older sister: "She deliberately flirted with the man I brought to a family wedding, right in front of me!"

That's enough to keep her living on the opposite side of the country, avoiding her sister and choosing to see her brothers or parents only when there's little chance Lenore will be involved. Still, she misses that bond of unconditional trust that she sees in other sisters. "One of my friends calls her sister cross-country *every* day to talk. She tells me her sister is her best friend, which I already sensed. I may be someone she pals around with, but I know I will never replace her sister. It makes me sad and envious at the same time."

Ginsberg offered an essential truth about sisters that she realized shortly after she ended a relationship with her lover: "At that moment, I also knew this: men leave, my sister would always be there."

Lessons Learned

According to Vern Bengston and his family therapist colleagues, the sibling tie is unusual in that it lasts longer than others, but normally involves a lower level of mutual obligation. During times of parental need, this sense of obligation increases, but more toward their parents than to one another. Not that siblings are united—tremendous conflicts can emerge over how much caring should be provided to Mom and Dad, and by whom. When caregiving demands become extreme, even the most compatible of siblings can have conflict, which I have witnessed time and again. (I attribute some of this to the high demands placed on families, especially women, for complex levels of caregiving at home, formerly provided by around-the-clock nurses in the hospital.)

Sisters can be caregivers, but they can also be sparring partners. Are sisters the testing ground for female rivalry and competition? Do women who grow up with one or more sisters learn to navigate the rocky road of RA better than their sisterless peers?

Women I've asked think so. Norma, a teacher of middle-school girls, told me she can almost pick out those who had sisters: "In some ways it's better for them, because they've learned to have conflict with their own gender. At the same time, they've mastered the 'tricks of the trade' in a way the other girls haven't."

The Mom Factor

The academic and author Melanie Mauthner notes that "the relationship between sisters is always deeply affected by the relationship each has had with their parents, especially their mothers. So there is always something of a triangle in the bonds between sisters and their mothers." She believes that mothers mediate the relationship between sisters, sometimes even aligning them against one another.

When roles are switched, and one sister becomes a caregiver or mother substitute to another, feelings are much harder to sort out. The next story describes a woman's attempt to resolve the complex relationship she had with her sister—and, by default, her mother.

My Sister's Religion
Leigh Perham

My sister fell in love with the junior minister at our church at sixteen. Compelling in that intensely attentive way that encourages girls to trust men, Terrance always had a half-smoked cigarette between his fingers. We did not care about Christ's sacrifice for our immortal souls, we cared that he noticed our new Shetland sweaters and blue eye shadow. The Youth Fellowship met in the rummage-sale living room of Terrance's house at seven o'clock every Sunday night. His wife, a feminist activist, haunted Washington, D.C., with busloads of other disgruntled women to champion causes from equal opportunity to armpit hair. Those of us condemned by our parents to weekly religious youth fellowship speculated about how Terrance had ended up married to a hairy-legged, army-booted activist who was always trying to provoke us out of our suburban cheerleader mentality.

At YF meetings, ensconced in his leather chair, Terrance would search our faces, inviting all of us to believe, not in God, but in him. After meetings the church ladies provided no-name-brand soda and cookies and the girls crowded around Terrance, high-strung hounds sniffing the boots of the master of the hunt. He listened to each of us as if we mattered, but I did not miss his hand drifting to my sister's bare shoulder, or his thumb as it hooked underneath her Peter Pan collar. It was evident to me that my sister had to be within the circle of his British Sterling scent, within the possibility of his touch—clear enough to make me look around to see if any of the other girls noticed.

They only noticed Terrance. Gentle, generous, and guilt-ridden, Terrance embodied passion for us and was the love of my sister's life.

"Someone is going to find out," I whispered when Mrs. Oxford's station wagon backed out of our driveway one night. "You don't even bother to hide it anymore."

"I love him," she whispered.

Despite the fact that he promised her a love filled with a passion foreign to his own marriage, Terrance could not summon the courage to act in the face of his Midwest, farm boy, Christian cornfield heritage. In her room next to mine, my sister wept for him, hugging her worn baby doll.

I wondered how my mother, a child psychologist with a stack of book titles beneath her Ph.D., could be so oblivious to her own daughter and the after-school sessions in the rectory. I was the one who garnered the blatant parental troubleshooting—skirts so short that the assistant principal sent me home on a regular basis from school, debates with teachers ending in multiple detentions, refusal to attend gym classes I deemed senseless, editorials in the school newspaper sparking angry responses in the editorial section of the local newspaper . . . and the time I ran away for two days.

I would sometimes sit on my sister's bed, the streetlight falling across the worn fibers of her navy blanket, listening as she whispered into the mothball-scented darkness. With some sympathy and some jealousy, I learned of her continuing pilgrimages to Terrance's bed despite her pain and desperation.

My mother should have been the comforting one, but there was nothing to be done. As a therapist, she provided counsel for a hundred and fifty dollars an hour in the office beneath my sister's bedroom. My sister used to throw her stuffed animals out her window into the snow just to get a rise from the sobbing patients huddled on the couch below, but only I noticed.

Although my mother never confronted my sister over Terrance, eventually she must have drawn her own conclusions, because one summer she sent my sister off to an overnight camp in Maine as a crafts counselor. My parents were going out of the country, so I was the one who received the call a few weeks later.

"Your sister has had her stomach pumped. She will be fine, but you better come and get her." It turned out that my sister had been treated in the emergency room after taking an entire bottle of aspirin.

I would have to drive from Boston to rescue my sister from Maine. It would mean leaving my boyfriend, warm in my parents' bed, and returning into forests, which I had never liked. Individual trees in the park were okay, but not woods.

When I arrived, the doctor took a chewed pencil from beneath his limp mustache long enough to speak: "You should consider getting her some help."

Help! "Well, no shit. Tell me something I didn't already know."

Unsure of what to do about a sister who had attempted suicide, I put her in the car and brought her back home. I sure as hell did not want to be her caretaker for what was left of my summer, but I decided not to call my mother and father in Europe. I did not want my parents on the next plane home, and I did not want a summer of psychoanalytical bullshit sending my boyfriend fleeing from my bed in search of a less complicated vacation break. I thought my sister might ask for my mother, but she didn't.

I kept my sister at home for three endless days. She wouldn't eat, take a shower, or come out of her room. With dirty hair stringy across her face and shoulders hunched around her Laurie doll, she scared the hell out of my boyfriend.

In the end, I gave up and called Terrance. He came, very much the competent minister. He gathered her into his arms, brushed her hair away from her swollen eyes, and let her cry. The sobbing was the first real sound she had made in three days. He fed her soup, packed her clothes—all the while talking to her with the gentleness of a man handling an injured bird.

"What are you going to do with her?" I demanded.

"Whatever she needs me to do," he replied. Despite knowing what I knew, I hesitated only momentarily because I did not want to care for her—nor did I know how.

My sister spent the remainder of the summer in the rectory behind the church. I had my summer vacation, and she had the last of her only love.

When Terrance's wife unearthed his secret, she was seven months pregnant. Guessing correctly that Terrance's affair with my sister was not a momentary lapse in judgment, she issued an ultimatum. At seventeen, my sister would have followed him to the cornfields of Iowa, even to his God's heaven, but Terrance's wife held his unborn child as ransom. She packed up her banners and slogans and prepared to return to the safety of the Midwest. Terrance would have to sacrifice my sister or his child.

In the end, whether courageous or cowardly, he followed his child and let the cornfields swallow him back. My sister was abandoned by Terrance, abandoned by God, and abandoned by love. She had no appetite for anything more. I do not know if my sister ever told my mother what happened. I never did—until now.

Leigh's story captures almost every emotion sisters can feel for each other: love, anger, resentment, jealousy, frustration, and loyalty, however begrudging. Like Renae's story in chapter 1, a relationship with your sister can be more important than any other, for better *and* for worse. When a sister void exists, you may search throughout life for that special other who understands, accepts, and loves you as only a sibling can. Sometimes you're lucky enough to find her.

PART THREE

In-Laws and Others

12

Mothers and Sisters, by Law

The sisters and mothers we grow up with aren't the only ones who challenge us. A brother's wife or a husband's mother can thrust families into a state of chaos and disrupt previously happy relationships. While virtually any female relative can buzz into a woman's life like a Queen Bee, using a variety of hurtful behaviors to wound, in-laws seem to provoke a special brand of venom and rivalry, even when husbands (the brothers and sons) get along fairly well. The lack of a blood tie may make the situation worse, since women may not be inclined to give in-laws the same benefit of the doubt as they would other kin.

Bothersome Behaviors

Dr. Bree Allinson, the author of the book *How to Deal with Your Mother-in-Law*, is a therapist who works with many women experiencing relationship problems. Curious to know if there were specific types of problems or pleasures, she polled one hundred married women about their relationships with their mothers-in-law. Her results showed that women believed:

- Their mothers-in-law were nice initially, then changed a little (60 percent).
- Their mothers-in-law changed for the worse when they realized their sons were getting married (65 percent).

▌ Their husbands (the sons) were unaware of any hostility directed at their wives (70 percent).

Here are some of the examples of bothersome mother-in-law behaviors Dr. Allinson received:

▌ Blaming the woman but not the man for having premarital sex

▌ Not inviting the fiancée to occasions all other family members were invited to

▌ Showing up late to the wedding

▌ Keeping wedding gifts

After the marriage, faux pas included:

▌ Interfering

▌ Excluding the new daughter-in-law

Each of these behaviors sounds remarkably like the stockpile of relational aggression strategies we've already discussed. The in-law relationship is different, however, because the parties involved were usually strangers to each other before the couple's romantic involvement began.

Here are some stories of mother-in-law missteps that have been shared with me:

▌ Tracy's mother-in-law bought Christmas gifts that only her son would obviously enjoy, but addressed them to the couple.

▌ Barb's mother-in-law organized meals so that the men were at one end of the table with her, and the children at the other with Barb.

▌ Mary's mother-in-law went into hysterics when her son informed her he'd be spending his birthday with his wife only.

▌ Manipulative but long-suffering Rita let her daughter-in-law Sydney know it was okay not to visit every week. (She wasn't going to be around much longer anyway, so why not get used to it?)

Bad Beginnings

Sometimes warning signs begin to flash before a bride takes her first step down the aisle. The following excerpt from an interview with

Wendy describes a relationship destined for challenges, but one that could benefit from some "preventive health" intervention.

Wendy and her fiancé, Joe, live close to both of their families, so there were many personalities to please as they planned their wedding. The most challenging, however, was Wendy's future mother-in-law. Shortly after the couple became officially engaged, a conflict arose when Wendy was asked what she thought about a highly charged political issue and she politely disagreed with the prevailing opinions. Her innocent remark ("That's just my opinion") led to a full-scale female family feud, with Joe's mom calling him late one night and asking him to come over and discuss his relationship with Wendy. Here's part of what followed the next time Wendy and Joe's mom met face-to-face:

> Joe told his mom, "Next time we have an issue, I think we just need to sit down in the beginning and talk about it when it is all fresh in our mind and then everybody that is concerned should be there."
>
> So she looks at me right away and says: "You mean to tell me that I am not allowed to talk to my son unless you are around?"
>
> I said, "No, nobody said that. What Joe is trying to say is that if you have an actual issue and it concerns me, we should all sit down and you can talk to me and we will try to work it out because there is no point in talking to Joe about me. What is he supposed to say?"
>
> Joe's mom didn't hear that and kept focusing on her initial concern, saying, 'That's ridiculous, that I can't talk to my son unless you are around."
>
> She was actually yelling and going off on a tangent about Joe's grandpa and how my parents raised me, and how she doesn't like them because of how they raised me. I told her she doesn't even know my family, but she just kept ranting.
>
> Then she said, "I'm going to wait for Susan [Joe's adult sister, who is five or six years younger than him] to come home."
>
> So Susan finally came home, and all Susan said to Joe was: "I feel like I am losing a brother, like I can't talk to you anymore."
>
> Joe said, "Susan, we were never close, but you know, you're my sister and if you need to talk to me, you can always talk to me, but it's not like we talked and went and did things every day. We were never really that close."

In this situation, Joe tried to blend Wendy into his existing family, rather than breaking away, creating a new family, and notifying his parents after the fact. His strategy backfired as his mother and sister threw up one roadblock after another. (Joe's dad was completely supportive of the engagement.) The situation became further complicated by a subtle rivalry between Wendy and Susan, who had young daughters close in age. "Susan started saying that my daughter is bad and her daughter is good. I had my daughter's party in March, and a week later she had her daughter's party. Joe's brother's girlfriend, Holly, told me the whole time Susan was decorating for Krystin's party, she was saying how she was going to outdo me and how her party was going to be better than mine."

The overt competition over whose children were best, along with a subtle competition for Joe's affections, continued. Even Holly got involved:

> Holly had not been a part of the family very long. The weekend before Easter I met her for about the third time and we were kind of talking, and just out of the blue she says to me, "If I have to hear about what happened with you, Joe, and his mom one more time I am going to puke."
>
> I said, "What do you mean?"
>
> Holly told me Joe's mom brought up the previous argument that happened with me and Joe and his mom. Joe's mom had been telling her everything.
>
> Holly told me, "I have only been a part of the family about four or five months and right away she started going off on this tangent about this argument and about you and how rude you are and everything else. I told Matt, 'I don't know what to expect from your brother's fiancée. I am really afraid to meet her.' Joe's mom made you into this really horrible person before I met you, and I was afraid to even meet you. Then once I met you, I asked Joe's mom, 'What's wrong with her? She is really nice.' From then on, every time I would talk to you, Joe's mom would say to me behind your back, 'So what did you think of her? So what did you think?'"

Wendy was completely overwhelmed by the situation and told me, "I was floored. I couldn't believe things had gotten so out of hand."

The women in this situation were immersed in a no-holds-barred RA battle that involved:

▌ Provoking guilt (manipulation)

▌ Verbal harassment

▌ Gossip

▌ Rivalry

▌ Rumors

All of their conflict was peripheral to the relationship they shared with Joe. As Wendy talked further, I discovered that Joe's mom and dad had divorced when he was in high school and that he was the only one of her four children who elected to remain with their father, for very practical reasons—he didn't want to change high schools. Nonetheless, the details of the "female family feud" Wendy shared with me suggested that Joe's mom had never gotten over his earlier choice, and that she now considered his pending marriage to be another rejection of her.

The circumstances surrounding Wendy's situation shaped the way each woman responded:

▌ Wendy's previous marriage and having a young daughter made her concerned about Joe's dependability.

▌ Joe's regular practice of stopping over to see his mom every night until he met Wendy had created a ritual of sorts that signaled his affection for his mom.

▌ A sister-in-law-to-be (Susan) who was also divorced with a child, but dependent on her mother rather than independent like Wendy, would inevitably lead to comparisons and possible resentment.

Although divorce and stepparenting will be discussed separately, it is clear that a greater likelihood of conflict exists when the family is split: old wounds resurface, new alliances are formed, and the needs of former in-laws, who share a biological tie with any children from the marriage, must be taken into consideration.

Her Little Boy, Your Big Man

A line from the play *Daughter-in-Law* by D. H. Lawrence summarizes the mother-in-law dilemma well: "How is a woman to have a husband when all the men belong to their mothers?" Ayelet Waldman describes how she handled the delicate process of dividing the man from his mother in a bittersweet essay published in the book *I Married My Mother-in-Law*. Now a mother, Ayelet admits to feeling an illicit pleasure over her own young son's stated intent to marry her, but she remembers believing it was her "job to step between her [future mother-in-law] and her son." In subtle ways, Ayelet staked her claim on her husband's affections over the years. Then the arrival of her own sons changed many things, including the realization that her mother-in-law was not a rival, but an ally, joined in mutual love for all the children they shared.

Few women entangled in wife–mother-in-law RA are conflicted about their feelings.

"Think about it," said my friend Lenore. "You've got a little boy who is at the center of the universe for two women. Both will do anything he wants in order to be 'top dog.' They may scratch each other's eyes out, but to him they're both sweet as pie. It isn't so different from those high school competitions over the star quarterback."

The popular television show *Everybody Loves Raymond* offers a banquet of relationally aggressive behaviors between Marie, Raymond's mother, who still coddles her son as she might a little boy, and Debra, his wife, who expects him to step up to the fatherhood plate. It's easy to imagine either of them as the Queen Bees of yesteryear, although their styles of aggression differ. To the men involved, it's entertaining and a source of great humor.

Sharing Space

Tatiana Boncompagni recalls an experience that changed her relationship with her mother-in-law forever. Sharing a country house seemed like a pleasant opportunity to spend downtime with in-laws, but instead of rest and relaxation, the cozy home became a battleground.

First, Tatiana expanded the arrangement to include her own parents. Then her mother-in-law announced, "I am the Queen," and instructed Tatiana and her family to do as she commanded while at the house. In the therapy session that followed, her mother-in-law complained of feeling disrespected; Tatiana felt ordered around. She and her husband decided to spend Christmas alone and lonely, which led to a desire to reconcile. They visited the therapist again, and, for the sake of family unity, Tatiana did everything asked of her.

A new problem developed when Tatiana's brother-in-law's girlfriend took on the role of bully in the mother-in-law's absence; then Tatiana's son was born and ties to the country home got tenser. In a three-page note, her mother-in-law requested that baby paraphernalia be kept out of sight.

More arguments and e-mail battles escalated the conflict to the point where Tatiana and her husband moved their belongings out and gave up visiting. Reflecting back, she recognizes the real reason for the conflict: both she and her mother-in-law were struggling to establish themselves as the main woman in her husband's life.

The Velvet-Gloved Duel

The reporter Sari Botton has also written about the antagonism that can exist between mothers and daughters-in-laws, saying, "We all know the archetype: the critical, meddling, demanding, and even evil matriarch who never quite got over the loss of her son to another woman. She terrorizes his wife by interfering in their marriage or, worse, by trying to prevent it." Botton points out that even the wife of the current president of the United States recently compared her mother-in-law to "Godfather" Don Corleone.

Sometimes, the animosity between mother-in-law and daughter-in-law is so intense it leads to marital discord. "My mother-in-law was a nightmare," a divorced mother of two told me. "The first time she came to visit, she opened up all my cupboards and checked out what was inside, commenting as she did so. From that moment on it was constant criticism of my appearance, my parenting, and my relationship with her son. Sometimes I think if he had just stood up for me, our marriage might have made it."

A woman named Jeanette, quoted in Botton's article, agreed. "My mother-in-law is one of the biggest reasons my husband and I got divorced," she said. "The woman drove me crazy for six years. She kept a picture of my husband and his ex-girlfriend on display in her living room. She changed our bridal registry so that we would get the china pattern she wanted us to have rather than the one we wanted. Then she changed the menu for my wedding without even talking to us. She was always causing problems like that."

The Online Rant

The Internet abounds with Web sites where women can hash out their mother-in-law issues:

- http://messageboards.ivillage.com: A "Mean Girls Grow Up" thread describes mothers-in-law who try to break up relationships, gossip, use children as pawns, and put down their daughters-in-law.

- www.motherinlawstories.com: Includes incidents where mothers-in-law nearly punched their daughters-in-law, were critical, or treated some preferentially.

- www.ihatemyinlaws.com: Women complain about mothers-in-law who are stuck in the victim role, prefer other sisters-in-law, exclude, overcontrol, and gossip.

- www.foreverwed.com: Engaged women already in conflict with their mothers-in-law-to-be describe various forms of meddling in the wedding planning process and public declarations of disapproval over the match that get back to the fiancé. One future daughter-in-law wrote that her fiancé's mother pressured her to wear her wedding dress. Another particularly egregious post described a mother-in-law who sabotaged a woman's wedding plans by gleaning information on music and quotes to be used in the ceremony, then sharing them with her own daughter, who used them in her marriage ceremony three weeks earlier.

Culture and Ethnicity

RA struggles with in-laws are not only an American phenomenon. Struggles with sisters-in-law, like those with mothers-in-law, may be universal. At www.paklinks.com's "GupShup" site, women from Pakistan complain about sisters-in-law who are cunning, snide, intimidating, and prone to exclusion. Long-distance gossip and rumors are other strategies they used to cause distress.

Another culturally specific Web site for advice is http://qa .sunnipath.com, which provides a venue for other Muslim women to obtain help with in-law issues. One question posted involved a mother-in-law who probed into her son's intimate relationship with his wife, asking about sexual relations and other private details. Nazim Mangera, an Islamic scholar who responded, advised the woman that her mother-in-law was making hurtful remarks that the husband should put an end to, but he also told the wife that she needed to allow her husband to visit with his mother as he wished.

Ethnicity can itself create tension. The author Susan Straight, who is white, noted that when she first went to the home of her black boyfriend (later to become her husband), it was the women who responded most negatively to her. As the years progressed and she earned a place among the females of the clan, tensions lessened. Even after Straight and her husband divorced, she continued to visit on holidays, along with her daughters. In a twist of irony, she responded to a recent put-down about interracial dating from one of her sisters-in-law by pointing out that she, too, was blond. "No, you're not," they told her.

Kids Can Change It All

Many experts believe that childbearing changes everything, transforming women who were previously strangers, or even enemies, into allies. Mothers, daughters, and sisters who are born, or sworn, into relationships with each other may discover that the common bond of childrearing overrides conflict.

In other situations, children up the ante, creating more competition and even manifesting their own RA through conflicts with or between the sons and daughters of warring women. In this case, the "born into or sworn into" distinction of vulnerability doesn't seem to apply—a sister-in-law who preens about her children can cause just as much antagonism as the sister who gently reminds you that both she and her children have always gravitated toward academic excellence, while you and yours haven't.

According to Dr. Bree Allinson, sisters-in-law can be as bad as, or worse than, mothers-in-law. Some of the infractions she hears about are not so different from those with mothers–in-law, but they have a peer-to-peer type manifestation:

- Trying to be closer to the brother than his wife
- Being mean to children
- Excluding the wife and/or her children
- Betraying confidences
- Gossip

Dr. Allinson actually warns that although you might want to trust your sister-in-law who is close to your own age, you shouldn't, because she will always be more loyal to her family. Her opinion may be supported by data from the second part of her poll, where daughters-in-laws reported that:

- 26 percent have had verbal fights with one or more sisters-in-law.
- 32 percent believed their sister-in-law would never like them.

Just Leave Me Out of It

Emmy tells the story of her sister-in-law, who "stole" the name she had picked for her firstborn, ironically, a name that would have made him a "Junior," carrying on the tradition her husband, the oldest, had been groomed for ever since he became his own dad's namesake. Although Emmy's husband took the behavior in stride, Emmy was sure the move was part of an ongoing competition her sister-in-law had introduced into their relationship as soon as Emmy married into the family. "She even pushed her kids up front in the family portrait so they'd be standing right next to my in-laws,"

Emmy complained. "Now, every time I look at that picture it reminds me of her overriding the photographer's careful arrangements."

As an in-law, it can be tempting to get caught up in a preexisting drama between sisters. As a relative newcomer to the situation, your loyalty can be tested by subtle pressures to take sides, just as middle schoolers do during sports.

Blood Is Thicker than Water
Fiona Dundee

"You're more of a sister to me than they are," sobbed my sister-in-law Cindy, after another female family feud pitted her four sisters against her, leaving her feeling isolated. "I'm not going to let them control me anymore. I'm going to stand up to them and make them leave me alone!"

As I hugged her, I felt honored, trusted, and appreciated. At the same time, my late mother's cautionary words kept running through my head: "Always remember, Fiona, blood is thicker than water."

Several days later, Cindy and I were chatting on the telephone when she casually mentioned that her daughter was going to her younger sister's home for the day so Cindy could have her hair and nails done. I was surprised that so soon after her outburst about her sisters, Cindy was again taking favors from them. There seemed to be a pattern, whereby Cindy's requests to her sisters for help resulted in their exerting more control over her life. Repeatedly and vociferously, Cindy asserted that such control was unwelcome.

A short time later, all four sisters were in an uproar over the fact that Cindy's daughter now sported sculptured, painted nails like her mother's. They called Cindy an irresponsible parent, a spendthrift, and a bad example to her daughter. Cindy ranted and raved at them in return, then called me crying about how mean they were. Next, the two older sisters called me, each complaining bitterly about Cindy's irresponsible nature; both displayed frustration at my reluctance to become involved.

I was confused. If Cindy truly was tired of her siblings' attempts to control her, why didn't she just cut off ties with them or at least minimize the opportunities for friction? When her husband was transferred to a neighboring state, I thought the feuds would lessen, but it was exactly the opposite, because by this time, e-mail had made its grand entrance. With message forwarding, all five women could now hash out their differences freely and unabashedly over the Internet for the rest of the family to read. To save my sanity, I deleted the messages without reading them and begged the sisters to drop me from the list.

Over the years, numerous similar situations played themselves out, seemingly without any real resolution. Most often, the four sisters would gang up on Cindy, although there were times when they would go for one another's jugulars as well. Cindy would regularly call or even visit to ask my advice on how to handle her sisters, but she always failed to follow what I offered.

At times, it would seem that Cindy was on the verge of breaking away from her sisters' power, but then she would be drawn back into the fold, and the scenario repeated itself over and over. On rare occasions when I mentioned the details of a particular conflict to my husband, he appeared disgusted, as if he had been through this for years. Not once was he able to shed any additional light on the intricacies of the girls' relationship, except to say that he believed there was no changing them and that he was tired of receiving their calls at work.

Fast-forward to last month, when Cindy's daughter, now almost eighteen, threatened to leave home and enlisted her aunts' assistance. For several days, the telephone wires burned up as each sister called the other and Cindy called me. Everyone's goals seemed at cross-purposes. True to form, after hours of pleading, yelling, name-calling, and recriminations, all was forgiven. My niece never left home, the aunts did not have to help her run away, and life settled down again until the next incident.

These days, I no longer try to advise Cindy, even when she pleads, "What do you think I should do?" I recognize that nothing among these family members will ever change. They have even succeeded in recruiting their oldest niece into the drama, and she is learning the role quite nicely.

My mother was right. Blood really is thicker than water, and female family ties sometimes bind in a way that an outsider may find difficult or impossible to understand.

Webvent

As with mothers-in-law, there are sites where sisters-in-law can vent their spleen online. At Baby Center (www.babycenter.com), one woman describes her sister-in-law's manipulative behavior, which involves dropping off her children for free babysitting. (Several respondents complained of the same problem.) At the Known Bitcher site on www.ezboard.com, one post describes a sister-in-law who gives preferential treatment to other nieces and nephews, while another shared the scheming of a sister-in-law to trap the poster's husband into online infidelity. An acerbic message described one woman's sister-in-law as "a total bitch from hell" who employed a classic RA strategy I call "take-backs": saying something mean and then pretending you were just joking. Other RA behaviors mentioned were spreading rumors and playing family members off against one another. There was even encouragement to become "bigger bitches" than sisters-in-law, using many of the same tactics that offended the posters.

What Lies Beneath

Understanding context and motivation is an important RA prevention strategy. For example, I have two sisters-in-law. The one married to my only brother lives fairly close and has been part of my life for many years. The other (married to one of my husband's two brothers), is an e-mail pal, keeping in touch regularly with notes and phone calls. We rarely get to visit face to face, since, like my first sister-in-law, she lives in Texas.

With only this minimal information, it's easy to see how family structure and history are bound to play a role in our relationships. One expert I spoke with assured me that sisters will never get along with their own brother's wife because of "territorial issues" (think back to chapter 4 where I discussed evolutionary psychology/ biology). This is especially true if there's only one brother.

Fortunately, this hasn't been the case for me, but I warned you there are always exceptions to rules. My brother's wife is someone I connected with immediately, perhaps because she was a career woman like me and had a sense of humor that I enjoyed. Our geographic proximity meant that I saw her frequently, but we weren't able to spend any extended time together, so our conversations were often superficial. She gravitated toward my next-youngest sister and her children at family gatherings, probably because of the closer relationship my sister had with our brother.

With time, things began to change. Family illnesses led to more meaningful conversations, and the artistic talents of one of her daughters fit well with a Club Ophelia project. These events caused a shift in our relationship, and I began to feel a more direct connection with her that has grown steadily stronger.

My other sister-in-law has been a bigger presence in my life, because my second husband comes from an all-male family. Our first meeting was a positive one, too, although we are completely different people. As an only child and one of the only two daughters/sisters-in-law on this side of the family, she made it clear from the beginning that our relationship was special for her. She was one of my strongest supports during the early years of my daughter's teenage struggles. Never judgmental about my parenting or my daughter's behavior, my sister-in-law always offers a willing ear and keeps to herself the confidences I share—a great gift to give the mother of a troubled child.

Another difference in my tie with that sister-in-law is our children. My three are the only cousins her children have, so she has always gone out of her way to treat them well and to reinforce their ties through cousinhood. Consequently, my son made a solo visit to Texas to see them, and he has expressed similar feelings of closeness to her family.

Two women, both sisters-in-law to the same person, and yet the relationships are very different. It's easy to see how the context of each situation could have turned our interaction in a completely different direction. If, like the expert I spoke with, I felt the need to guard my brother against outsiders, or if his wife had wanted to exert her potential power as the wife of the only male offspring (a big deal to my parents), our lives would be very different. The same holds true for my Texas sister-in-law: distance or a number of other issues could have led us to a different kind of connection. I'm so thankful it didn't, and I hope this book will offer strategies to prevent or correct potential or actual snags in relationships with in-laws.

13

Daughtering,
the In-Law Way

Recently I found a card my oldest son had sent me a long time ago that apologized for some misunderstanding we had had. I've forgotten the specifics of the disagreement, but not his signature: "I will always love you. You are #1 <ALWAYS>." Even back then, I knew that someday, I wouldn't be the number one woman in his life—at least not in that same sweet-little-boy way as when he was growing up.

Two Women Who Care about
the Same Man

Given that both of my sons are married, I was discouraged by the notion that women share the "Take my mother-in-law, *please!*" philosophy of comedian Henny Youngman. Dr. Terri Apter, an internationally recognized expert on women's relationships, was inspired to study female in-laws after musing on feelings of being smothered by her own mother-in-law. Her conclusions? The daughter-in-law/mother-in-law relationship bears many similarities to the volatile female adolescent years of testing and hypersensitivity between mother and daughter.

Dr. Apter's work in this area began with observations of twenty intact families, which led her to conclude that the female in-law relationship was the most troubled, although mothers-in-law seemed to have less animosity toward their new "daughters" than vice versa. Her next study involved interviews with twenty mothers-in-law and thirty-two daughters-in-law who had been in a relationship with each other for at least one year.

In the paper Dr. Apter wrote to describe her findings, "friendship at an impasse" was the theme. Mothers-in-law generally didn't understand the reasons for their uneasy relationships with their daughters-in-law. (The husbands of the mothers-in-law were also interviewed, and they generally agreed with their wives, describing their daughters-in-law as "difficult.") Dr. Apter also admits that many of the complaints of the daughters-in-law were hard to understand—one participant was bothered because her mother-in-law just sat and watched her when she visited. Other complaints Apter received referred to mothers-in-law being too cheerful, intruding by doing too much housework, and praising the daughter-in-law for being a good wife (therefore implying that the expected role of the daughter-in-law was to be a "good wife").

Dr. Apter calls this situation a tragedy, since there is clearly an opportunity for a fulfilling connection between two women who care about the same man and who cherish the same children. Maybe this is one female relationship predisposed to doom, but I prefer to think not. Understanding the context and motivation of each woman involved can help prevent needless tension and conflict.

In an article by Sharon Jayson, experts suggest that turf wars often cause difficulties between mothers-in-law and daughters-in-law. Writes Jayson: "Mothers-in-law say they feel rebuffed by daughters-in-law who take their comments the wrong way. Daughters-in-law say their husbands' mothers are judgmental and overly critical. Marriage has suddenly created an instant family in which the only common interest is the man they either raised or married."

The Numbers

Susan Shapiro Barash, a women's studies expert and the author of *Mothers-in-Law and Daughters-in-Law: Love, Hate, Rivalry and Reconciliation*, says in her book that mothers-in-law have also been daughters-in-law, and should therefore appreciate the sensitivity and challenges of the relationship. Her belief is that the most ·

intense conflicts are going to occur between the mother of a son and his wife.

A survey she conducted with 150 women revealed that from the mother-in-law's perspective:

- 60 percent thought they got along at least fairly well with their daughter-in-law.

- 40 percent felt the daughter-in-law was a good mother.

- 40 percent felt the daughter-in-law was a good wife.

And from the daughter-in-law's perspective:

- 63 percent said they got along with their mother-in-law.

- 30 percent said sisters-in-law included them.

- 58 percent said children changed their relationship with their mother-in-law.

- 63 percent were excluded from mother-in-law/sister-in-law plans.

The conflict may simmer when a woman crosses the line from girl-friend to fiancée, and after marriage it can burst into flames. Not to mention all of the daughters-in-law's family members, who come as a package deal along with her—each with the potential either to disrupt and cause drama or support and offer rewarding new connections.

How It Plays Out

Rosaleen Leslie Dickson, the Internet "Great-Granny," compiled a book of challenging scenarios called *The Mother-in-Law Book*. In it, she shares these "disappointing daughter-in-law" situations:

- A mother-in-law is disappointed with her daughter-in-law who is "demanding and disrespectful" despite the mother-in-law's generous emotional and financial support. *The RA Dynamic:* Unequal power and expectations, manifested in rudeness.

- The daughter-in-law-to-be doesn't want any of her new hus-band's family at her wedding, from mom to brothers. *The RA Dynamic:* Exclusion and humiliation.

▌ A daughter-in-law came into the family's life during a time of conflict, and the mother-in-law didn't even know her son was engaged. *The RA Dynamic:* Withholding important information.

▌ A daughter-in-law suddenly refused to see her mother-in-law but had six pages of complaints against her despite their rare contact. She was so angry she refused to accept a Christmas present from her mother-in-law. *The RA Dynamic:* The silent treatment as manipulation.

▌ A grandmother whose son is divorced loves her grandson and spends time with him whenever she can. Her former daughter-in-law seems to hate her and criticizes her constantly, despite her efforts to soften her daughter-in-law's heart for the sake of the grandson. *The RA Dynamic:* Gossip and resentment.

My observations suggest that when a mother has many sons and especially when she has *only* sons, the integration of a daughter goes more smoothly. Sometimes, too, mothers are grateful to women who straighten out a wayward son.

"My Mark was a real 'problem child,'" Nancy said, describing her youngest son's history of drug abuse. "Even his older brother couldn't talk sense into him. Then he met Jennifer, a real 'no nonsense' type. She was better than any rehab program we sent him to. Now he has a kid and is taking evening classes to become a lawyer, and working during the day as a teacher." Needless to say, Nancy has a special affection for Jennifer.

The Story of a Mother Misunderstood

A sad story I heard contradicts the previous theory. Ellie's situation with a "distressing daughter-in-law" was made all the worse because she had only one child, Ted, who was her pride and joy. For twenty-four years she "lived life for him," working two jobs so he could go to college and then supporting his ambition to attend medical school. He bought her thoughtful gifts for Mother's Day and her birthday and made a special point of coming home for at least a day at Christmas and Thanksgiving, even when college or work took him far away. After graduation, Ted, a good-looking boy with a ready smile, came back home and took a job as a paramedic to earn money for medical school.

He told Ellie, "You don't need to work extra anymore, Mom. I appreciate all that you've done, but I'm an adult now, and I can earn my own way."

Then Ted met Vicky. Vicky was a clerk in the emergency room at the hospital where Ted worked, and she quickly became a serious girlfriend. Unlike the other women Ted had dated, Vicky was interested in Ellie and made a point of coming along on each of Ted's home visits. Ellie welcomed Vicky into her life and even invited her on a few "girls-only" outings.

"I'm so lucky," Ellie told her sister. "Vicky is a great influence on Ted. She's helping him save money for medical school and study for his MCATs. And when I asked her what she loved most about Ted, she couldn't stop talking about his kindness and dependability."

It would have been impossible for Ellie to anticipate what happened next. Ted and Vicky became engaged, and at a special celebratory dinner, Ellie met her son's future in-laws for the first time. Before the dinner could start, Vicky suddenly developed an excruciating migraine and asked Ted to get her a taxi home. She insisted that the others continue with their meal. This left Ted in a bind, but after ushering Vicky off, he returned to the table, clearly subdued.

Somehow the casual dinner conversation between Ellie and Vicky's parents, Helen and Sam, turned to belly rings, when their waitress's short top revealed that she had one.

"I never really liked them until I saw Vicky's," Ellie said, after Sam commented on it. "But hers was so cute I decided they were sort of neat."

Helen and Sam paled noticeably.

"Vicky has a belly ring?" Helen said in shock.

Ted quickly changed the subject, and everyone seemed to forget about the awkward moment, at least until the next day, when Ellie was wakened by a call.

"We won't be coming over for breakfast," Ted informed her. "Vicky still isn't feeling well."

"What about Sam and Helen?" Ellie protested. "I'd still be happy to have them. I made your favorite egg casserole."

"We'll get back to you," Ted said curtly.

It was the last time Ellie would speak to her son for months. Despite frequent calls, letters, and e-mails, he refused to tell her what had gone so wrong between them.

Ted and Vicky were married a short time later, an event they informed Ellie about through a mailed photograph of them posed outside a small chapel in Las Vegas. Thanksgiving and Christmas passed with no word from Ted, despite the package of gifts Ellie mailed to the couple.

Ellie was so confused and heartbroken she went to see a therapist, where she described what had happened in great detail, trying to find an explanation for the sudden estrangement. On her birthday in February, a curt note arrived from Ted telling her he was going to be interviewing for a medical school near his hometown. He agreed to see her briefly but warned he would not "tolerate any grief."

At that meeting, Ellie learned what had caused the long-ago rift: Vicky's parents had been upset with her for getting a belly ring, which led Vicky to explode at Ted for his mother's innocent mistake.

"But I thought they already knew, and I was trying to be nice" Ellie protested, sobbing. "Please forgive me for anything I did wrong."

Later she wrote to Vicky, apologizing and asking for another chance, but her daughter-in-law never replied. Ted explained in an e-mail that Vicky wanted no contact with Ellie because of what had happened.

Clearly, Vicky is, at a minimum, the bully. Perhaps she was threatened by Ted's close relationship with his mother, or maybe, Ellie's therapist suggested, Vicky never learned to interact with women in a healthy way. Regardless, her treatment of Ellie not only inflicted a deep emotional wound but shattered a potentially amicable family life. Had Vicky been a young woman Ellie encountered at church or at the gym, she could have quickly decided to avoid her in the future—but that wasn't an alternative in such a small family.

The story of Ellie calls to mind the words of my cousin, who is the mother of two sons. She told me an older woman gave her valuable advice when her sons were young: "Be nice to their girlfriends—they could end up as your daughters-in-law. Find something to like about them—even if it's just the way they breathe."

There are times when a mother-in-law can become the lost parent a woman yearns for, as happened to Marsha. Estranged from her own mother, Marsha discovered that her mother-in-law, Selma, was the kind of nurturing parent she longed for. Her frequent hugs and compliments turned out to be a panacea for the mothering void in Marsha's life.

"Selma's the *best*," Marsha said, smiling broadly as she discussed the relationship.

"We've Always Done It That Way"

Turf issues between mothers-in-law and daughters-in-law can also occur over holiday traditions. Great energy goes into planning get-togethers, scheduling visits, and arranging for all the relatives to be together, and for women, the expectations that accompany any family celebrations can layer additional stress onto already hectic holidays.

The questions of whose family gets visited and when are complicated further by divorce. I knew this was always a source of tension for me, but I grew to appreciate that a child, too, has to contend with these pressures as I watch younger women with multiple sets of relatives to please. "Making the rounds" on holidays can also become a race against time for those from very large families who live close to each other, or those with former in-laws they must add to the list of visits.

Then there's the whole kin-keeping drive, which comes out in full force during the days when we take off from work and expect to celebrate with our loved ones. My family is a case in point. Traditionally, even after her children married and left home, my mother made most of the arrangements for the holidays. She would have meals planned for weeks in advance, along with sleeping arrangements and an activity schedule. Even when a particular event like a family reunion wasn't being held at her house, she was still "information central," keeping track of who was coming, when they were arriving, where they were staying, and what food they were bringing. I used to find her compulsiveness excessive, until my own family was launched and out of the house. Now I do the exact same things, because they seem a necessary part of keeping my family connected.

Nourishing the Body

Special foods associated with holidays hold significance for both men and women, but they can position mothers-in-law against daughters-in-law, and vice versa. (I'm lucky that all of my relatives can outcook me.) Traditional family dishes can have tremendous emotional meaning for women, as Tina, a newlywed, learned. She recalls the first time she invited her husband's family for Christmas dinner. Her mother-in-law took a look at the meal she had prepared and appeared ready to faint.

"Where's the turkey and stuffing?" she cried, eyeing Tina's carefully prepared ham and green bean casserole. Tina, whose family had never eaten anything *but* ham and green beans for Christmas, was just as stunned. While none of the men commented on the menu, that incident introduced tension into what had been an otherwise pleasant visit.

As I discovered in my work with eating disorders, for men food is nourishment, but for women, the selection, the preparation, and the presentation of food has deeper significance. It's a way of family continuity (no one will ever replace my mother's potato salad), expressing care (she makes it especially for me on certain occasions), and a sign of love and nurture. Food is nurturing made visible.

Blending the many traditions of families can take negotiation and compromise, almost as a metaphor for larger RA issues. Aunt Minnie may try to manipulate you into cooking a traditional Thanksgiving dinner for twenty people when you're eight months pregnant, but if your sister-in-law wants to bring enough soul food to feed an army, you have a great opportunity to model positive relationship skills.

What about situations where multiple sisters-in-law are blended into an existing family? Whose traditions should take precedence? Sometimes a happy solution occurs, as with Alyssa, where everyone's favorite rituals and dishes blended to create a new and diverse tradition. "I bring southern, my sister is gourmet, and my sister-in-law is organic. The men don't care—it's all just food to them. The hardest sell was my mother, who still insists on an occasional meal where she prepares all her traditional dishes."

What about You?

Could you be part of a destructive relationship with your female in-laws? Consider the following statements to get an RA score for your relationship.

1. When I'm with my mother-in-law/daughter-in-law, I sometimes forget she is my husband's mom/wife and I relate to her as I might to another woman.

2. Before I'm about to see my mother-in-law/daughter-in-law, I mentally review all the qualities about her that irritate me, and prepare to deal with them.

3. When my husband/son talks about his mother/wife, I screen his comments for any implied criticism of me.

4. I sometimes suggest that my husband/son should do something special for his mother/wife.

5. I often question who comes first in my husband/son's life—me or his mom/wife.

If you answered yes to questions 1 and 4 and no to questions 2, 3, and 5, chances are you're an easy-to-get-along-with mother-in-law or daughter-in-law, and are secure about the affections and loyalty of your son or husband. If you answered no to questions 1 and 4 and yes to questions 2, 3, and 5, check your behavior to see if you may inadvertently be coming across aggressively to your in-law.

Daughters-in-law and the emotional territory that comes with them can be a pleasant surprise or a deep disappointment. On both sides of the relationship, there is potential for aggression, affection, or a combination of the two. How you respond to each other is fluid and subject to change, no matter how deep-seated the resentments and difficulties may seem. Women, like girls, want to have positive connections, and they rarely enjoy animosity. If the *only* person you change is yourself, you'll still be better off than in a situation rife with RA, where each encounter is a battle and every interaction fraught with tension.

PART FOUR

Not Quite Family, Definitely RA

Family, More or Less: Extended, Extra, or Estranged

In chapter 1, Renae described the women she adopted into her life as "fictive kin"—those without a blood tie but who were important to her emotionally. For Renae, a godmother and an aunt became strong maternal figures in her life, giving them the same privileges and expectations that come inherently attached to blood family.

At the same time, we often have "pseudo kin" who are related to us only distantly or legally and are not considered true family. In-laws and stepfamily can be relegated to this category, along with lots of other "hangers-on": your mother's favorite cousin who is the Gossip Queen of the kitchen, or your daughter-in-law's mother, who puts the drama in mama. Each is connected to us, and yet we often accord them an uneasy status somewhere between acquaintance and kin.

Then there's the issue of nontraditional families where the setup is ripe for relational aggression. The HBO series *Big Love* presents a fictional story of three Mormon wives married to the same man, although only the first wife has legal rights. While polygamy has been outlawed in the United States, stories about this practice provide further data on some of the inherent differences between men and women described in earlier chapters, morality issues aside.

Yes, there are a few places where women have many husbands (polyandry), but polygamy is far more prevalent and continues in both remote areas of this country and in other countries.

Sharing a Husband

On the Web site Principle Voices (Power in Education, Advocacy, and Communication for Equality, www.principlevoices.org) there is a message board debating the pros and cons of polygamy. A summary of the postings suggests:

- The motivations for this practice are religious, enabling women to achieve a blessing from God.

- Monogamy is less successful than polygamy, where divorce is rare because there are many more people to support both the struggling couple and their children.

- Plural marriage brings out both selfishness and humility in men and women.

- Polygamy encourages women to look to God rather than their husbands for fulfillment.

R.W., fifty-eight, was born into the secretive Kingston church and lived there for thirty-four years as the second of two wives. She bore eight children in thirteen years. During her time in the compound where she lived as a sister-wife, she was so poor that she was on and off food stamps and collected recyclable aluminum cans for money. Then, in 1992, she was excommunicated for questioning what she saw as the church's harsh treatment of women and children.

She now says she agreed to live most of her life as a polygamous wife because her mother thought she'd get religious "credit" and therefore more "celestial glory." Polygamy, says R.W., offers the only true path to the "celestial kingdom," which according to the Mormon church, is the highest level of heaven.

Here is her story:

My husband's first wife was my older sister. It might seem odd to other people, but when you're in that sort of group it seems

completely normal. Your thinking, doing, and being are all controlled by the church.

The marriage changed my relationship with my sister pro-
foundly. She was eight and a half years older than me, so it was
very, very hard for her. She didn't know how the first wife typically feels, as no one had talked to her about it. She became
depressed, angry, hurt, and jealous. In polygamy, the first wife
thinks she's going to live "God's law" by having a "sister-wife,"
and it turns out to be easier said than done. My sister blamed
herself for not being able to please God.

We all lived together for eleven years in the same household,
then I lived elsewhere and our husband commuted between the
two of us. We alternated nights, and I was dutiful and never
refused him. It was very formal and sterile, because my marriage
to him had to be secret because it was illegal. My kids—like quite
a few other kids in our church—didn't even know who their
father was.

I was very strong, having grown up competing with four
brothers. I was able to do it, but I was so very lonely. I had no
affection, no attention from this man. Intimacy was never talked
about. I remember I'd shower at night and I'd just cry in the
shower so no one could hear me then. It was horrible. I never had
male companionship. I never loved him. When I was pregnant,
he wouldn't even ask when the baby was due; never a word.

Another Mormon wife, Vicky, said that her sister-wives consciously interacted in a welcoming and cordial way because they saw
it as a way to please the husband and God, but their inner emotions
still raged.

The feelings of jealousy and resentment are kept inside and we
pray to God to rid us of those feelings because it makes us sin-
ners for feeling that way. Two situations in particular made me
feel jealous and resentful.

There is competition inherent in the hierarchy of the wives.
The first wife was in charge, sort of a wife that was made CEO
with power over all the wives. Jealousy would manifest itself
when one wife and her children had more material things or
more time with the husband. Daughters would also get jealous
of other daughters if there was an imbalance in work responsibilities, which often happened.

Dorothy Allred Solomon, in *The Principle*, her memoir of growing up in polygamy, portrays a classic setup for rivalry and hostility: sixteen women living together and competing for the romantic attention of one man. She describes the domineering behavior of Aunt LaVerne, her father's only legal wife. In response to Aunt LaVerne's open ridicule, Solomon's mother, Ella, simmered with resentment but felt powerless to act.

Solomon recalls one type of competition where the mothers tried to "outmartyr" each other, going to extremes to sacrifice more and make do with less. She also discusses "The Law of Chastity," which helped to reduce jealousy somewhat because it allowed a wife not to have sex when she didn't want to or couldn't conceive.

Solomon's situation was similar to R.W.'s in that her mother's twin sister was also married to her father. Despite the low stature of all wives but the first, it was women who were in control of the home and the family, but often they, like the women from sub-Sarahan Africa, undermined their power by working against one another. Solomon gave as an example the many strategies women would use to usurp one another's scheduled night with the husband, causing tears and resentment. There was also gossip and bitterness because one wife came from a more aristocratic Mormon family and felt she was better than the others.

Solomon felt that her father secretly enjoyed having the women quarrel, especially over him, but for the women, the fights were "gut-wrenching wars of body, mind, and spirit." Each woman's worth was set by the number of children she produced—and even among the children, RA continued.

A Cast of Characters

The definition of "family" can be stretched in other ways. Depending on the size of your clan, there can be many or few female relatives, each with a unique connection to you by virtue of being born or sworn into your family. The positive and negative interactions you have with a distant cousin-in-law who lives next door will, of course, be dramatically different from those with a sister located on the other side of the country. The twice-a-year meetings with the venomous mother of your son's wife will pass more easily than everyday drop-ins from your sister's husband's sister, who doesn't know you well but loves to cause trouble.

Yet at some point, each person must decide how far their loyalty and leniency extend. Who do you share a special bond with, and who don't you? If a woman is related to you in some way, however remote, must you accord her special consideration as a family member? Following is a story from a woman who wondered about these same things.

Same Name, Different Game
Chris Fox

My mom was bullied by my aunt Delia before she even married my dad. At my mom's wedding shower, my aunt, supported by "her" side of the family, gave my mom a candy dish and left a ten-cent Woolworth price tag on it. That sort of bullying escalated until my aunt decided to join her cousins' fraternal lodge. The cousins were active and well-known members, and my aunt wanted to be a member, too. Coincidentally, my mom and my aunt had the same first and last names and both belonged to the same Protestant church. That particular branch of the church was very strict and forbade members to join fraternal lodges.

My aunt joined her lodge, and all was fine until the pastor started to hear rumors from conservative members of the congregation that "Delia Hammond" had joined a forbidden organization. He went to my aunt and asked if it was true. She denied it and was horrified he would think that of her, then told him it was her sister-in-law (my mother) who was the guilty party. He then came to my mother and asked her. Of course, she denied it because it simply wasn't true. The pastor, faced with the dilemma of knowing that one of them was lying, chose to believe my aunt, because, as he explained, he had known her from childhood, he had confirmed her, and he believed she wouldn't lie to him.

He threw my mom out of the church.

I remember as a very young child asking why my mother was always crying and why my father was so upset. It ruined our family forever and tore apart whatever tolerance had been there before.

Years later, my mom got a call from one of the cousins asking for her help. My aunt Delia was suffering from breast cancer and needed someone to drive her to and from her chemotherapy appointments. My mom said she would be glad to drive my aunt wherever and whenever she needed to go. Her only condition was that my aunt, who had shunned us for years and even refused to look at me when she saw me on the street, call and ask herself. My aunt refused to "lower" herself, did not get chemotherapy, and died of breast cancer sometime later.

It has always been my belief that my aunt knew exactly what she was doing when she joined that organization so many years ago, and that perhaps the rumors might initially have been started by her, too. What she couldn't have known was that when she needed my mom at the end of her life, she would be unable to back down from her bullying, and she would pay a terrible price for it.

The RA in this story was as real and pervasive as the breast cancer that ended Aunt Delia's life. Although she was an in-law and an aunt, her power to wound beyond her immediate sphere of influence was every bit as intense as with blood relatives.

In the following story, this same point is well illustrated. Although the abuse between distant relatives was removed from the author, she still felt the pain of the exclusion, the put-downs, and the silent treatment that occurred decades earlier.

Tragedies
Ruth Jacobs

Since I am eighty-one, my grandmother is long dead, but I often think of her good qualities and also of her not-so-good qualities. Grandma got guardianship of my brother and me after my mother died when I was ten and my brother two. My father had proven to be an incompetent, even abusive, single parent, and Grandma rescued us from him and refused to let him see us.

Her younger sister, our great-aunt, told Grandma she should let our father see us and Grandma got very angry at her sister. She refused to see or even talk on the phone to her again. She would also have nothing to do with her sister's children, which left her sister hurt and sad.

I liked my great-aunt and sometimes walked with a friend to her store to see her, but never told my grandmother, who had only nasty descriptions of her sister. When I grew up, I continued to feel very bad about this rift between sisters, especially after my grandmother was widowed and could have used a sister's companionship.

Because of my grandmother, I could not invite my great-aunt to my wedding. Later in life, when I became a Ph.D. sociologist, I often brooded that there might have been some sort of intervention that would bring these two sisters to reconciliation. But, at the time, as a little girl, I did not know how to do it.

While any member can hold grudges that divide families for decades, the impact is different for women, who experience a deep sense of grieving and loss, even if they are not directly involved. On some level, this severing of ties seems to signal a personal failure to maintain connections, prompting even distant female family members to feel responsible for finding a way to end the conflict.

Saying Good-Bye for Good

By now it should be apparent that women work hard to maintain their family connections, even when abuse, mistreatment, or illegal arrangements exist. Therefore, estrangement, the most extreme example of family fragmentation, can destroy those involved, because it represents the ultimate failure of female connections.

An Internet search for writing about estrangement reveals that most of the postings come from women. Laura Davis, in her book *I Thought We'd Never Speak Again*, describes the painful process of separation from her family, which occurred after she raised allegations of sexual abuse. She says, "When we lose a relationship that is precious to us, the fabric of life is torn."

Carol Tuttle is a master energy therapist, an author, and a spiritual teacher. At age thirty-four, a series of depressions led her into therapy, where she was encouraged to confront her family about past sexual abuse. What followed was a series of traumas that led to a complete reorganization of Carol's life. Her husband, who worked for her family, quit his job, and they moved out of their home ten miles away from relatives. To a person, her relatives sided with her father and ceased contact with Carol.

"My mom never actively disowned me, but she did so passively, aligning herself with my father and not speaking to me," Carol says. Her brothers' wives also elected to adopt their spouses' point of view.

Carol admits she was initially angry with her mother for the "disowning by default" and "choosing" her husband over her daughter. Carol, although geographically distant, tried to maintain communication with her mom, who made it clear she would not have a relationship separate from her husband, Carol's father.

And so Carol began a new life, encouraging her children to have strong bonds of friendship with each other since they now had no relatives on their maternal side. In 1993, she wrote *The Path to Wholeness: A Personal Approach to Spiritual Healing and Empowerment for Survivors of Child Sexual and Spiritual Abuse*, which told the story of her family and her past as a Mormon church member. This was an endeavor that allowed Carol to describe her healing process.

She comments, "My new work and life was all about healing, and yet there was a disconnect inside me. With some more therapy, I began to realize that my life had been better than my dad's, and I felt I could create some movement in my family, so I approached him and asked for forgiveness. He responded right away, but my mother was more tentative because this had had such a big impact on her and had caused tremendous heartache." Carol went on what she calls "a six-month probationary period" to reconnect with her mom, who adopted a "let's just move on" attitude.

"I couldn't ignore what had happened," Carol says, "and so we talked through things and it was tender, but I accepted the validity of her experience. My sisters-in-law took the position of 'no one wants to talk about this,' which was a real trial. I never felt close to my sisters-in-law, but I thought well of them, although to this day they aren't interested in my real life and never ask about the books. Still, motherhood is a great common ground, and I really did want my children connected to their relatives."

Carol notes that her father-in-law and mother-in-law had great compassion for her during the estrangement, and when she made headlines because of her book, they were clear in their support. Her relationship with her mother-in-law was close, and Carol admires her many strengths and considers her a mentor, but she could not stop longing for the same kind of connection with her own mother. As a teacher and guide, she hears many stories like hers and notes that most are from women.

The therapist Mark Sichel is one of the few men who have shared a memoir of estrangement in his book *Healing from Family Rifts*. On the Web site mentalhealth.about.com, he says that although statistics on estrangement are lacking, the situation is "an increasingly frequent problem." He describes the circumstances of one client whose mother disowned her after she had a mixed marriage. Another daughter cut off contact with her mother after her parents divorced. Sichel feels estrangements may occur more often because we are freer with our emotions and convictions, and that the rules for cruel behavior have changed. Laura Davis, on the other hand, attributes estrangement to the different perceptions of family members. She says, "Each of us builds our own life story around events that are shared differently."

Estrangement can even be a generational phenomenon, with rifts passed on from one set of relatives to the next. This most often seems to occur through kin-keeping females. "My aunt and my mom cut off contact years ago, so I never see her [the aunt] either," Tamara told me when describing her maternal side of the family. She also hasn't pursued relationships with that aunt's children, even though they live close by.

Reconciliation may be impossible, or it may occur on a continuum of choosing to forget and moving on, agreeing to disagree, or actually becoming closer. For Carol, the process was a slow one, but she persisted, saying, "I knew I had to win back everyone's trust."

Tips for overcoming estrangements between mothers and daughters are offered at www.pioneerthinking.com. Most could apply to any estranged relationship:

- Try to appreciate the context of the other person's life.
- Develop special mother-daughter (or other) traditions.
- Go into therapy together.
- Join a discussion group.
- Accept the ups and downs of relationships.
- Recognize that choices have consequences.

Most experts believe reconciliation is not only possible but important. Sichel notes that "the most important reconciliation is the one you make with yourself."

Stretched to the Limit

Family ties can be fierce or fragile. Across generations, women can unconsciously give their relatives permission to be abusive, but the cycle is sometimes broken by a younger relative who is willing to step out of the bystander role and end a hurtful situation.

The Invisible Sister
Caitlin' Jeffrey Pause'

Attempting to write an essay that details the cruelty of women who share a family name is difficult, even treacherous. I wonder what damage my words will cause for my mother and her sisters, and I worry that exposing our family secrets and calling a bully a bully will simply bring more pain to my mother. Or perhaps what I write will damage my mother in other ways, bringing light to the treatment she endures from her sister, and causing her shame for such allowance. I've finally decided that telling my story is so important that while it may bring questions and tears, it may also bring healing by raising the consciousness of readers and expressing emotions long kept silent.

My mother is the third of eleven children and the second of five girls. Her youth was shaped by the traditions and culture of Catholicism and her Irish heritage, as well as by her many brothers and sisters. My mother and her cohort of older siblings grew up in a much different household from that of the younger children, who enjoyed the comfort of money and a secure future. They never knew the difficult times of spreading food and resources to tend to several children on a tight budget, or having to share clothes and textbooks.

As one can imagine, eleven children makes for cliques and groupings within the siblings. My mother became allies with her older sister, and the lines in the sand were drawn. My aunt (the second-youngest daughter) has been a bully in our family for as long as I remember. I used to worship her when I was younger. She was powerful, making decisions and speaking in a loud voice during all conversations, a force to be reckoned with, her size as well as her desire to be in charge and share her opinion overwhelming.

At a very young age, my aunt nicknamed me "Dogface" and purchased doggie cola, doggie biscuits, and even my very own dog bowl to eat out of (never on the floor, but at the table in place of a regular bowl). She found this funny and encouraged the rest of the family to participate in the teasing. I took these actions as tokens of her love for me. As I grew older, however, I began to resent my aunt's behavior, but it was difficult to find my own voice with hers shouting so loudly in my ear.

I chose to spend the summer of my eighth-grade year with her and other members of my extended family in California. I left my parents' home a fresh spirit, looking for answers and eager to explore. I returned home to Texas a defeated soul, crushed under the weight of my aunt's forcefulness. Everything I believed, according to her, was wrong, stupid, and immature. Everything I wanted to try, to learn, to experience, was wasteful and foolish. My spirit destroyed, it took years for me to find my self-confidence and self-efficacy again.

While I suffered at the hostile hand of my aunt, my mother bore a bigger brunt of the bullying. Now that I am older, I refuse to allow my aunt to speak for me, or for my mother. I refuse to allow her to bully my mother in my presence, and I continue to do what I can to build my mother's confidence and help her see that she deserves better. My mother suffers from low levels of self-esteem and confidence. Now well into her fifties, she still cowers and cries at the cruelty shelled out by her bullying younger sister. I try to shield her, but there is only so much a daughter can do.

Sometimes we stay in relationships out of obligation, and sometimes we choose the path of forgiveness and love. For Caitlin' and her mother, changing two generations of bullying will not be as simple as making a choice and following through. "Not simple" does not mean unimportant. In fact, putting an end to relational aggression that has persisted for a lifetime may be the most critical lesson she, her aunt, and her mother can learn and share with other women in the family.

15

Carebearing and Carewearing

The care and keeping of families can be a nearly full-time job for many years—consuming much energy and causing much frustration. As women age, these roles shift, and as the roles shift, so does the power within the family. Consider Rheta, the hub her husband and three children revolve around. Mandy, the youngest and a new mother, lives close to Rheta and is the most involved in her life on a day-to-day basis. The other children and grandchildren receive equal attention from their mother and grandmother, even if it requires long travel or exhausting days of babysitting.

Rheta is also expected to be a conduit of information, updating each set of family members on news about the others—meaning information often gets passed along second- and thirdhand. She also is responsible for planning reunions, birthday milestone celebrations, and holiday get-togethers, and she is the point of contact for lists of who should be invited to bridal and baby showers. If anyone has a question relating to any aspect of family life, they call Rheta. Does Rheta enjoy all this responsibility? Her daughters sometimes wonder, because she becomes especially irritable around the time of holidays, when her clan automatically assumes she will prepare Thanksgiving and Christmas dinners for the extended family.

However, an interesting change is taking place as the oldest daughter, Heidi, is approaching midlife. Heidi has copied her mother's address book, which contains current contact information for all family members, as well as a record of birthdays and anniversaries. She has also begun to take a more active role in planning get-togethers and has started her own traditions involving the family. The once thorny relationship between mother and oldest daughter has mellowed, and although they skirmish from time to time, Heidi is the first person Rheta calls with new information or questions. While both Heidi and her relatives defer to Rheta as the matriarch of their immediate family, there is a subtle acknowledgment that this role will be passed on to someone else in the future—perhaps Heidi?

Care Needing, Caregiving, Careworn

Sometimes a daughter isn't quite so willing to step forward and take over the lead role in her family, or any other. As health-care resources shrink, family members are expected to pick up the slack for "quicker and sicker" elders, but not every frail patient has a daughter or a daughter-in-law eager to provide the support they need. And what if that parent or aunt or in-law was one you never got along with?

"My mom and I were never enemies, but we weren't close either," Sue, a client of mine, once confided. Her eighty-six-year-old mom, Anna, was in a stage that I call "care needing," struggling to live on her own but reluctant to enter any kind of assisted living facility.

"It must be tough to have her turn to you for help since you're the only child," I commented.

"Tough?" Now Sue was angry as she spoke. "She's never given me a bit of support in my life! She watched me go through a divorce, cancer, and a bunch of other problems and just assumed I was doing fine without her. In fact, she made some pretty ignorant comments about me and bad-mouthed me to the rest of the family.

"Now she wants me to give up my job and move to New York to take care of her because she's sick! I wouldn't mind so much if she just came out and asked, but it's the guilt-provoking phone calls and manipulative letters that get to me. She even wrote to my aunt and said I was so self-centered I refused to answer her phone calls, which is so not true! On my birthday, she sent me a check for five thousand dollars and a card that said, 'Although you don't care about me, I will always love you.'"

Difficult Adults Are Difficult Elders

Although many women (and men) believe that relationships in old age become calmer and more placid than in the younger years, more often than not, little changes. If your ties to your mother in your younger years were conflicted and relationally aggressive, they aren't likely to magically improve as the two of you mature, barring an extraordinary event.

Another reason conflict so often occurs around the issue of care-giving is that the need often arises when midlife women are at the pinnacle of their careers or personal lives, able to focus on them-selves for the first time in years. In the meantime, their mothers are in the process of letting go of worldly accomplishments and begin-ning to focus on accepting what is. Two women with such differ-ent priorities will be challenged to have a conversation, let alone share living space. Tracy found this out when she moved back home during a hiatus between jobs.

"It seemed an ideal solution at first—I was broke and she was lonely after the death of my father and some health problems. The first two weeks were fine, but then she got really upset with me for reasons I don't understand. She called my other sister and told her that I was so lazy I slept in every day and never helped with house-work! She failed to mention that I work night shifts and usually wake up to find all the work done. My sister called and screamed at me for taking advantage of a 'sick old lady,' so now she and I aren't talking either. My life is like one big cold war."

It's difficult to draw a line between reasonable requests and rela-tional aggression, as Irene discovered when her mother, Lou, suf-fered a serious heart attack and required complete nursing care. Initially, Irene was happy to help Lou and felt she couldn't do enough. As Lou recovered, however, she became more demanding of Irene, sending her on repeated trips to the grocery store and pharmacy that sometimes seemed meaningless. She criticized everything Irene did: the way she parked the car in the garage, the meals she prepared, and even the brand of paper towels she bought. With anyone else, Irene would have seen this behavior as illness-related, but with her mom she felt propelled back to her teen years, when everything she did was wrong. Soon, Irene and Lou could barely have a conversation that didn't involve a cruel comment or subtle snipe.

Sibling Rivalry in Extremis

You, like many others, might think that as adults you and your siblings will be able to confront the crisis of elder care with maturity and grace. Would that it could be so. More often than not, in my experience, the kinds of conflicts you may have had with your sister (more so than with brothers) during childhood are likely to rear their ugly heads again when caregiving needs arise. Who does what? Who is best qualified? Who does Mom want to live with? The list can be endless and the battles bitter—but they're not really about the surface issues. Underneath the hurtful put-downs and accusations are sisters who have spent a lifetime in a caustic competition for their mother's or father's or approval and love.

Consider what Trudy has to say:

It's not that I wanted to take care of Mom—she and I have always had a challenging relationship. She could have been a lot nicer to me when I was growing up, but then again, she was a single parent with four kids to raise. Who knows how I would do in similar circumstances?

When the police called and told my brother mom had been found wandering in the neighborhood without knowing where she was, my sister-in-law called me, as if it was understood that I "would take care of things." My brother's a busy engineer while I'm a stay-at-home mom. It made me angry, but out of guilt and some sense of obligation I brought her to stay with me.

Mom started doing loopy things like leaving the oven on and losing her purse (we still haven't found it). The doctor diagnosed her with Alzheimer's disease, and I thought okay, this is it, I've reached my limit. I thought it was time for my sister and brother to start helping out, so I called a family conference. My sister-in-law "spoke for" my brother, reminding me that my parents had given me a down payment for our house and suggesting that I "owed" it to Mom to take care of her. My sister, who lives in the same town but isn't married, told me she was trying to make partner in her law firm while I was just a mom. "What better way did I have to spend my time?" was the message I got. When I challenged my brother, he just shrugged his shoulders and said he thought Mom should go to a home.

So I went to one of those places that specializes in Alzheimer's disease and took a tour. I told myself, yeah, I'm going to do this, Mom will be okay. My kids are just entering high school, and I want to be part of their lives while I still can. On my way out, I happened to see one older woman crying and asking the nurses where her children were, and my heart—and my resolve—broke. How could I think of turning my mother over to strangers, this little old lady who had devoted her life to the kids, in her own way?

The upsetting thing is my sister and brother feel no responsibility at all, but on the rare times when they visit my mom, she lights up like a Christmas tree, thrilled to see them and full of questions about their jobs. When I suggested I could use some more help, my sister acted put-upon, just like she did in high school when I wanted to borrow one of her sweaters or skirts.

Deciding who will be a caregiver, and all the associated details, often occurs during a crisis, when emotions are already tense. Add to this the perceived obligation to nurture, common among women, and the conflict can escalate.

Scene One, Take Seventy-Six

Often the struggles that occur during the illness and death of a family elder bring into play a family "script" that has been in existence for decades. The bully will continue to be aggressive, and the victim will receive mean-spirited messages delivered in ways that are designed for maximum hurt.

Consider these situations described in greater detail on a caregiving Web site:

▌ A younger sister (the family black sheep) who came around to see her elderly parents only when she needed money. The mother gave her money, even though she didn't have any to spare. Manipulation and perhaps guilt provoking were the RA behaviors used to take advantage of a relationship.

▌ An adult woman who drives one hour twice a week to take groceries to her elderly parents when her sister lives within minutes of their home and won't help. Again, either the silent treatment from the nearby sister or her quiet manipulation and guilt provoking was an RA lever to avoid responsibility.

▌ Struggles between an eighty-five-year-old woman and her daughter over how the mother's money will be spent. In reading this entire message, a power play was clearly ensuing. The mother was intimidating her daughter with threats of disinheritance if she didn't "shape up," while the daughter was manipulating her mother to give her money and threatening to withdraw affection, more classic RA.

"My cousin just couldn't stop criticizing me for the care I provided for my mother after her stroke," Rhonda, a middle-aged woman who was both a full-time employee and the caregiver for her frail mother for five years, told me.

As she spoke, it was clear she was still distressed, years after her mother's death. "She would arrive at the house and begin bullying me around, saying things that were frankly hurtful. 'Why don't you comb her hair this way?' 'Can't you find something nicer for her to wear?' 'You need to feed her the kind of food she used to cook for you.' No man would do that."

Further questioning revealed that Rhonda and this particular cousin had had a lifelong history of acrimony, not much different from their interaction in the caregiving phase of their relationship. However, Rhonda felt particularly wounded because her cousin's relationally aggressive comments were directed at the care she was providing for her mother, and they struck at the core of her feelings of obligation and competence. Being judged as deficient in a family caregiving situation seems to strike at the heart of a woman's identity, and is her Achilles' heel in the same way that deficient parenting would be.

In the midst of what should be a loving gesture to an older member of the family, horrible conflicts between women can arise. I saw many of them in my time as a nurse practitioner. The woman who first opened my eyes to RA between female relatives was Deanna, the adult daughter of my patient Patricia, a seventy-eight-year-old woman who had suffered a serious stroke. She was dependent on others (that is, Deanna) for help with day-to-day activities she had always done for herself. The first time we met, Deanna described the full-time care she was providing for Patricia. She'd been "on the job" for only a month, but already the signs of strain were there: dark circles around her eyes, a sad expression on her face, and posture that told me she was worn out.

Deanna's husband, Frank, had just retired in the hopes they could finally fulfill a lifelong dream and take the cross-country trip their adult children had been bugging them about. Then Deanna received a midnight call from a hospital in Florida informing her that her widowed mother was seriously ill. She flew to Florida, as did her younger sister Norma, who lived in California with her husband and teenage son. At Patricia's bedside, the two sisters discussed what to do with their mother once the hospitalization ended. The discussion quickly escalated into an argument.

"Norma thought Mom should be put in a nursing home and never considered having her come live in California," Deanna told me, recalling the scene with rancor. "She accused me of wanting to save money so we'd have an inheritance, and left after a day, telling me the problem was in my hands since I didn't like the solution she came up with.

"Growing up, we didn't have the greatest relationship," Deanna admitted, "but my mother did take care of me, so I decided it was only right that I reciprocate, especially after I visited some of the facilities the hospital recommended."

Focusing on the present, Deanna sighed. "Every day there are new problems: the urinary tract infection, the walker that broke, the medication the pharmacy insisted wasn't covered by her insurance. When I call Norma and try to talk about Mom, she thinks I'm hinting at getting money from her to help with expenses. I'm not—I just need some support."

Norma's behavior was topped by Aunt 'Nita, Patricia's sister, who made weekly visits weekly to check up on Deanna. While Deanna might have welcomed able-bodied 'Nita's visits if she volunteered to help out or even give Deanna a free hour, that didn't happen. Instead, Aunt 'Nita spoke almost exclusively to Deanna's mom, referring to Deanna in the third person:

"Is *she* giving you extra fluids like I suggested?"

"Has *she* taken you to the doctor about that sore toe?"

"Did *she* tell you I called to check up on you this week?"

Deanna had learned not to challenge 'Nita when she was a teenager and her aunt had ridiculed her new bra in front of the entire family one Christmas. Still, desperate for relief, she tentatively questioned 'Nita about her willingness to pitch in and keep Patricia company from time to time. In return, she got the same silent treatment she had often received in childhood.

Deanna, like many of the women I would see in the years that followed, was involved in carewearing, which is my name for extreme caregiving. Each day, there was a demand to provide varying degrees of emotional and physical support for an infirm elder, often at the expense of other family members. The situations varied as much as the individual women involved, but all reflected back to the concept of kin-keeping and child caring. There seemed to be a very short lapse of time between the launching of one's adult children and the assumption of caregiving for an older parent.

The Caring Imperative

Women in families are almost always the ones to step forward and bear responsibility for the care of a frail or debilitated elder, even if the person is an in-law. (Men help more often through financial support.) Often middle-aged and beginning to recognize their own mortality, they will caregive until they are exhausted and even then feel they haven't done enough. For many, there is often a need to let go of the "supercaregiver" complex, which drives women to the point of exhaustion. Frequently I heard women who spent most of their day providing care for an elderly loved one say they felt guilty for not doing more.

Dealing with a "pseudocaregiver" (Mall 1990) who makes minimal contributions to avoid being accused of not helping at all is another challenge that many caregivers face. At other times, women who appear to shirk their daughterly obligations are in reality unable to step into that role due to other obligations or sheer squeamishness, and they feel plenty guilty about it. What looks like nonchalance and neglect can be deceiving—but the daughter who is exhausted from providing hours of care may not understand her sister's qualms about dealing with the illness of a loved one.

Another interesting caregiving issue is how often childhood roles are resumed during late life. For Deanna, a lifetime of being the caregiver for whatever went wrong in the family may have conditioned others to believe she really didn't mind this role. By considering the possibility that the current situation may be a replay of lifelong patterns, women can look more objectively at their relationship with, and obligations to, an elderly family member. In a win-win situation, caregiving strengthens family connections rather than weakens them. Performing care from a sense of love and affection rather than out of obligation can facilitate this (Pyke and Bengston 1996). The following story is another illustration of a female family feud that fractured relationships—almost beyond the point of repair.

To the Rescue
Gwen Roberts Tyndale

I ended a relationship with my beloved elderly aunt Peggy two years ago, after my mother was diagnosed with paranoid schizophrenia at age sixty-five. She was involuntarily committed to a mental hospital by the police. It was an extremely emotional and painful time for me.

At the hospital, my mother's psychiatrist asked if I knew any history about my mother's family. I didn't, so I called and e-mailed my mother's two older sisters, Peggy and Anne. I also asked my cousin, Anne's daughter, for information. Cagey responses came after I tried to confirm stories my mother had told me about a male cousin who had committed suicide.

Vehement denials came up like coffee in a percolator. They denied that there was any kind of mental illness in the family. I insisted that I knew there was. I wasn't looking to blame, but it was taken that way. My mother was the prettiest, the smartest, and evidently the weirdest.

Here is an excerpt from the e-mail that ended it all for me:

"We have all been taken aback by the fact that she has not gotten her act together. I had thought she had gotten a grip on life but she is still up to her old tricks. Do not know of any suicides—maybe you are thinking of someone else. Maybe my brain is atrophying also.

"We all have our limitations. Your mother always had delusions of grandeur and I figured it was just in the makeup of the person and was not catastrophic. Enough of that. Am afraid I cannot add any more to what you already know. Do not know what the doctors are looking for but that is your problem and theirs."

In retrospect, my aunts might have perceived me as a bully. I kept up the e-mail exchange of questions, perhaps longer than I should have. Maybe I should have let up on the questions and just accepted their answers.

Less than eight months after my mother was diagnosed, my aunt Anne died of a heart attack. I was politely uninvited to the funeral. I had the task of telling my mother while she was in a nursing home that her closest sister had passed away, and that the funeral was already over.

Up until the hospitalization, I took refuge in Aunt Peggy. I never had a close relationship with my mother and often saw Peggy as my second mother. She had sent care packages to me in college, made and bought things for me, and confided in me. She listened to all my complaints about my mother's bizarre behavior.

Something about this hospitalization crystallized my commitment to my mother. I took offense at comments Aunt Peggy made in her e-mails that referenced my mother's "wing nut" personality. It was all true, but it hurt even more during this time. So I had to cut off communication to survive. It was a relief not to deal with her, but on the other hand, I felt great sorrow over losing her.

Now that I am not in the throes of anxiety, anger, and self-pity, I see things differently. Aunt Peggy recently sent me a Christmas card that I think was an olive branch. I have been spending time going back and reading her e-mails, thinking about how I am going to respond to her card, and I think soon we will reconcile. I just don't know exactly what I should apologize for.

Feeling protective of and responsible for your mother's well-being is often a trump card that outweighs other motivations. Like Gwen, many women rush to defend or explain the behavior of a mom they may not have been emotionally close to.

The advance of technology further complicates the situation. Cyberslamming or online RA can occur when communication is terse and lacking the body language cues women depend on. When e-mails are the sole means of contact, especially between relatives who have been out of touch, there is further risk of misunderstanding.

What We Inherit

Unfortunately, caregiving crises aren't the only kind women (and men) deal with in later years, but again, the kin-keeping role of women shapes their responses to failing health, dying, and death in subtle and surprising ways. While Gwen may have offended her aunt by ceasing e-mail contact, she was the recipient of put-downs, open insults, and exclusion from a cherished relative. She also missed the chance to attend the funeral of another relative she cared about. There was hope for reconciliation, but many times there is not. All too often, I hear about bitter battles that arise after an elderly family member dies, often over the most inconsequential possessions and, almost always, fiercely fought by women, as the following story illustrates.

Situations with Sisters That Involve a Female Family Feud
Miriya Kilmore

Mom's sobbing woke me. "I have to go. I have to go right now." My father tried to comfort her as she frantically dialed the airport, trying to change her flight.

She'd been fast asleep when a dream changed her world. "Dad said I have to hurry. I have to come right now."

A quick call to her stepmother confirmed her worst fears.

"He had a stroke an hour ago. They don't know how long he'll live."

Mom was on the first plane in the morning. My grandfather died an hour after she took hold of his hand.

I'd only met him once. A kindly man, he let us romp through the pastures of his two-hundred-acre farm and explore the island in the middle of the river. A lifelong equestrian, I loved his big barn, with its smell of hay and old leather.

Before my mom could return to meet with family and divide up her father's memorabilia, her sister rented a truck, filled it with his belongings, and drove home. Mom was furious. Phone calls and letters raged to no avail. Jennifer was determined to keep her booty. Mom was determined not to speak to her again if she didn't share.

Mom's mourning centered on her father's harnesses, which surprised me. She hated horses and never went near ours. Yet she would have conceded everything else Jennifer snatched if only she could own the horse collars and harnesses that once adorned the necks of her father's team. It wasn't to be.

Jennifer died without acknowledging her sister's request. Her daughters ignored Mom's pleas too, even when they knew she was dying from breast cancer. My cousin Debra, Jennifer's youngest daughter, attended the funeral, at last bringing the collar and the harnesses. Debra handed them to my youngest sister, Kathy, who turned them over to me, saying Jennifer wanted me to have them. I don't know if that is true. It's just as likely that I, the family scapegoat, received them only after everyone else turned them down.

Although I treasure these items, the feud behind them keeps me from full enjoyment. Even worse is the knowledge of the legacy of a sister feud continued into the next generation.

Disparities in longevity have led some to call aging a feminist issue. Caregiving for an elderly family member is also unique to women, who are much more likely to take on this responsibility, even if they suffer declines in their own income and health because of it. Women who are caregiving for a fragile elder are much like their younger counterparts. They cluster together in the same way as parents of infants, seeking support and advice on issues such as nutrition, sleep, and medical care.

It's the Same Old Song:
You and Mom at Midlife

There can be tensions between mothers and daughters as well when roles are reversed and mothers find themselves relying on daughters who may disappoint or surprise them. (Sometimes the "ideal" daughter shrinks away from caregiving and the rebellious child steps forward and does a wonderful job.)

I remember visiting an older woman I'll call Lindy, who lived in an urban area where she was being cared for by her daughter, Nancy. Their cluttered apartment seemed poorly arranged to accommodate a fragile elder who needed a walker to get around, but it had been Lindy's home for many years, and she was reluctant to move.

Nancy lived with Lindy, and while their quarters weren't spotless, it was clear that Lindy got her medicine on time, was kept clean and comfortable, and had opportunities to go out to the movies or shopping at least once a week. Still, Nancy showed no affection for her mother and seemed almost mechanical in her interactions.

The tenor of our visits changed when I happened to stop by one day when Nancy was out running an errand. Lindy told me she felt Nancy had never forgiven her for divorcing her father many years earlier and marrying a man who then deserted the family, absconding with all the life insurance money the first husband left.

Sensitive to the issue of abuse, I listened to Lindy describe Nancy's "silent treatments" and mocking behavior: "Sometimes she uses this baby voice to repeat what I say, just to be mean."

Lindy didn't want to move out of her apartment, nor did she want Nancy to leave. Authorities would not consider the situation abusive: with too many older patients needing beds in too few facilities, there was no overt mistreatment that would move Lindy to the top of the list, even if she requested that. (You might think it would be easy to find alternative care, but baby boomers beware—services for the elderly look impressive on paper, but they are often nonexistent when you really need them.) Counseling with Nancy revealed that she felt Lindy was nasty to her, too, using guilt to keep her tied to the apartment when she really wanted to accept at least a part-time job.

Even after death, the potential for sibling rivalry involving a parent can persist, as the following story shows.

The Obit
Essi Simpson

They were just as I left them the day of Mom's funeral service . . . photos from the old country, bearded men, women in black dresses, their hair covered as required of Orthodox Jews—my mother's relatives. Only she could identify them, and now she was gone. She was the last of the family who came to America, where "the streets were paved with gold." I sat in a fog of sadness, and tuned out. I forced myself up. There were things to do.

The mail . . . I hadn't opened it yesterday or today. I could tell by the shape of the envelopes that most were cards. I was intrigued by one from Shirl. She'd gone back to Arden the day after the cremation. The envelope felt almost empty, like it might be a check or a one-page note, but not a letter. It was a clipping from the paper. A few lines. An obit about my mother. As I unfolded it to read "Mrs. Gordon is survived by a daughter, Shirley Marsden," my jaw tightened. A daughter? She couldn't have said "*A* daughter." Not my only sister, my twin sister; it must be a mistake. But why did she send it? Anger seeped into my confusion. I was burning. I stood, the old photographs rustling as they scattered. I needed water, anything cold to "cool" my feelings. It is a horrible mistake, I muttered as I telephoned her. I took a deep breath.

"I got the obit, Shirley. Is it right?"

"What do you mean?" she asked.

"Shirl, is it okay? They made a mistake, didn't they? Did they make a mistake?"

I heard the little noises she makes when she needs time, but was she upset? Hell, no.

"Did you write it or did they? How could you send it? Why did you send it?" My questions shot out, and I recognized that my voice was distorted by anger, forced from a throat that was knotted with growing rage and hopelessness.

"How could you write it? You left me out, you kicked me out of the family. How could you do it?"

I waited. Finally . . .

"I guess I was just so upset," she said.

"Did I hear right? What did you say?"

"I guess I was just so upset" she repeated weakly.

"Bullshit!" I snapped in anger and despair, banging the phone down. This time my sister had outdone herself. I was through. It was hopeless . . . hopeless.

But time numbs.

A week or so later she called. "I haven't heard from you."

"Did you expect to after that obit?" I countered. "Until you take some responsibility for it, I can't talk to you. Don't you realize what it said . . . how I'd feel?"

"I'm sorry. I talked to my therapist, and she thought I could have been that upset."

"Do you understand why I'm making 'such a fuss' as you put it?"

"It's not an obituary," she said. "Didn't I tell you, it's a death notice? They are different. They're for local people, and they don't mention relatives living far away."

This was typical Shirl: avoid, evade, duck. My shoulders drooped. "You've been trying for years, Essi," I told myself, "give it up."

Over the next weeks when we talked, I stopped pushing. I heard one of my mom's old sayings: "It's like trying to get blood from a stone." I was trying to heal as the weeks passed. Shirl phoned.

"I've been thinking. Maybe it was unconscious stuff. Essi, I don't want to hurt you, I love you."

"That helps. I've wondered about that," I acknowledged, believing it was as good as it would get. The hurt is scarring over, but I've learned to live with scars. I live with my sister.

These sisters had shared so much and were divided by animosity, and yet found a way to reunite during a time of grief. In the months that followed Essi's story, perhaps she and Shirley discovered that they could heal their relationship and replace aggression with affection and sorrow with support.

16

Really Forced to Be Family: Divorce

Although divorce severs relationships, remarriage holds the promise of new opportunities to create a family. However, when children are involved and a new wife must be in close contact with both her predecessor and that person's offspring, "forced to be family" takes on a new meaning. (Usually the ex-wife is just as wary of her replacement and the effect she may have on children from the previous marriage.) The greater the number of people involved in the divorce drama, the more clashes in expectations and perceptions are likely to occur, and, in direct proportion, the intensity of relational aggression can spiral out of control.

Dylan Evans, a senior lecturer in intelligent autonomous systems at the University of the West of England, authored *Introducing Evolutional Psychology* along with the illustrator Oscar Zarate (imagine a graphic novel or a comic book approach to the topic). Dr. Evans believes we marry a particular person because we believe he or she would make a good mate and parent to our future children, not because we love his existing sons and/or daughters. If a woman were to have her own children to add to the mix of a new romantic partnership, it's natural that her protective drives would be biased toward them. Evans's views offer a reasonable explanation, perhaps not politically correct, for why remarriage and stepparenting are such challenging endeavors.

Sharing the Man and His Clan

It's not surprising that many bitter stories have come my way from women who had a problematic relationship with another woman because at some point in their lives, they both married the same man. No one expects the current and the former girlfriends of a star quarterback in high school to get along, especially if the split from the boy was acrimonious. Regardless of the flaws or rude behavior of the husband (or boyfriend), it's guaranteed that the current girlfriend or new wife will almost always be the target of the ex's venom. (I did a podcast on this topic with the award-winning author Lisa Cohn, at www.stepfamilytalkradio.com, audio name "Step Moms and Their Husbands' Ex-Wives.)

Throw in ex-mothers-in-law, partisan sisters, and an array of other extended former family members, each with his or her own agenda in support of the biological mom or dad, and you can imagine what verbal violence might result. (That's assuming the parties involved don't have mental health issues on top of whatever sparks might be flying between previous and current partners.)

Ripe for RA

In her book *It's Not My Stepkids—It's Their Mom*, the author Karon Phillips Goodman compares an ex-wife to "the soap opera character you love to hate and can't kill off." She argues that a stepmom has very little real authority over a biological mom, who will always have number-one status with her children. At the same time, current and ex-wives share an uneasy legal status that could connect them forever via the man and the children they share.

When I began teaching, my oldest son attended a day care center at the university where I worked. It was a wonderful place, but the adjustment was rough for both of us. There was a huge plate-glass window facing the parking lot, and for some reason, the lead teacher felt it would be helpful for my crying son to be held up there so he could see me pull away each morning, leaving him to his destiny in a world of terrifying three-year-olds. If I hadn't been dependent on my paycheck, I would have ditched work and plucked my screaming son out of his captor's arms; as it was, I put my car in reverse and went to my office.

Later, when I had to surrender him to a stepmother, I often felt that same sinking feeling in my stomach, with hundreds of "What ifs?" percolating through my mind. I wasn't so abnormal; when mothers find themselves supplanted by another woman, it's threatening, even if the new stepmom just won an award for outstanding parent of the world (perhaps more so in that situation). There is often a mixture of fear ("Will she care for my children?"), envy ("She gets to care for my children"), and resentment ("Why does she want to care for my children?").

One ex-wife openly admits to jealousy because her kids seem to like their stepmom better. "She's younger and more fun," she says. "And, like a mother bear defending her cubs, my worst side comes out around her."

"I'll never forget the day when my daughter's stepmom told her that I had walked out on her dad because I didn't love him or her," says Sharon, whose daughter is now grown and the mother of her own child. Decades later, Sharon's bitterness is still evident.

The new wife, Linda, had a different story. "Sharon made it clear she wasn't interested in her daughter until it came time for her to pay alimony. She was running around with other men until my husband took her to court. Then suddenly she decided she wanted to be 'mother of the year.'"

Whose story tells the complete truth? No one—most certainly the participants—will ever know. It's only now, twenty-six years after my divorce, that I have begun to see many things that I could have done differently. (My current husband was smart enough to provide lots of moral support and avoid emotional explosions, which was exactly the right approach.)

Women Speak Out

Lisa Cohn, the author of *One Family, Two Family, New Family* and a cohost of Stepfamily Talk Radio (www.stepfamilytalkradio.com), says that after divorce, many, if not most, of the issues that come to her attention involve women. One of the biggest problems she hears about is the first wife–second wife relationship, where intense aggression can be very subtle.

The usual means for achieving more peaceful relationships is to try to get the various parties together to talk face-to-face, but this becomes difficult given the typical pattern of undermining, bad-mouthing, and trying to make one another's lives miserable in various ways. On the rare occasion when Cohn hears from men, she finds that they write to discuss having a hard time with an ex-wife over their children.

Cohn says, "It is really difficult for women to have their children away from them half of the time, and to allow other women into their lives, especially as a mom. It's on a very primitive level: I gave birth to this kid and raised it, and now I'm expected to let another woman take my place?"

Cohn also offers online stepfamily advice in a weekly column. She recalls a situation where a woman went from being the first wife to being an ex-wife, and she felt very threatened by the new step-mom, especially when her son came home smelling like the other woman's perfume. Another of Cohn's question-and-answer columns at Philly Women (www.philly.com/mld/philly/living/people/women/columns) described a situation where a mother went so far as to copy the stepmother's hairstyle, dress, and decorating style.

This situation will be further aggravated when children are drawn into the battle and used as indirect weapons against the mom or stepmom. Consider the following situations:

- Michelle shares custody of her ten-year-old son, Todd, with her ex-husband, Mark. After each visit to his dad's house, Michelle grills Todd about his stepmother, Anna. She warns him not to trust Anna because Anna is threatened by how much Mark loves Todd and wants his dad to stop visitation because she thinks Todd is bad.

- Stepmom Trish tells her husband's two teenaged daughters that their mother was having an affair, which caused the divorce. She points out each new boyfriend the girls' mother dates, and raises her eyebrows when the relationships don't last.

- Mom Alicia refuses to let her ex-husband's new wife, Lisa, pick up their daughter, Candace, for custody visits. She also won't acknowledge Lisa, and refuses to say hello or speak directly to her. She refers to Lisa as "your dad's new wife" whenever she has to talk about her to Candace.

▌ Ann admonishes her five-year-old daughter, Marissa, that she should never call her stepmother "Mom" or any other affectionate term. When she drops Marissa off for visits, she shares her dictate with both Marissa's dad and his new wife.

▌ Carmen is the mother of two grown daughters. Although she walked out on her husband twenty years ago, she can't stop the flow of bitterness she still feels toward him, and she regularly indoctrinates the girls with the flaws of both their dad and his new wife. The daughters are then confused by Carmen's sweet persona when all of the players in this drama are forced to be together.

The Ex-In-Laws

Relatives-in-law can exacerbate the situation further by refusing to consider a second family to be a real family, or by treating stepchildren with rudeness or indifference. The most common complaint I've heard relates to mothers-in-law who won't acknowledge children from a new marriage as their grandchildren.

Cohn frequently hears about this, too. Ideally, all women involved should work together for the well-being of the children, and men should take a stand, but that ideal rarely occurs. No doubt, men have their share of burdens postdivorce, but it's usually the women who bear the brunt of hostile coalition building between former and new wives. Blending together various female family personalities is sometimes like whipping up a milk shake and other times like mixing cement.

Step-grandparents must also find a niche, says Dawn Miller, author of a column on life in blended families (www.thestepfamilylife.com). She shared her own experience on her Web site and gave me permission to reprint part of it here:

Like every mother of the bride, my mom was delighted to hear that I was getting married. My parents liked my fiancé and were happy for us, but my mom was especially excited about her three new step-grandchildren. Finally, she was about to become a step-grandma.

My mom is June Cleaver incarnate. In her mind's eye, she saw herself playing games with one stepkid, giving another advice, and baking cookies with the third.

Mom was ecstatic. I was terrified.

With the boys at eighteen and fourteen and my stepdaughter at twelve, I worried how receptive they would be to a whole new set of step-grandparents.

So I sat her down and said, "Look, Mom, please go light on the kids. Give them space and don't push it. They already have two full sets of grandparents, and they will need time to adjust. Don't expect for them to treat you like regular grandparents."

She looked hurt. Crushed even. I had popped her bubble with blended family reality.

Extended family members may either support or turn against the first mom after a divorce, regardless of their previous relationship with her. At times, in-laws keep pictures of the first wife on display, which bothers stepmoms. They might think their in-laws are favoring the mom over her, and wonder: "Is that because they want to stay close to the children or because they don't like me?" At other times, an ex-wife can find her image cut out of photographs and all evidence of her existence erased from the in-laws' lives.

Again, for the sake of the kids, hopefully the grandma can get along with both the stepmom and the mom, but all three are in a potentially tense situation. I remember well how different the climates were at my son's two homes, and how clearly the lines of loyalty were drawn. Although my husband and I were careful to shield my son from the conflicts, I know he picked up on the tension. (I can't help envying my youngest sister, who is the one woman I know who has an easy, collegial relationship with her ex, who hasn't remarried.)

Another perspective on solutions to in-law issues is offered by Miller in her column "When Your In-Laws Act Like Outlaws":

There's no easy solution to in-law woes, but sometimes not going to an event is all you can do. There are lots of reasons people avoid socializing with their in-laws. Feeling like you are being judged and like you don't fit in is at the top of most people's lists.

Although many married couples have in-law issues, in a blended family situation in-law flare-ups can be volatile. Second wives often feel like they are tiptoeing around followed by the ghost of an ex-wife. In my case—it's literal.

My husband's ex-wife attends every party and holiday event held by my husband's large extended family—watching my every move, ensuring her children give their father (and me) none of the hugs we normally receive, and reinforcing that she will always have known my husband's relatives far longer than I have.

My situation is not typical. In a normal divorce, the ex-wife does not expect an invitation to Uncle Sam's birthday party or Christmas Eve dinner. Although postdivorce coparenting is quite popular, sharing holiday meals and extended family events is not recommended by even some of coparenting's staunchest advocates.

Although my in-laws claim her inclusion is for the sake of the children, it's apparent that that's not the driving reason behind why she attends every family get-together. It's not a two-way street. When her family is in town or holds parties for my husband's children, he's not invited.

The real reason is that to my husband's family his previous marriage is not over. One of my sisters-in-law put it quite well: only he divorced his ex-wife—they never did. The point was driven home to me repeatedly during my father-in-law's funeral, when she was introduced to guests as if she was still my husband's wife, and I was expected to stand in family portraits alongside her and smile.

To resolve the growing tension this was causing in our lives, my husband and I tried to identify a compromise that we can live with, one that preserves our relationships with his kids and allows me to get to know my in-laws a little better and without an ex-wife in tow.

My husband asked his siblings to support our request to find a "balance" at family events, and they agreed to clear invitations for his ex-wife before family events. He also talked to his ex-wife and explained that she might not be invited to some events—she was none too pleased. At first we thought our plan would work, but reality soon tore it to shreds.

Every request by an in-law to invite my husband's ex-wife to a family activity was prefaced with emotional pleas and manipulations. After never turning down a request, my husband hit his limit and asked his sister not to invite his ex-wife to a party.

It was a family going-away party for my niece. We figured that if his ex-wife was keen on spending time with her former niece that she'd go out with her for lunch or coffee, that there was plenty of opportunity to say good-bye outside a family event. We thought we were being reasonable. We thought wrong.

His sister took off her rhetorical gloves. First there were ugly barbs about the demise of his first marriage. Then the complaint that we were making things difficult and the jibe that I "would be accepted, but for my being too distant." She topped it off with the revelation that the family would rather have his ex-wife at gatherings than us, and that they would not support our wishes for balance.

So we made other plans.

It seemed easier than walking into an emotional boobytrap on hostile turf with an ex-wife in our wake. And quite frankly we had little desire to spend time with the in-laws at this point. For us our priorities are our marriage and our time with the kids. And those things work well for us right now. The in-laws can just stay outlaws for a while.

Stepsibs and Stepkids

RA can surface in its most virulent form between stepmoms and moms, but stepchildren can also be involved. There have even been extreme circumstances where a mom called state authorities for a protection-from-abuse order against a stepmom. One can only imagine the conflicting stories the police heard and the stress it caused the kids.

Loyalty issues in situations like this make children feel uncomfortable, but girls can also be jealous of the attention their dad bestows on his new wife, particularly if the divorce occurs before a girl has developed her own sense of self-esteem and sexuality. In the same way, female stepsiblings and their stepmoms can get into a contest with no winners: the father/husband will resent being forced to choose between two people he loves, just as any woman would.

Consider the stories of Tammy, Barb, and Lee Anne. Tammy says:

I am married to Tom, who had a daughter before we were married. I also had two children from a previous marriage, and then we had twins together. At first, my stepdaughter was very attached to her father and did not want to share him. After we had been together for a year and a half, she got much better at this. It also took some time for her to get used to the rules of our home because her dad was more laid back with her before I came along. Through consistency, love, and acceptance, we had open communication about our feelings and needs. We made sure that she had quality time with her Dad, one-on-one, and also with all of us as a family. It just took some time and patience. It is still challenging: I love all of them and spend time with them equally, but I used to catch myself favoring my birth daughter when they got into arguments. I realized this and prayed to God and he helped me love my stepdaughter and treat her like my own. To me she is my own now.

Barb says:

I have one sister from both my mother and father, and three half-siblings by my mother. My mother never remarried after she and my dad split up. My dad remarried when I was six. I have three stepsiblings who are all much older than me. My stepfamily is pretty close; the biggest conflict that seems to be a theme with my stepmother is her trying to tell my dad what to do. She used to tell him how he should discipline my sister and me and to be stricter with us. I also get mad when she attempts to control him in other ways, too. My relationship with my mother is close and nurturing. I feel like she has gone through a lot of life struggles that I can learn from. My stepmother is book smart and is a good source of support for information on schools and careers. Our relationship feels like it is superficial. I love her, but I dislike her at the same time.

Lee Ann says:

My dad and mom divorced when I was young, and my mom disappeared from my life. My dad married a woman with one daughter who is two years younger than me. We have had a lot of conflict, at first between me and my stepmom because I resented sharing my dad with anyone. After a while, though, I got used to her, and it was sort of nice to have a clean house and home-cooked meals, so I tolerated her. My stepsister is another case entirely. She is the original drama queen who has a way of getting every drop of attention available: she's sick or she's depressed or she's having trouble with friends. I'll see her crying one moment and laughing on the phone the next, as soon as our parents are out of the house. She also constantly sets me up as the bad guy and makes it look like I've been rude to her or mistreated her. I think what bothers me most are the holidays because my stepmom has a huge family and my stepsister goes out of her way to make it clear I'm not a "real" part of the family and don't know everyone as well as she does.

For each of these women, Relative RA is an everyday occurrence. Tammy faces manipulation, disrespect, and competition from her new stepdaughter. Barb must deal with rivalry and competition as well as conflicting loyalties. Lee Anne's challenge is to overcome the manipulative behavior of her stepsister, as well as her feelings of rivalry.

Common Clashes

Based on my reading and interviewing, there seem to be some typical scenarios where moms and stepmoms may clash:

1. School events, where a mom either refuses to allow the stepmom to come, or the stepmom is so intimidated by the mom she chooses not to go.

2. Holidays, which are made more stressful by jockeying for position with kids and debates over who will see which relatives and when. Even though relationships may appear cordial on a day-to-day basis, holidays often bring out hidden tensions.

3. Transition times, when new jobs or new homes throw a precarious state of balance off kilter as both sets of families try to adjust to changing circumstances.

4. Loyalty demands such that the husband in the middle is forced to take a stand and choose between his kids, his ex-wife, and his new wife (and possibly her kids).

5. Financial pressures and struggles between families over who should pay how much and for what.

Each of these issues can manifest itself in behaviors that are relationally aggressive, either directly between the individuals involved or on a larger scale with one family against another.

In an Ideal World

In a healthy relationship, women feel secure about themselves and their relationships with their children: a mom doesn't undermine a stepmom or vice versa, and neither feels the need to force children to demonstrate more love for her over the other. Usually kids want everyone to be happy, so they suffer the most when there are relationally aggressive rifts between their moms and stepmoms.

Karon Goodman cautions women to remember that this is a relationship that is going to last forever, so if either the mom or the stepmom says something negative or demeaning to the children, the kids will respect her less. She points out that adults have a great opportunity to role-model kindness and forgiveness to the kids through their interactions with each other. (Like most divorced women, I have to admit I never appreciated the fact that my situation presented such an opportunity.)

Goodman concludes, "It's a very tough situation, and not something a woman thinks about, because you don't plan to become a stepmom. It can be really hard, no matter what you do, because there are so many people to consider and so many things to control. Getting to the point where you can exist without conflict can take a long time. A good motto is to deal with what you can and let go of the rest."

What's in It for Him?

Jann Blackstone-Ford, a divorcee and stepfamily mediator and the director of Bonus Families and author of three books (www.bonusfamilies.com), suggests that some husbands may not want their current wives and their ex-wives to get along, so they create, facilitate, or tolerate an adversarial relationship between the two women. Blackstone-Ford notes that there is also a difference if the biological mom has remarried, because the situation is more balanced when both ex-husband and ex-wife have found new partners.

Karon Goodman has several suggestions for moms and stepmoms hoping to have a positive relationship:

▍ Set aside feelings of intimidation that might cause you to respond in an aggressive way.

▍ Show that you are reasonable by being willing to compromise—rather than issuing edicts, make requests in a factual, nonargumentative way.

▍ Be proactive in addressing issues, but don't assume that you know what the outcome will be.

▍ Solve one problem at a time and have more than one plan as backup. Offer new chances for a better dynamic, and don't take things personally

▍ Avoid losing your temper, and understand that there are times when you must be with the ex-wife, and that when that happens, her children will want to be with her.

▍ Focus on others, not on yourself or the mom.

▍ Keep a journal that offers you an outlet for expressing emotions as well for maintaining a factual record.

Making It Happen

Despite wonderful advice, difficult situations will still occur within families, with solutions hard to identify and harder to implement. Although children complicate a divorce situation further, even a childless divorce can bring out underlying tensions between family members.

Mistakenly, many divorcing couples assume their own family members will support them in whatever course of action they take, but this isn't always the case. When your own sister or mother sides with your ex-husband, it can add extra drama to an already difficult situation.

On the other hand, trying to maintain relationships with ex-in-laws you may have known for a long time can be challenging for women, who take family fractures to heart and engage in an ongoing search for solutions. Sometimes wounded feelings can lead them to lash out in anger when they believe they have been emotionally abandoned. Men can engage in the same behaviors, of course, but the perceptions driving them differ for reasons already explained.

The following story demonstrates how RA was used by one sister against another in a postdivorce situation.

Betrayed by My Own
Lane Johnson

My older sister, Jan, and I have had a somewhat competitive relationship (I'm four years younger than her, and the second-oldest of four kids.) While I tend to "take care of" the sister and brother younger than me, Jan and I have much more of a prickly relationship. For example, if I want to visit her spontaneously when I'm driving through her town, she'll always let me know if it's a time that's acceptable to her or not.

I think our relationship got worse when I divorced my second husband and a few years later began dating a white man. She was very disapproving of me having an interracial relationship as well as leaving my ex-husband, but never came right out and said it.

When my current husband and I got married, he was always nice to her, but she and her husband were always cool toward us. The first time she visited us in our house at Christmas, she left after staying only forty-five minutes because she wanted to stop at my ex-husband's home to visit while she was in town.

The final blow was when I found out that she was in town for a pastors' conference, and that she and her husband planned to visit my ex-husband, who happens to be black, like them. They discussed with him at length how they thought I had made a mistake marrying my current husband, but never came by to see me or even bother to tell me that they had lunch with him! I heard it all secondhand through a mutual friend.

When I asked her about it, she blew it off by saying she ran into him by coincidence at the mall and they had lunch. She insisted that I was being manipulative by not wanting her to be friends with him! I felt really betrayed by my sister when she did this, as if her loyalty was greater to my ex-husband (who had been incredibly abusive) than to me, and I don't believe her actions were prompted by caring at all.

The Truth Test

If you're in the midst of a stepfamily drama, you might get some insight on what is motivating the RA by answering these questions:

1. Is this behavior about *me* or about *her*?

2. Are her motives related to the welfare of her children?

3. Is there a lot of animosity between her and her ex-husband that's affecting me when it shouldn't have to?

4. Is there ever a time when we relate in a neutral or positive way?

5. How does she relate to other women?

6. Does she have other emotional and physical problems that affect our interactions?

7. How motivated am I to work out a relationship with her versus just having no contact?

8. Would she be willing to go to therapy with me?

9. Are our conflicts about specific situations or about life in general?

10. Am I comfortable with her being with my husband when I am not there?

Figuring out whether the conflict is really about unresolved feelings you have nothing to do with, discovering if RA is her standard operating procedure, and being honest about your own feelings are all strategies for gaining insight. Thinking outside the box to find novel ways to intervene are other steps to empower you and the ex, as well as demonstrating positive relationship skills to those in your family.

PART FIVE

Connected, Caring, or Coping

17

The Female Family Maintenance Plan

By now, you may be wondering if there's any hope for women to have cordial and rewarding relationships with family members. The answer is absolutely! Just reading this book is the first step toward improving your relationship skills as you begin to recognize that in our culture, women are the primary conduits for emotional experience (Surrey 1991). Belonging to, and feeling valued within, a family means something different to women, which is why most will go to extraordinary lengths to prevent female family feuds.

Long before tiny tensions escalate to full-scale conflict, there *are* actions you can take to prevent a relationally aggressive dynamic from dominating relationships with females in your family. Granted, you aren't going to be able to stop a longtime bully or a victim from living out their entrenched roles by educating them about RA, but you can create a shift, however small, in the way situations get played out. Even if you are the only one willing to change, that may be enough to alter a lifelong pattern of destructive interaction between you and your mother, your sister, or others.

Reaching a Diagnosis

Developing insight into the dynamics of your female family situation is a bit like the diagnostic workup you get in the doctor's office. Before a problem can be identified, different kinds of information need to be collected. If the problem is complex, more questions need to be answered; if it's simple, the job is a little more straightforward. For example, it takes more probing to detect diabetes than it does the common cold.

In health care, the best way to improve outcomes for any specific illness is prevention, hence the drive to exercise, control stress, maintain ideal body weight, and so on. The same principle can apply to RA: being proactive to eliminate risk factors and maintain healthy relationships is the most effective way to eliminate this dynamic. Obviously, when a mother's mean behavior has made you miserable for years, you're not going to erase the past, but perhaps you can shape the future.

The Family Script

I've mentioned the concept of family scripts; they provide a good place to start, much as a doctor will review what we call a PMH (past medical history) when you first come in for a visit. Just like the volumes of paperwork most health-care institutions require, gathering data on your family script can be time-consuming and even frustrating, but the process is essential.

What is a family script? Television shows, plays, and movies all have detailed descriptions of settings, dialogue, and context to guide the actors. Many therapists believe families function in the same way, but they are a bit more complicated. The master clinician John Byng-Hall, the author of *Rewriting Family Scripts*, has summarized many of the questions one might ask to get information for the family script. These include:

- Who are the "key" (actively involved) and "distant" (still an influence, but not primary) family members?

- How are connections (positive and negative) maintained among both key and distant members?

- How are problems negotiated?

- How is intimacy expressed?

- What are the life stories of members, and how do they relate to family stories?

- Who has power within the family?

▌ What intergenerational dynamics are in place?

▌ Which family traditions are shared by all, and which are unique to some?

▌ What expectations do family members have of one another?

After answering these questions, you can look specifically at the women involved, and perhaps you will see that the larger system you are part of is not always functioning in ways that uplift and affirm others.

The last, and perhaps most important, question to ask relates to expectations. Expectations can be both a liability and an asset for all parties involved. We all have certain beliefs that determine how we interact with others (such as the imagined and real sister concept, which applies to other relatives as well). Beliefs and expectations take a lifetime to develop, and they may differ dramatically. Think of some of the values that may be important to your older female relatives:

▌ Closeness and connection

▌ Respect

▌ Religion

▌ A husband's status

▌ Their children's success

▌ Material possessions

▌ Emotional and physical support from children, as needed

Whatever the list involves, review it closely to see how compatible your beliefs and those of your contemporaries are to those of your older female relatives. That will help you understand how you and your family members perceive everyone's role in the family script.

Each family is unique in its emotional closeness, and there is a continuum of degrees of connection, according to the therapist Peter Gerlach. While some are very intimate and bonded, others are detached and disinterested.

For example, as a military child my husband grew up having limited contact with extended family, so his sudden immersion in my family's frequent get-togethers (and all of the caring and challenging aspects associated with them) required a mind shift on his part. A friend who comes from a small family told me that initially, she, too, felt overwhelmed by all of her in-laws and just wanted to find a place to hide during their frequent get-togethers. You can see how differing expectations could fuel friction in these situations.

Expectations are influenced by myriad factors: ethnicity and culture, history, personalities, geographic proximity, socioeconomic status, and so on. Until recently, families depended on one another for both survival and a sense of group belonging, which is part of our universal need to affiliate. Gerlach believes that women have a stronger need for closeness and connection than men do, which is why Relative RA is more likely to occur among females.

Connected or Not?

If you've never experienced family closeness, you won't expect it, so assessing your family and evaluating how tight the connections are is important. Your past experiences have a strong influence on your expectations for existing, as well as future, relationships.

A typical problem Gerlach encounters is one person feeling offended by another person's apparent lack of interest in socializing. He gives the example of a blended family where the wife is not accustomed to socializing, but the husband is, so she does it out of obligation rather than desire. Resentment builds up as this "duty" becomes distressing.

After you have looked at what others would like from you, consider what you expect from them. Here are examples of some typical expectations that women have shared with me:

▎ Mothers should be nurturing and comforting.

▎ Sisters should be loyal and supportive.

▎ In-laws need to prove their allegiance to the family.

Should and other words such as *must* or *have to*, with an absolute attached to them, are problematic, because they imply the possibility of failure. By changing a few words, your expectations become more realistic.

▎ Mothers *might* be nurturing and comforting.

▌ Sisters *may* be loyal and supportive.

▌ In-laws *could* prove their allegiance to the family.

Practical or Not?

Ask yourself how your expectations might differ for male versus female relatives. Taking this kind of look at beliefs and values through the microscope of reality can be eye opening for some. If • what you want and hope for isn't realistic, you may be sending or receiving aggressive messages that are the outward manifestations of an inner disconnect. Following are some scenarios:

▌ Tessa believes her sister "should" take her side in any family disagreement. When, on occasion, that doesn't happen, she becomes angry and gives her sister the silent treatment for days thereafter.

▌ Ann is constantly hurt by her mother's preferential treatment of her younger sister, Jean. She thinks her mother "should" support her in the same emotional and material ways she does Jean, and she has fallen into an aggressive communication style with both her mother and her sister. Sarcasm and put-downs dominate their conversations.

▌ Julie's mother-in-law thinks she "should" be ingratiatingly polite to Grandma Nan, the family matriarch everyone caters to. Julie comes from a family where relationships have always been distant, so she hesitates to be part of the many gatherings her husband suggests they attend. When she does go, she rarely speaks to Grandma Nan, who now considers Julie rude and arrogant. Julie's mother-in-law responds by subtly lecturing Julie on her manners.

In each of these examples, no one is at fault, but conflicting •
expectations lead to negative consequences. Realizing this can •
unmask RA behaviors assumed to be rooted in hostility or dislike. •
If you're a Tessa, Ann, or Julie type, it's easy to see how the dynamic might be changed—or explained. In other situations, it isn't that clear-cut, as Millie, a midlife mother who continues to have a conflicted relationship with her own mom, told me:

I'm the oldest, and I left home pretty early and never returned. My sister, Sue, on the other hand, stayed close to mom and even bought a house down the street when she got married. Over the years my mother has gone out of her way to do things for Sue, either giving her things she doesn't want anymore, or providing free day care for Sue's kids, whom my husband and I refer to as the "superstars" because my mom brags about them constantly. When I try to talk to my mom about my feelings, she points out all the things she has done for me, which then makes me furious, because there's no way we've been treated equally.

Fed up with her frustrations, Millie began counseling, abashed to still be dealing with "mother" issues when her relationships with her own teenaged children had hit a problematic phase. She discovered those situations weren't unrelated.

I realized that my anger toward my mother was based in part on my feelings that she could have helped me more with babysitting my children, and that as a grandmother she should treat them like she does Sue's kids. I also unconsciously compared my kids to my sister's, hoping they would outshine them at something. My therapist pointed out that there's no way I will ever make either of those things happen, because I can't force my mother or my children to do things they're not inclined to do. That really changed my attitude.

Now, when my kids joke about their "superstar" cousins, I don't bristle like I used to. When Sue is given the living room furniture my mother no longer wants, I don't take it as a personal affront. That's the way it's always been, and that's the way it will always be.

Instead, I've found some older women who give me what I need emotionally, and other people to fill a "grandma" role in my kids' lives, so both they and I aren't so emotionally dependent on my mother.

Millie has come to recognize that what she expected of her mother wasn't realistic, and although she's changing herself, the struggle to craft a new way of relating is ongoing.

"I just accept that at seventy-seven, she's not going to change—it has to come from me," she concludes.

Millie has begun the process of shifting the dynamic with her mother, which had led her to respond in the past. Her put-downs, silent treatment, and gossip to other family members have tapered off, and Millie has a "relationship health promotion" plan in place for herself and her children.

Now Auditioning

The flip side of understanding and trying to accept the expectations of others is figuring out what they expect of you. On "The Family Myth" blog, Sadi Ranson-Polizzotti says that we all play a role within the family, even if it's not based on reality. She goes on to note that in her family, it was often girls who took on, and were subject to, the family myth.

What role do you play in your family? Are you:

▌ The perfect daughter, who never does anything wrong, and fulfills your parents' goals and dreams by pursuing a career you didn't really want or marrying a man you didn't really love?

▌ The caretaker, who automatically steps forward to volunteer your services whenever a need arises? You live to give, but often at your own expense.

▌ The rebel, who has been in trouble since high school, acting out in ways guaranteed to keep the family energy focused on you?

▌ The success story, who floundered earlier in life but overcame obstacles and has now gone on to flourish?

▌ The bully, always on the offense and known for acerbic comments, manipulation, silent treatments, exclusion, and a number of other relationally aggressive tactics?

▌ The victim, receiving whatever aggression is heaped on you without protest and often not even realizing you have stepped into a role that makes you a convenient target for relative RA?

If you have been typecast in one of these or any number of other roles, it's easy to see how gossip, competition, jealousy, resentment, anger, and other energy-draining emotions can cause you and your female relatives to interact in unhealthy and unsatisfying ways. In turn, you may experience conflicting feelings about your role and be burdened by the expectations that come with it.

Now that you've considered both sides of the expectations and roles among female relatives, the next essential piece of information is how you typically respond to these expectations. A helpful way to explore this is with a quick internal assessment.

A Relative Relational Checkup

Think about a particular female family member and note which of the following are typically true of the time you spend with her.

1. I feel truly relaxed and enjoy myself during our time together.

2. I dread getting together with her.

3. We laugh or smile a lot.

4. Before I speak, I check what I am about to say in order to avoid offending her.

5. I leave feeling grateful she is in my life.

6. When I think about her the day after we've been together, my blood pressure soars.

7. Our relationship is very similar to the ones I have with my friends.

8. If I suggest we follow up our time together with a meal at my house, she almost always refuses.

9. When we part, I am happy to know she will be at the next family gathering.

10. She continually "one-ups" me, so I need to be on my toes at all times.

11. If there's a family decision to be made, she and I work well together.

12. She brings out the worst in me, no matter what I do or say.

13. I can think of at least three things I like about her.

14. If I didn't have to spend time with her, I wouldn't.

15. I ask her for advice on a problem or seek out her opinions.

16. I am never my "true self" around her.

17. She and I have resolved past conflicts without excessive hurt to each other.

18. I can never forgive her for some of the things she has done to me.

19. I trust her with a secret.

20. She is my enemy.

Now add up (separately) the number of odd- and even-numbered items that apply to your situation. As you might have guessed, the even-numbered items indicate a conflicted relationship where RA may manifest itself overtly. To get some insight into how other women respond to you, go back over the list and see if you can figure out what they might say if they were responding with you in mind.

Other Influences

Just as women express their fondness for one another through social relationships, hostility can emerge through interactions with family members. If the situation is extreme, maybe you can play detective and discover the reasons beneath that tension, whether you are the angry aggressor or the tormented target. Underlying gossip, exclusion, competition, and other types of RA are some kinds of conflict, which in families is often directly connected to expectations.

Female family members in particular are bothered when they view a relative as "different" in some way, which may manifest itself in hurtful behavior toward that person. Again, this is linked to expectations—Deborah Tannen points out that women find it important to see similarities in order to establish connections. A woman who enters the family and is strikingly different from everyone else is going to have a harder time feeling accepted. Her relatives may wonder what it says about *them* to have someone so unusual in their midst.

Troubling Topics and
Radical Responses

Our expectations can lead us to have particular vulnerabilities or triggers that set us off more quickly. To see what yours might be, evaluate how the following comments from a female relative would strike you. (Choose a relative you are close to and care about, then repeat with one you are more distant from or even whom you dislike.) Rate each comment on a scale from 1 to 10, with 10 being the most hurtful and 1 the least:

"Are you still having a hard time paying your bills? Maybe you should think about getting a job."

"You look like you've gained a few pounds since the last time I saw you."

"What made you get a haircut? I always liked your long hair."

"Boy, is your house always such a mess!"

"Why don't you try giving your kids a 'time out' to see if they'll settle down? That always worked for me."

"What is that odd flavor in your casserole? I can't quite identify it."

"You're brave to wear such a short skirt!"

"So, I heard you got passed up for a promotion again."

"Pregnant again? Are you crazy?"

"We took a vote and decided your husband is the laziest man in the family!"

"Maybe you need to do a little financial planning and budget your paycheck better."

"Gosh, your daughter just learned to say 'Mama'? Mine was speaking in sentences at that age!"

"You know, it's never too late to get braces."

"I'd never let my husband go golfing with his buddies every weekend like you do."

"Here, let me scrub off that countertop before you start cutting any salad on it."

"Your friend Marcie sure is a snob, isn't she?"

"Your sister's picture was in the newspaper for that award she won. I always knew she'd be the shining star of the family."

"Aren't you a little old to be wearing cutoffs to a family reunion?"

"Your husband is a real lush, isn't he?"

"I never realized how small your house was. How do you fit everything in it?"

This is an interesting exercise to go through for several reasons. First, it can help you identify whether some topics upset you more than others—if you find that you're more hurt by the items that deal with your appearance or your children, you will have some valuable information that can reshape your responses. Second, understanding your "hot spots" can help you sort out how relationally aggressive you view your relatives: clearly, some of the statements are phrased in ways that are more acerbic and humiliating. Third, it can help you see how you respond to different women—you're more likely to give some latitude to those you trust. For another variation, ask yourself if a man making the same comments might evoke a similar response.

In an attempt to use the information you've just gained to improve family interactions, the next time you find yourself in the midst of Relative RA, think about your responses to this little survey. Then step back, take a deep breath, and remember that each person is unique and bound to have a different effect on you, which is what makes family life so interesting.

The Power of Words

It can be helpful to spend some time processing a distressing Relative RA situation through reflection and writing. Allow yourself adequate time to record your thoughts either in longhand or typing, and ask yourself the following questions:

▎ What has your past relationship been like with this woman?

▎ Describe a fond memory of her if you have one.

▎ Reflect on the most recent hurtful event. What happened? Be specific about time, place, people involved, and preceding events.

▎ What relationally aggressive behaviors were used?

▎ Describe in as much detail as you can how you responded. If appropriate, how did the other woman respond?

▎ What went on in the hours and days after the incident? Did she contact you, or vice versa? Did feelings of upset and hurt continue to distress you? What did you do to begin processing the situation?

▎ What options were present for addressing the situation that you may not have seen at the time?

▎ What plan can you put in place for the future? Think about both your next encounter as well as those in the more distant future.

Set your narrative aside for a few hours or a day or however long it takes for you to be able to think about the incident with some neutrality, rather than with hurt or anger. Then review what you wrote, highlighting emotion words that convey positive or negative feelings. (For example, *upset*, *furious*, *confused*, or *angry* would be negative emotion words, while *relieved*, *grateful*, or *satisfied* would be more positive.) You can be creative with colors and symbols if that's your style.

Review the list of the words you've identified, and see if they fit a theme that resonates with you. Was this incident related to an otherwise stressful time in your life, or was it part of the script you and this other woman have played out for years, if not decades? Draw any conclusions you can from this review process.

Next, force yourself to identify at least a few positive qualities about the person or people causing the conflict. If you talked to someone who knew her but didn't have the emotional baggage you do, what would they identify as her good points?

Then think about what part of her challenges you most. If you are the aggressor in this scenario, why does this particular woman

evoke such a strong response? As a victim, what keeps you on the ·
receiving end of her wrath?

At this point, you have enough information to make a choice.
You can use your newfound insights to:

1. Do nothing, but know that you understand the dynamics
   underlying Relative RA and choose to accept the situation
   for what it is.

2. Change your behavior using the information you've garnered, either with the goal of changing hers, too, or just to
   empower yourself. (Note: You might think there's a third
   option of changing *her*, but in reality you have no control
   over your relative. The only shift in her behavior that's likely
   to occur will come after you or others interact differently
   with her.)

Regardless of your choice, the next chapter will help you move
forward with a therapeutic plan for the future.

18

The Transformation Treatment Plan

Once you've reached a "diagnosis" of your Relative RA situation, the next step is to create a treatment plan. This will be specific to the roles you and other women play, and the expectations that accompany them. As is almost always true in medicine, there are several parts to a treatment plan, and several different therapeutic options.

Peace Treaty

While there are specific strategies you might want to pursue depending on your circumstances, a few ground rules can apply to almost any situation. First, think proactively. Before your next contact with this person, decide how you will act and set some rules for toning down the anger or hurt you naturally feel (there's a chance they're in the same emotional state). Decide what you will tolerate and what you won't, and include an exit plan, even if it's only to walk around the block by yourself, make a trip to the bathroom, or call a sympathetic friend on your cell phone (out of hearing range, of course).

Next, from the initial point of contact, take charge and set the tone for the encounter. If there's a group involved, it's a little more challenging, but adopt a one-on-one approach. Try giving your RA relative an honest and appropriate compliment before there's an opportunity to get into a tangle. Go back to the list of positive qualities you wrote about if need be, but the next time you see her, make the first words our of your mouth uplifting ones. Think: enter praising.

For example, if cousin Lilly always calls you "the runt" and makes fun of your clothes and hairstyle, disarm her at the next family gathering. Before she can get you in her sights, seek her out, give her a hug if that's the accepted practice, and tell her you saw a movie the other day with a funny actress who reminded you of her. "She was really something—you even look a little bit like her." Chances are Lilly will be so surprised by your taking control of the conversation and the pleasantry that she won't be quick with the criticism. (Clearly, whatever you say should be true, but it can be something fairly neutral.)

If flattery isn't your style, you may elect to steer clear of her, either figuratively or literally. Stay a room away from her, and remain engaged in animated conversation with the person nearest you. If your RA relative approaches, politely excuse yourself and get a glass of water, rescue your toddler from Grandma, or help to set or clear the table.

The "broken record" strategy I used to teach in my classes on assertiveness is another helpful way to distance yourself emotionally without offending: you simply repeat a stock phrase to everything that is said and refuse to be engaged in a diatribe. Possible responses include "Is that so?" "Let me think about that," or "That's really something." You can say them as many times as needed while the relative is going through her rant, with a pleasantly interested expression on your face. Other replies that get the focus off you and back on the other person include; "Explain that," "Tell me," "Educate me," "How so?" or "Say more." Each gives you time to mentally regroup and frame an appropriate response. For aggressors, this might be all you need to switch off a reply that would have been hurtful; victims can buy time and allow the bully a chance to run out of steam.

Even if her verbal grenade is launched in your direction, it will fall flat if you use this technique to free yourself from the role of a waiting target. Raise your eyebrows, look her in the eyes briefly, and tell her you'd rather talk privately about that subject. Repeat as often as necessary.

You've identified triggers you may need to avoid, but beware of hers. In general, too much of anything can provide fertile ground for female feuds: too much alcohol, too much food (and food preparation), too much close contact, and so on. There may even be certain conversation topics that spark an aggressive vent of simmering emotions—avoid them. Hostile Aunt Harriet probably won't take kindly to your suggestion that she should come to your new church, where they practice "real religion," and nasty niece Nancy isn't going to respond pleasantly to a sarcastic comment about the politician she campaigned for.

As a rule of thumb, don't gossip. That doesn't mean you can't or shouldn't share news of another's misfortune or accomplishments or seek help with a relationship conflict. However, twisting things out of context, passing along secondhand information, and involving others in a personal conflict so they'll take your side are almost guaranteed to worsen the problem. Discuss specific hurtful issues with your spouse and the person directly involved (or trusted non-kin), and don't count on another female family member to pass along a message or mediate on your behalf.

Remember, too, that each time your family gathers, there are many generations of women present. You, and your bully or victim, are role-modeling relationship styles for everyone else, perhaps giving younger women subtle permission to assume the role of victim, bully, or bystander.

Twenty Tips toward Tranquility

In addition to the "big picture" game plan, some specific strategies you might pursue include the following:

- Get to know your relatives in a different way—as individuals rather than actors in particular roles. Listen to their family stories, not as fodder for gossip but as a way to begin understanding who's who and what's what. Find out who they are in addition to their relation to the rest of the family: what hobbies they have and their favorite movies and books.

▌ Anticipate, and don't get caught up in, the drama dangled in front of your face. If your sister challenges you to a verbal duel with a statement like "You *always* suck up to Grandma so she'll leave you her pearl necklace," you now have a repertoire that offers you any number of neutral responses (see the previous section), after which you can walk away.

▌ The right kind of humor never hurts. In my family, should one of those carefully coached nieces or nephews declare, "Aunt Cheryl is my favorite aunt!" I'm pretty sure another woman will be quick to ask about the size of the bribe behind that statement.

▌ Deal with issues one-on-one and during times of calm. Make •
it a policy to stay pleasant in the moment, but have a follow-up conversation to defuse a hurtful situation: "I don't understand why you would point out that I'm on my third marriage at a family reunion. Educate me." "When you said I let my kids 'run wild' at Thanksgiving dinner, it seemed like you have some concerns about their well-being. Let's talk about that." "I'm sensing I've done something to offend you—but I can't figure out what it is. Can you tell me why you didn't speak to me at the anniversary party?"

▌ Put it in writing. Share what you've written, but be factual rather than emotional, and keep other people in the family out of it. Remember, too, that letters and e-mails can be freely circulated, even if you ask that they be kept private.

▌ Give others the benefit of the doubt. Maybe your daughter-in-law, sister, or niece isn't the most polished person when she talks to you, but she probably doesn't mean to offend. If she misspeaks, it may be because she's nervous.

▌ Focus on the positive. Aunt Rhoda may be the family victim who automatically takes on a passive role in any situation but complains about it later. Nonetheless, she is your aunt and she clearly cares enough to invest the energy to stay connected to the family. Where else is that true?

▌ Try to uncover the underlying conflict triggering an RA response. Gently explore clues as to why your relative acts the way she does. Could she have difficulty relating to women in general or is it you specifically? If you are the bully, what redeeming qualities are there about her that might enable you to change the dynamics, even slightly? Has she, perhaps, been caught up in an RA drama in the past, either in or outside the family, and could this be driving her current passive or aggressive behavior?

- Recognize that you can't change or control anyone but yourself. Altering your own behavior often serves as the best strategy for overcoming the RA style of another woman.

- Polish your communication skills. Avoid inflammatory words, show that the speaker has your full attention, ask if you've gotten the correct message, pose questions, and try to turn spats into chats.

- Listen before leaping in to respond. Keep your expression and body language neutral, and let others know that they have your full attention. If you're really upset, take a deep breath or count to three before you reply in order to better process what's just been said.

- Have a time limit when you're with a woman who upsets you. Knowing you will be in her company for three hours and not a minute longer can help you stay calm. When things are really tense, until the conflict is resolved, the less time spent together, the better.

- Get to know family members you may not have spent time with previously, and use them as a buffer, or if you can, expand the size of the gathering, for an even bigger "neutral zone."

- Cue someone in to intervene when you signal that an RA drama is boiling. Have the person ask if they can talk to you about something or otherwise help extricate you from the situation.

- Change the dynamics, whether it be the seating arrangement at the table or the kinds of games you play—get together at a local pool rather than at someone's house. Activities and structure tend to reduce aggression.

▌ Have some positive self-talk in anticipation of the encounter, and beware of seeing the words and actions of others as hostile when they may not be intended as such.

▌ Change the subject, or try to distract her (kids and pets are great for this).

▌ Ask your spouse/sister/mother or some other helpful ally to stay by your side at all times to help curtail an episode of RA. Whether you're the bully or the victim, that support person can help you avoid a destructive drama by either intervening or removing both of you from the dialogue.

▌ Busy yourself with food preparation, child care, kitchen duty, or chatting with a lonely elderly relative so you won't be available to get involved in a word war.

▌ Take a sabbatical from her. Accept that sometimes you may have to limit contact or even walk away from a relationship. It doesn't have to be permanent, but a vacation from family can allow you time to make decisions without the emotional pressure of constant conflict.

Male versus Female, Again

In their book on dealing with difficult people, Arnold Sanow and Sandra Strauss, the authors and facilitators of Get Along with Anyone workshops, offer suggestions that are relevant to resolving RA conflicts. Some of their observations about gender differences can help you plan your strategies for dealing with RA:

1. Women value quality and want to talk about relationships and feelings, while men talk to get information.

2. Women pick up on conversational nuances and are more tuned in to body language.

3. Women talk about problems; men offer advice and solutions.

4. Women use input from others to make decisions; men come to conclusions independently.

5. Women tend to diminish their achievements; men exaggerate theirs.

6. Men avoid seeking help and directions; women ask for them straightforwardly.

7. Men focus on external events, women on internal.

8. Men confront face-to-face; women are covert.

Keeping these differences in mind as you develop your plan can help you address particular gender issues that are important in communication.

You may eventually decide to bring in other women or men as part of your plan, but this can be risky if the others are family members, too. That strategy should come after you've exhausted plans A, B, and C. If the RA relative is your mother-in-law, your spouse may have to intervene on your behalf and set some boundaries. Your older sister may run interference with your bullying mother, but keep in mind the words of Dr. Leonard Felder: "Most of our difficult relatives have developed prickly layers and defensiveness to keep their inner psychological wounds a closely guarded secret." If you can't break through, chances are that others won't be able to, either. (Making a tentative overture to end an estrangement is the one situation where an uninvolved family member can be helpful.)

Sometimes younger female family members can be a great source of potential solutions or support, and you may find your relationships with them a soothing balm for the caustic comments of others. You can also enlist their advice in solving the problems at hand, if appropriate, but be careful not to draw them into the conflict. Rather, consider them a resource for better understanding of your RA relative. This recently happened to two of my friends, who came to a new appreciation of, and tolerance for, their sisters after conversations with their nieces.

The other option for your plan is to accept the person for who she is and recognize that the best you can do is surrender your expectations for a positive relationship. That decision in and of itself can move you from a passive or aggressive stance into a neutral one.

Home for the Holidays

Special planning needs to take place to prevent the holidays from becoming "hellidays." Aggravated by the excitement and stress of extra activity, these are peak times for kitchen wars to escalate. The journalist Bob Morris writes about the extreme emotions that can surface during the holidays, noting that get-togethers are often a time when people feel free to vent their spleen at a captive audience. "Duck the holidays," he suggests. He believes that coming together with people you may otherwise see rarely and being confined with too much alcohol and food can be a recipe for disaster. If you must confront, the psychiatrist Gail Saltz suggests you do it in private.

The columnist Martha Beck from *O* magazine believes it is possible to enjoy the holidays when you're with your family, even if they're difficult. To begin with, she counsels readers to understand that although your family *should* treat you well, it doesn't mean they *will*. A key step is freeing yourself from the expectation of, or need for, approval and love. She says, "Paradoxically, you get this blessed feeling by not grasping for it." Her final admonition is to give yourself the feelings you think you need from kin.

In an amusing story from the book *I Married My Mother-in-Law*, the author Susan Straight recalls the effort—and payoff—required to blend into a family that differed not only in personality but also in skin color. Even after she and her husband divorced, she continued the Thanksgiving tradition of visiting his home, where men gathered in the driveway to barbecue and women gravitated to the kitchen to prepare their own signature dishes. She says, "I stayed away from family gatherings for the first two tough years after we broke up. But I missed the company of my other family, and my three daughters needed the stories and the ribs and the cobbler." Sometimes, surrounding your children with family whom they will only see a few times a year can be worth whatever problems you feel you might face.

Another source of holiday conflict can occur when married couples come from different ethnic backgrounds. The *New York Times* journalist Benedict Carey describes the increase in mixed marriages since 1990: they account for a third of Hispanic marriages and Asian marriages, 13 percent of marriages to black Americans, and 7 percent of marriages to whites. He believes the arrival of a culturally different new partner is felt most keenly during the holidays, which are already a time of tension. Sometimes, the newcomer is a buffer, but at other times he or she is a catalyst. He concludes that holidays are probably not the best occasions to introduce someone new, especially if they are of a different ethnicity. If it's inevitable, preplanning, time limits, and structure can be helpful.

The parenting coach Terry Carson responds to a reader's question about another holiday dilemma: sisters who have different parenting styles. She suggests:

1. Think about what memories you'd like to create ahead of time.

2. Talk to your sisters about parenting styles and how you can best support each other.

3. Take time with your own family.

4. Focus on what you're enjoying about the time together.

The End Result

Families last a lifetime, so think of the big picture and ask yourself these questions: Have I ever made a mistake? Have I ever been given a second chance? Of course, we all have, so why not extend the same opportunity to the woman, or women, in your family you've had a conflict with? Plan to forgive, wipe the slate clean, and agree to start over. It may be undeserved, but treat other women as you would like to be treated, even if they can't or won't reciprocate. You will benefit, even if others don't.

19

A Time to Act

Jean Baker Miller and Irene P. Stiver (1997) believe women use their power to enhance another's resources and strengths; in other words, power grows as it is used. Trying to end female family feuds can seem like a no-win situation: any option is less than ideal because the only reason the other person has a relationship with you is that you're a family member. In reality, you can intervene to empower not only yourself but also those women around you who are caught in relationships they find challenging, conflicted, and even cruel.

With a plan in place, however, you now face the "put up or shut up" dilemma. The difficult dynamic you are entangled in will continue, unless it becomes legal to divorce a sister or a mother, but even after "diagnosing" and planning for change, the prospect of taking action can seem frightening. As you motivate yourself to implement the steps to alter the destructive dynamic you've somehow become stuck in, consider these pros and cons:

▮ Timing. Is this the right time to act? The offenses of a sinister sister-in-law or a meddling mother can be tolerated once a year, but if she's your next-door neighbor, the incentive to begin your plan soon is more pressing.

▮ Place. Consider the best environment to take even a small first step toward change. Should it be in your house, out in public, or in a neutral setting?

▮ People. Who else should be involved? You may need an objective outsider to provide wise counsel, since in the heat of a conflict it's normal to feel so beaten down or worn out that your ability to be objective or optimistic is lost.

▌ Motivation. How much are you willing to invest in having your choices prevail? Depending on the scope of the problem, the energy you expend trying to fix things might be greater than the energy you'll spend dealing with it for a lifetime. Ask yourself, "On a scale of 1 to 10, if 10 is most important, where would this issue rate?"

▌ Confidence. Use the same scale to measure how confident you are that you can actually bring about a meaningful change, however small, in the behavior dynamics. Low numbers on both scales might suggest it would be wise to find other ways of dealing with problems or waiting for another time to try to change the situation.

▌ Others. Are you willing to risk alienating others over the issue? If your family network is dense, it's likely that taking the initiative toward change is going to extend beyond you and the woman or women involved. That makes the stakes higher.

▌ Your spouse. If relevant, what does your spouse or significant other have to say about the issue? If you're married and your husband's family is the source of the problem, how does he feel about your taking action to end the RA drama? The one area of universal agreement among those with personal or professional expertise is that men need to be willing to place their loyalty to their wives above all others in the family hierarchy.

▌ Professionals. Are families other than your own affected by the conflict? Is this a multigenerational, multifamily conflict that will take require the expertise of others to resolve? If so, you may need the help of an experienced professional to help implement your plan.

Realizing Your Role

If you are a witness or a bystander to relational aggression, you may have the easiest course to follow, either by addressing the conflict directly or indirectly. If bully sister Rose torments victim sister Lydia, your objectivity can help penetrate surface behaviors and recognize that Rose has had a lifelong resentment of her younger sister's role as the "baby of the family whom everyone takes care of."

Understanding this, you might ask Rose privately, "So, what's it like to be an oldest sister in this family?" or you may find ways to give her the nurturing she feels Lydia "stole" from her. Perhaps boosting Rose's self-esteem or complimenting her independence will open a dialogue about her feelings.

For victim Lily, it may be a matter of asking some of the same questions: "So you're the baby of the family. What's that like?" and then helping her to recognize untapped strength and independence.

Aggression Undone

If you're the aggressor, always fuming when you're with your family and constantly in the midst of drama with one of them, take a deep breath and consider what your behavior is costing you. Imagine how committed other women have to be to continue kinkeeping when family get-togethers involve one person being sliced and diced by another (you). How do the younger members of your clan view you, and what legacy are you passing on?

If you're the victim, you may feel your only choice is to accept the verbal slings and arrows of others, but there is a middle ground between accepting abuse and severing relationships forever. It's also worthwhile for you to consider the lessons you are implicitly teaching others—that it's okay to let a relative mistreat you because she's family. This is the very dynamic that is likely to destroy family togetherness rather than reinforce it.

Perhaps the best motivation for taking action on your plan is the following story, which illustrates that it's never too late to heal old traumas, even when a mother is elderly and frail.

Twelve Pounds of Reconciliation
Brenda Nixon

For weeks, we had ogled, held, and cuddled a four-pound miniature dachshund with stout paws and short, soft brown hair. The tip of his tongue dangled from his mouth in an innocent, "Love me" sort of way that pulled on my heartstrings.

"He's too cute!" I cooed.

"We already have a dog!" my husband objected.

"I know, but this one is special. He must be here for me. I can't resist."

My husband wasn't thrilled about the addition of another dog, and a puppy to boot, but my excitement and certainty helped him agree.

In the wee hours of the morning, I heard slight whimpers downstairs. I tiptoed down to see about our puppy. When he saw me, his cries ceased and he wagged his tail and yelped with playfulness. I took him out into the cool backyard to do his business.

Then it hit me. An ominous thought: "This isn't right. I can't keep him!"

The feeling hovered over me, and I sensed a heavenly force telling me to give this puppy to my elderly mom and dad.

This is ridiculous! I thought. I can't give them my puppy.

The compulsion would not leave, though. My dad was slow and shaky on his feet, and my mom and I had not communicated well for years. I was annoyed and resentful toward her, and it seemed we argued when together. Long periods elapsed between our forced, perfunctory meetings, and now she was overwhelmed with decisions about my dying grandmother, Dad's failing health, and her growing limitations.

But my heart ached from years of ugly communication and tension, and I felt cheated out of having a warm, wisdom-laden mom. Just weeks before, she misunderstood something I'd said, and I became the target of her angry words as she shouted at me as if I was a disobedient toddler. I wasn't feeling particularly benevolent, yet I couldn't shake off this impulse to give the puppy to her.

Later I told my husband, "I have to do this. You know I'd been praying for a way that we could get along better."

"But they won't want a puppy," he replied in disbelief over my change of mind.

"Yes, but I have to follow my conscience."

On a sunny spring day we drove the hour to my parents' house with the little dachshund contentedly riding on my lap. From his mouth jutted the ever-present tongue as I stroked his soft ears, feeling a mix of anticipation and sadness.

We pulled in the driveway and jumped out of the car.

"Here! Happy Father's Day, Happy Anniversary, Happy Birthday, and Merry Christmas," I said as I shoved the puppy into their arms.

They stood there silently amazed, and then Dad asked, "What's this all about?"

"It's for you," I said. "I also brought you a kennel, puppy food, collar, and leash, and he's had his immunizations and is housebroken."

They began to examine him like a newborn.

"Oh, look at that tongue," Mom said.

"He's cute," added Dad. "What should we call him?"

Our conversation was pleasant. We talked, laughed, tried different names, and watched their puppy explore his new home. There was a cease-fire that day and our drive home was optimistic, although I missed the little fellow.

The next day, I phoned to ask about the puppy. Mom told me of his antics and said, "I think he'll be your dad's dog. He seems to favor him." Then on the next call, "Now he's following me around the house."

"I take him when I go for my walk," Mom told me. "Your dad holds him to watch TV."

Months passed, and one day my husband commented, "Your mom is less stressed with a new life to take care of. Maybe there's something to this pet therapy."

Since then, the gloomy subject of Grandma and selling the property has come up but doesn't dominate our conversations. Mom and Dad have a new interest. We talk rather than argue, laugh rather than leave in a huff, and I tease Mom that she buys more treats for the dog than she ever did for us kids. I no longer feel anger toward her—instead, I stand amazed and refer to this dog as our twelve pounds of reconciliation.

Not every woman can be wooed by a pet, but underlying this story is a willingness to give the gift of self. Taking action to prevent, confront, change, or cope with aggressive behaviors used in female family feuds may be the most significant relationship investment you make with other women.

When You Need to Confront

Sometimes your plan will include having a one-on-one discussion with the relative who has caught the two of you up in an RA drama that just won't end. (If there's a group involved, talk to each person separately to avoid a "you against them" scenario.)

Having a confrontation is different from "getting to know her." Your purpose is to talk things out, to get to the bottom of the conflict if you can, and to avoid another outburst of RA—from either yourself or her. It's a process that should take the following points into consideration:

▌ Don't postpone the conversation until feelings fester and explode, either as a long-tormented victim or a lifelong aggressor.

▌ Prepare and rehearse what you will say. As discussed previously, certain words are almost guaranteed to incite—avoid them, and substitute a respectful request, which is usually received better than a command or an ultimatum.

▌ Make the confrontation as nonthreatening as possible—have it in a private and neutral setting (that is, *not* your house or hers) and at a planned time. If you can arrange to talk when you aren't in the midst of conflict, all the better.

▌ Open the discussion with something positive, such as your desire for a polite relationship (at a minimum) or your respect for her contributions to the family.

▌ Share your perceptions as factually as possible: the only person you can speak for is yourself. Acknowledge that they are just that—*your* perceptions. Ask for hers.

The hurts of a female family situation poisoned by RA may never heal, despite our attempts to do so. Following is the story of a woman who, at age fifty, still recalls her situation in a stepfamily.

Words Will Ever Hurt Me
Denise Kincy

I sometimes wish a decision I made at the tender age of six had been a different one, but I was a strong-willed child, raised by my grandma after my mother left when I was a baby. When my daddy married again, I was determined to be part of a "real" family, so I ran away from the babysitter's after school and beat on the door of my dad's house, crying and pleading with my stepmother to let me live with them. I see now that I gave her no choice, but what was a sixteen-year-old girl supposed to do with a six-year-old kid?

The answer, unfortunately, was to resent and demean that self-confident little girl, turning her into an insecure, frightened, and bewildered person. Nothing I did was right: I was a liar, too skinny, and stupid; even the dishes weren't washed correctly when I did them. Once my daddy and my stepmother had three children of their own, I became a built-in babysitter.

Where was my daddy in all of this? I never told him because I might have been sent back to my grandma's. Although she loved me more than anyone else, she was an old woman, and I wanted a mother.

I have suffered for that long-ago decision, and for my silence. I have a poor self-image and have spent years trying to erase the old tapes that play in my head, saying I am no good, I am stupid, I am too this or that—all negative claptrap that is untrue. Searching for someone to make me see the beauty that resided within me, I turned to men.

About ten years ago, on a quest for inner peace, I decided to confront my stepmother. I envisioned a cleansing, picturing us putting the past behind us and becoming closer, because on some level, I did love her and just wanted an apology.

In hindsight, I suppose an invitation to lunch was the wrong way to go about confronting her. The consensus of my stepmother and my youngest sister was that I had set her up. I finally got up the nerve to ask why she did and said the things she did to me. Her denial was so strange: what was I talking about? She never did any of that. Needless to say, the lunch date was a disaster.

Not long after I got back home, my stepsister called. She cursed me out, screaming and yelling over the phone. The end of my feelings for the only family I had known came when she said, "You were never anything but a burden to Mama."

How do you deal with that? At first, you hide. You beat yourself up. You decide that everything you've been told about yourself is true. Then you realize what utter bullshit that is. You were only a kid, wanting to be loved, needing a mother.

I got over it, or they think I did. I still go to Thanksgiving dinner, I smile, I laugh and act like everything is fine. But it's not.

I have a great life, a wonderful husband—finally—and my sons are grown, but still, at fifty, I wonder—will I ever be able to lay this baggage down?

In this story, Denise tried to do all the right things to resolve the residual conflict she felt, but different perceptions of the past prevented a satisfactory resolution. Still, she has taken the initiative to let go of troubling issues that she has carried single-handedly for many years. Hopefully, her writing will further empower her and others in similar situations.

Think of even the smallest change in yourself or in the RA relative as a positive outcome, and as, perhaps, the beginning of bigger changes. Your rewriting of the female family feud script will be a contribution to the next generation of relatives, too.

20

Special Strategies for Mother or Sister RA

How does one find resolution when there is no overt physical or emotional abuse to bring to the therapy session? An ongoing pattern of relationally aggressive behavior can wear a deep groove in your psyche over a lifetime, but describing specific hurts that need to be healed can be difficult.

Moving On with Mom

If you hope to end the RA way of interacting that has characterized your relationship with your mother, change is always possible. Iris Krasnow describes this process as "death of the fantasy mom and birth of what is real." Usually, there comes a time when every woman who has been wounded by RA needs to resolve her issues, either by letting go of what has already happened or working through it in the present so that negative interaction patterns learned in childhood don't persist in our own offspring. (The same holds true for men, of course). There are a number of strategies women can use to make peace with their mothers.

A Female Family History

Look at your mom's history of relationships with her female relatives. You may discover that just as you ask, "Why doesn't she care about me?" she at one time may have wondered the same thing about you. It's also possible that she was the very child to her mother that you are to her and once confronted the same issues you do now.

To see if this might be relevant, ask yourself these questions:

- Was my mother bullied or mistreated as a child?
- Is my mother currently the target of everyone else's aggression?
- Have there ever been times when my mother showed affection to me?
- Could other family circumstances (divorce, for example) have led my mother to bully me?
- Does my mother's self-esteem lead her to feel good or bad about herself?
- Are there any "safe" topics my mom and I can relate around, like children, pets, or careers?
- Have I inherited any traits from my mother that are positive?
- What traits of hers am I afraid of inheriting?
- Is there anything about my mother I admire?
- Are there other people who might be helpful to me as I try to change my relationship with my mother?
- Are there any positive female role models in the family for me and my mother?
- Could my treatment of my mother be a problem? If there's conflict between us, am I the one who initiates and perpetuates it?
- Are there any signs my mother is willing to change her interaction style?

If you can answer yes to some or all of these questions, consider yourself at the beginning of a program that can help both you and your mother in different ways: you can step out of an interaction dynamic that is hurtful to you, and she will be relieved of the pressure of continuing a pattern of behavior that requires a lot of negative energy.

Other Mother Strategies

First, recognize that concepts such as "right," "wrong," "good," and "bad" aren't helpful when referring to either parents or children. Every mother makes mistakes, and every child does things they regret. The task is not to show who gets first prize in the wrongdoing arena, but rather to look at what exists today that needs healing.

All too often, a dead end is reached because it's too threatening for a mother to admit she might have erred in her child-rearing practices, just as a daughter is intimidated by the thought that she may not have achieved the dreams her mother had for her. As a result, both refuse to let go of blame, take an objective look at the situation on hand, and try to work through it.

Second, use the kind of positive confrontational style described in the previous chapter that will help both of you grow and learn more about each other, rather than punishing, provoking, or enduring more RA. Taking steps to smooth out the communication and connection between you can be slow: a lifetime of bully/victim dynamics aren't likely to be transformed with one heart-to-heart conversation. To improve your chances for change, do some thinking and writing ahead of time. (See the writing exercises suggested at the end of chapter 17.)

Clear your brain of clutter and set a series of small, realistic goals for yourself.

- Have one ten-minute conversation where you don't feel victimized.

- Write one honest note that conveys your hope for a better relationship.

- Spend one evening together doing something pleasant that distracts you both from each other (watch a movie, go to a museum, shop for shoes).

- Take her to lunch and avoid controversial topics.

Knowledge is power, but there are other factors involved in creating change. Recognize that a good deal of energy, motivation, and persistence will most likely be needed on both sides. If you've just had your first child and are ready to explode in frustration because your mother repeatedly points out your inadequacies as a parent, it's probably not an opportune time to tackle a relational overhaul.

A Caring Confrontation

Talking things out with your mother is likely to be more successful when it is a planned process rather than a spur-of-the-moment activity, even though most communication is not that deliberate. Go slow to avoid making either of you feel pressured or tense about the task at hand. Jot down a few notes and review what you've written before the confrontation is about to occur, and keep these points in mind:

1. Start positive. No matter how aggressive or passive your mom has been, don't launch into a diatribe of complaints the instant your conversation begins. Talk about the weather, her new shirt, or some other pleasantry, then ease into the tougher topics by finding one thing about her parenting that you are grateful for: she kept your family together during hardships, she made sure you had the opportunity to go to college, or she always remembered your birthday. Even something as small as the great Halloween costumes she made you or the time she let you have a dog is better than nothing.

2. Be careful not to start off the discussion from a victim/bully stance. Monitor your expression and posture so you don't convey that attitude nonverbally—women have antennae for the unspoken message beneath the words being said.

3. Keep the conversation focused on the goal you have set. If Mom tries to change the subject and discuss the beautiful and expensive hand-knit sweater your sister just gave her, steer her back to the topic on hand: you would like to work on your relationship with her.

4. Give a few factual examples of the RA behaviors that bother you most—either yours or hers. If it's the right time to brainstorm, try to come up with ways to avoid future encounters that hurt rather than help. Avoid attaching a value judgment to the behaviors and acknowledge that this is the way you feel—you can't speak for anyone else in the family.

5. Talk about your past and present expectations of her, see what she thinks, then check out her expectations for you.

6. Confrontation is a two-way street. She may have her own list of ways in which you used relationally aggressive behaviors to hurt her; if she listens to you, you owe her the same courtesy.

7. Don't expect one conversation to bring about a complete overhaul in your interaction style. Keep the communication open and ongoing once you've broken ground and laid the framework for this kind of discussion.

At any point, if the discussion gets too emotional or heated, end it gracefully. "I'm going to have to stop now," "This seems like a good time to end today," or "Maybe a break would be a good idea" are all ways to exit without causing further upset. It's also okay to agree to disagree: there's one subject my mom and I are likely to differ on forever, but rather than try to convince each other who's right or wrong, we accept that our opinions don't mesh, and let it rest.

Back to You

Each conversation with your mother about touchy topics may get easier, or, as you delve deeper, more difficult. It's good to have some anti-RA strategies in mind for yourself, whether you find yourself on the passive or aggressive side of the fence:

1. Be proactive. If her bullying or victim behaviors overwhelm you, think of a Plan A, B, and C for coping. (For example, leave, talk it out, ignore it, or get help from another relative.)

2. Feel comfortable having boundaries and knowing that when your mother says hurtful things, it's more a reflection of her negative feelings about herself or some aspect of her life than of your personality traits.

3. Keep working on your listening and communication skills. Make sure you each understand what the other has said, and don't assume malicious intent.

4. Find other older women who can bolster you with RA-free relationships, and turn to them in times of trouble. They'll

help validate your talents and strengths, and you won't have the emotional baggage about your relationship that is inevitable with mothers and daughters.

If your mom isn't interested in "growing" (or if after a discussion you feel you aren't either), something helpful is still learned: by mutual consent, the status quo is going to continue. However, whoever is willing to change will control the future: that person can decide to develop new coping strategies, be more open with her feelings, or even take a hiatus from the family while she forms a new game plan.

Accepting an Impasse

Based on Iris Krasnow's advice, there are many approaches to improving a relationship with your mother, even if you're the only one interested in changing. Here are some practical tips she offers:

- Accept her for the person as she is, not the image you have built up.

- Forget more than forgive.

- Don't miss the final chance to reconcile your relationship— who was right or wrong won't matter when she's dead. (Krasnow spoke with women whose mothers died before they had a chance to reconcile and said that the lost opportunity haunted them forever.)

- Keep in mind that perceptions are just that—your view of how things happened. Her view of the same event may be dramatically different.

Sometimes, one break in the action, however slight, can provide enough motivation to allow both of you to see positive possibilities for the future. Visiting an interesting new tea shop and discussing the collection of teapots rather than all the shortcomings you see in each other can open the door to other patterns of interaction. Some neutral alone time can work wonders: going to a movie and realizing you both adore the lead actress gives you something to build on that has nothing to do with the time she humiliated you in front of your least favorite aunt by commenting on your failure to finish college.

Being asked to spend some special "alone time" in order to work on your relationship can be an indirect compliment to your mom that will prime her for more positive exchanges down the line. Little things can lead to a willingness to take on bigger challenges, such as having a discussion (not an argument or a debate) about ways in which your relationship could be improved. (The expression "Rome wasn't built in a day" is a gross understatement. Rome wasn't built in a decade, or even a century!)

Changing Your Comfort Zones

Sometimes it seems easier to stay in our familiar roles, even if they aren't very fulfilling. It can also seem strange to have to renegotiate your relationship with your mother when you're both adults, but there are three good reasons to persevere in your quest for a bully-free relationship with your mom (or to savor one that already exists).

First, negativity takes on a life of its own. As your mother ages, it's likely she'll be more, rather than less, RA-prone than she is right now. I can't count how many times a middle-aged child asked me why their elderly parent was so disagreeable. "Tell me what she was like when you were younger," I would prompt, and inevitably I'd hear that Mom had been pretty disagreeable then, too. So, the goal here is to help your mother end a pattern of covert aggression and learn some affection—for herself!

Second, you, too, deserve to feel good about who you are. Being bullied and abused by your mother or living in a state where you are constantly angry and acting aggressively toward her can have a direct effect on your emotional and even physical health, showing up as depression, low self-esteem, and other unhealthy mentalities. Even if she is offended by the idea that she needs to change, you've tactfully laid your cards on the table, which can empower you to take other steps to shift the dynamic. The next time she gives you the silent treatment for going to your child's soccer game instead of driving her to the podiatrist, you'll know that you've opened the door to share that this is the kind of behavior you were hoping could change.

Third, think of the next generation of women and the kind of role model you are being to them. Do you want your daughters, nieces, or other relatives to learn jealousy, humiliation, gossip, and a host of other negative behaviors from observing you and your mom?

Sometimes sorting through all this information can make it clear that there's little, if any, hope of making changes at this time. If this is the case, your task is to let go of the hurtful input you get (and got) from her and find other ways to fill the mothering void in your life.

Farewell Isn't Forever

How do you let go of one of the most important relationships in your life? The options are limited only by your creativity, but here are some of the suggestions I've received:

▌ Limit contact with your mom to a minimum. If she has a good relationship with your children that you want to preserve, sign her up for regular babysitting and have your husband be the main liaison who greets and dismisses her.

▌ Take a "mom sabbatical"—spend some time without her in your life and see if that makes matters better or worse.

▌ Reframe her behavior so that it's easier to say good-bye—imagine her playing out a script that was written long ago in your childhood, again and again and again. It's going to continue for as long as you have contact with her, so anticipate and accept it.

▌ Find an ally you can talk to instead of your mom at get-togethers (but don't let a riff *about* mom ruin your good time anyway).

▌ Stop seeing her completely. If she causes you too much pain and suffering, take a healthy step away from her and find a mother substitute who would love to spend time with you.

▌ Correspond in writing only, but preferably not by e-mail, which can seem impersonal.

As painful as they may be, RA conflicts and tensions can also prompt emotional growth, long after the younger developmental years have passed. Even if you're the only person who does the healing and growing, that counts for at least one positive outcome.

Sister-Specifics

If you and your sisters are the ones caught in a bullying type of relationship, many of the tips offered for mothers apply, with a few differences. First, recognize that your tie to your sister often involves the expectation of friendship and loyalty different from the unconditional love of a parent. Second, since sisters are usually at about the same age and developmental stage as your peers, it can be harder to understand and deal with your feelings for them. Third, if you have many sisters, some may be supportive and some not. Therefore, you may deal with unique issues, such as finding two or more sisters aligned against you. Finally, your mother's relationship with each of you may be the underlying source of conflict. Favoritism or deliberate setups can cause one woman to turn on her other siblings, when the real issue is her parent.

Some thoughts to keep in mind as you work to change the sistering dynamics in your life:

- Connections to your sister are automatic on one level, but in need of care and upkeep on another. Just because she's your sister doesn't mean she'll understand when you regift a sweater you wore once and didn't like—her RA rage can have a basis in something you did without intending to hurt.

- Each sister relationship is unique, but comparing your sister Abby, who never calls or e-mails, with your best pal's sister, who does, can set you up for either wounded feelings or angry outbursts. In the same way, if you have several sisters, don't use one as a standard for the others.

- Knowing the dynamics of a sister situation is helpful. Melanie Mauthner, the author of *Sistering: Power and Change in Female Relationships*, describes three types of sistering relationships, noting that power is key in each one: a fixed relationship not open to change, mini-mothering (not by choice, usually), or a fixed relationship open to change. These roles are not necessarily determined by age or birth position, she notes. A younger sister can intervene to protect an older sister from bullying (as happened with Renae and Casee in chapter 1), or the family "baby" can mother the firstborn.

Mauthner's study of thirty-seven sisters revealed that fourteen were best friends, thirteen were close, and ten were distant. One sister commented, "A sister is a sister you have to live with all the time. A friend you can just leave." However, feeling forced to maintain contact with a sister who treats you aggressively follows along with the same kind of expectations in the "Good Daughter" and "Good Mother" myths.

▌ When examining your relationships with your sisters consider the question of power. Ask yourself:

> Who has the most power, and why?
>
> Is she willing to share her power or even surrender it?
>
> Do I want the same power I think she has?

Power can be related to the perceived affection of parents, material goods, connections to other family members, birth order, knowledge of family ups and downs, or any other factor, such as geographic proximity or resemblance to another family member. Recall Trina's story in chapter 1 and the ways in which each of the six sisters battled for power: being the rebel, the outcast, the attentive daughter, the information controller, and so on.

Keep in mind that power relationships and sistering relationships can and do change over time, which then shifts other kinds of interaction. The mother of a first grandchild may find herself displaced by the mother of the next grandchild, who becomes the family namesake. Suddenly, one woman has more power than the other.

▌ Giving up the notion that you must be close to your sisters can be very healing. You may need to appreciate the positive ties you do have and minimize the ones that are lacking, since unlike the role of mothers, sisters aren't mandated to love one another.

▌ Undoubtedly, friends can serve as sister substitutes, as previously described in Dr. Susan McHale's research. Therefore, cherishing your friends and allowing them into a sistering role in your life can compensate for what might be missing in your relationship with your real kin.

▌ Although sisters, like mothers, can change their behavior, most likely *your* response to a sibling who can't let go of her RA relationship style will be the one most amenable to adjustment.

Examining the beliefs and expectations you have about and for your sister and questioning whether they are realistic can be another healthy step toward change. If your sister thrives on belittling you at every public gathering, is it likely you are going to change her behavior overnight? Probably not. Is she ever going to be the best friend/confidant sister you see your girlfriends have? Again, not likely.

Knowing this, you can begin relating to the real person your sister is, who may be the next-youngest and constantly challenged to keep up with you, or the "baby" of many children, striving to establish her place in the family.

Conflict as the Norm

The author-memoirist Debra Ginsberg wrote her book *About My Sisters* to share the nuances of her life as one of four sisters. She remarks on the ambivalent nature of female sibling relations, noting that although she once got into a physical fight with a sister, she also finds her happiness dependent on them.

Conflict with sisters is more the norm than previously realized. Believing that RA behaviors such as competition, jealousy, setups and put-downs, exclusion, manipulation, and many others are the hallmarks of a bad relationship could alienate you from your sister unnecessarily. As with mothers, outward behaviors don't necessarily indicate inner feelings or values.

Your goal is to find ways to resolve conflict without hurting each other, either as the aggressor or the target. Pinpointing key triggers for trouble, sitting down during a time that is relatively turmoil-free, and coming to some agreement about how to declare a truce involves the same process with sisters as with other relatives.

Despite the temptation to involve your mother, a one-on-one approach is better.

Then and Now

Time is often the best remedy for troubled sister relationships. That may not help in the moment when relationships are trying, but it does offer hope for the years to come.

Dr. Harriette McAdoo of Howard University points out that maturity can help sisters who don't mesh as children become close in adulthood. An example is the sister relationship between Debbie Allen (TV producer) and Phylicia Rashad (of *The Cosby Show*), where rivalry was part of their adolescent angst. Now each has been successful in the same arena, so there is less need to compete. The pop music group the Pointer Sisters also admit that their childhood fights were sometimes vicious, but with age came less competitiveness and jealousy.

Then there are the exceptions. Donna Hogan, the sister of the late Anna Nicole Smith, publicly chastised her sister for flagrant ambition and failure to offer support in a time of need. Estranged for many years, the two related to each other only through a third party: the media. Tragically, any opportunity to reconcile was lost forever when Anna Nicole died. It's a grim lesson but one that might lead others to consider one more effort to reconcile before it's too late.

Sister Substitutes

In her book *Sisters: Devoted or Divided?*, the author Susan Shapiro Barash suggests that women without satisfying sister relationships may search for someone outside the family to fill the relationship void. Her book also points out that women who have no sisters may not have the same positive peer skills as girls who grow up in a family of women.

If you've tried all the suggestions offered to this point and met a roadblock, one alternative is to find "sister substitutes." They may not share a blood tie with you, but they can fill a void. Aunts, cousins, pen pals, roommates, and any number of other women can become substitute sisters—more than one of my only-child girl-friends has used this strategy successfully.

If your sisters won't buy into your exciting new plan for change, that doesn't mean you can't come up with other ways to cope on a situation-by-situation basis. Here are just a few possible responses to typical RA behaviors between female siblings:

- If she's jealous of your success in career or romance

  Point out her accomplishments.

  Consider men and work to be taboo topics.

  Mentally reframe her envious comments as a reflection of her own lack of self-esteem.

- If she likes to manipulate you

  Practice saying no before you see her—use one word and leave it at that.

  Look at your own past willingness to feel guilty or obligated toward her, and decide to end it.

  Shrug off the small demands and ignore the big ones—maybe you don't mind fixing her a glass of iced tea even though you've just settled into a comfortable spot on the sofa, but you do mind watching her children while she goes out to a party. Read up on assertiveness strategies and use them.

- If she undermines you

  Figure out her methods and confront her with the facts. If she gossips about you to others, let her know you know, and then work on making yourself immune.

  Enlist the help of other female family members to support you, and gain satisfaction from your relationships with them.

  If there is a theme to her sabotage (for example, her kids are always better than yours) make her feel more secure by agreeing that yes, her son did get an A in physics while carrying a twenty-two-credit course load, which is a wonderful accomplishment. Tell her she must be very proud of him.

Sister Sabbatical

Sometimes your only choices are hard-core ones, especially if children or spouses become the unwilling victims of a sinister sister. Your first loyalty is always to them, so if barbs begin to fly, you may need to remove your loved ones and yourself from your sister's firing range. You can also train yourself to develop a thick skin to her, either by conscious effort, therapy, or just avoidance.

The idea of a sabbatical, or time away, can apply to your sisters as well as to other family members. Spending a few weeks or months without contact may offer both of you the chance to remove yourselves from an emotionally charged, and possibly venomous, situation. While this happens, you'll also have the opportunity to discover whether your life is better with or without her.

21

Special Solutions for In-Laws and Exes

When a female relative or in-law seems intent on hurting you, many of the principles that have helped women deal with RA in other areas can be applied to the family-in-law situation. For example, the Web site weddings.syl.com/honeymoonto marriage/motherinlaw offers advice on how to promote a positive relationship with your mother-in-law. Some of these potential strategies can be modified to include all in-laws:

- Do some detective work early on and find out what your new in-law is like before you meet. Ask your husband-to-be about his mother's hobbies, traditions, and so forth.

- If appropriate, send a small gift or a card for her birthday or some other occasion, even if you haven't met. (Make sure it's okay with your boyfriend or fiancé first.)

- Show respect and approval of her relationship as your husband's mother or sister.

- Remember that you all want your husband's happiness. Don't compete, but cooperate to achieve this goal.

- Ask your prospective in-law for some advice. It will make her feel as if you respect and value her.

Loyalty and Longevity

While in-laws are technically family, sorting out issues and conflicts with them is different than with blood relatives because the loyalty issues aren't as clear-cut. Whose feelings should be given priority? Who do you owe allegiance to? If your sister-in-law's bully mother takes a dislike to you and decides to make you an open target in a word war about your lifestyle, how should you respond? Reflect back on some of the previous chapters about expectations and action planning to see if you can answer those questions.

Also consider the matter of longevity, which might influence who should intervene. Your spouse has spent a lot more time with his family and knows them far better than you do in most cases. For this reason, Lee Wilson of the Family Dynamics Institute suggests that "in-laws will probably react best to requests from their son or daughter," so it's reasonable to discuss the situation with your husband and involve him if appropriate.

For Moms-in-Law

Dr. Bree Allinson is the therapist who wrote *How to Deal with Your Mother-in-Law*. She cautions that your mother-in-law will never love you as much as she loves her son, which may lead her to try and sabotage relationships, especially if she feels threatened by you. Her suggestions for mothers-in-law and daughters-in-law who are interested in developing a more positive relationship dynamic follow. My additions are in parentheses.

- Remember that daughters-in-law are not daughters, and mothers-in-law are not mothers. (Adjust your expectations accordingly, and find out what you each expect of the other.)
- Avoid giving unsolicited advice on child rearing. (I would add, be careful how you phrase things even when your advice is asked for.)
- Keep in mind that each of you might be jealous or resentful of the other. (This can be especially true if you as the mother-in-law are close to her mother in age.)
- Often the husband or son finds himself stuck in the middle

and pressured to "choose" between two women he cares about. (Never make your husband or son choose between the two of you.)

▌ You can't force a mother-in-law or a daughter-in-law to do anything. (Keeping the channels of communication open and having a good relationship are the best ways to create a win-win situation for both of you.)

▌ Let bygones be bygones. (Hanging on to past hurts or disappointments will continue to destroy the present.)

▌ Enjoy the moment. (Create a lot of moments to enjoy by recognizing your mother-in-law or daughter-in-law for who she is, separate from your husband or son.)

▌ Live and let live. (Follow the "house rules" when you're there, and expect the same in your domain.)

▌ Pick your battles. (Better yet, prevent them.)

Dr. Terri Apter also has thoughts about what might help promote better relationships between mothers-in-law and daughters-in-law. She says good intentions can't always minimize friction, since families are in a constant state of change. Instead, use communication skills that help maintain neutrality and preserve boundaries. Be respectful so that when conflicts arise, you avoid verbal mudslinging. Finally, don't feel as if you must be a friend to your mother-in-law or daughter-in-law, especially in the beginning of your relationship with her.

Therapy for Toxic Relationships

Susan Forward, a family relationship expert and the author of several best-selling books on toxic relationships, suggests that issues with parents-in-law may be more challenging than issues with a sister or other in-law because younger in-laws are closer to your own age and you can relate better to them. She also notes that unsettled issues with your own parents may replay as similar issues with parents-in-law. If these problems aren't addressed, a marriage can even be shattered by the fallout.

Dr. Forward's typology of parents-in-law includes both fathers and mothers, but it illustrates the types of challenges that a daughter-in-law may confront if she marries into a family of critics, controllers, rejecters, engulfers, or chronic chaos seekers. Believing that "it will get better when . . ." (we get married, they get to know me, I have a child, and so forth) is most often faulty thinking. Instead, a plan for what to say and how to act will more likely help you reach a state of peace, and if they fail to respond to your attempts to change, Dr. Forward says, "No answer is the loudest answer of all."

Problems with mothers-in-law often begin before the birth of a child and may escalate thereafter, according to Elizabeth Lea, M.S.W. A new mom's anxiety about her parenting can cause her to feel vulnerable. Therefore it's important to talk things out before one of you blows up, Lea suggests. She also recommends presenting a united front with your spouse. Try to have your husband present when discussing issues, and keep the conversation focused on one specific topic rather than an entire problematic relationship. Sometimes it takes a lifetime of persistence to resolve challenges with relatives, but the outcome can be worth it, as the following story demonstrates.

Silence Really Can Be Golden
Marilyn A. Gehner

I met my mother-in-law for the first time the night before my wedding. I'd pushed for opportunities to get to know her before that, but when pressed, my fiancé told me that he'd had two previous relationships that ended once the women met his mother. He didn't want that to happen again. I was naive enough to think that it would be different this time, but my future husband wasn't taking any chances.

Her behavior was pleasant enough at the rehearsal dinner. She reminded me of a librarian, with her hair tied in a tight bun and her dark-rimmed glasses, and the way she politely shook my hand when we were introduced.

But the next day on the way to the wedding ceremony her demeanor changed.

"Let's get this circus on the road," she said as she got into the car.

My heart sank. So much for optimism. I held my tongue and

let the moment pass. Why would I want to cause an argument with her just thirty minutes before my wedding?

I didn't see my mother-in-law again until six months later, at Thanksgiving. I had a glimmer of hope that her inappropriate remark was a onetime thing. Unfortunately, she orchestrated a real fiasco by inviting my husband's former girlfriend over for coffee while we were there.

My husband asked, "Mom, why did you do that?"

She responded, "You two got along so well!"

"That was then and this is now—I'm married."

I wanted to pack my bags and go home. If a friend had done something so inappropriate, I could and would have, but this was my husband's mother. It was important to me to keep things civil, so I didn't say a word to her. Instead, my husband and I chose to stay upstairs for the duration of the ex-girlfriend's visit, but I was convinced my mother-in-law was trying to sabotage my marriage.

Following dinner, my husband and I showed a video of our trip to Canada. The only thing my mother-in-law could say was, "How unfortunate you look so fat" (referring to me).

I held my breath and gritted my teeth. I sure wasn't going to be calling this lady "Mom." Still, I was locked into the relationship.

I wish I could say that I handled all future encounters with my mother-in-law with the expertise of a psychologist. At times I really struggled, because she continued to make cutting remarks, and it looked like her behavior wasn't going to change.

How could I uphold my dignity yet not feel like a victim? I decided to set limits on my reactions and boundaries on my emotions. When she became critical, I would often leave the room or say, "Whatever you think." Instead of giving in to my emotions of hurt or anger, I questioned (to myself) why she acted the way she did. Was it only that she felt threatened by my relationship with her son, or was there more? Her verbal attacks seemed to be a way for her to feel powerful, but often they weren't really about me. Understanding this empowered me to repel her attacks and feel stronger as a person. While difficult at first, I found that the "keep silent" strategy worked best, and as a result, her remarks got less strident.

I also embarked on a campaign to "kill her with kindness" by sending her cards and gifts. When my husband and I visited, I asked about her collections of angels and shells. This not only disarmed her but began to foster a connection between us. The expression on her face softened during our conversations. She even made me a shell mirror for Christmas one year.

Five years ago, when my mother-in-law became gravely ill, I assisted with her care. One day, my husband went home to rest, and I was left alone with her in the hospital. I was giving her ice chips when she turned her head and looked at me. "Thank you for being so kind during my illness," she said.

"You're welcome," I answered. A moment or two later, she stopped breathing. I sat and reflected in the quiet before the nurse arrived. Wasn't it ironic, I thought, that I was the one to be with her when she spoke her last words, and that they would be kind ones directed at me? Despite our challenges, my silence really had been golden: it had led to this golden moment with her.

This wise woman employed several strategies that can be helpful in other types of female family feuds:

1. Give second chances and start anew. Don't assume each encounter will be like the previous one.

2. Refuse to engage in a word war, even when it would be understandable to do so. Find a neutral phrase that will allow you to exit the conversation gracefully: "Thanks for sharing that," "You really feel strongly about that," or "Everyone is entitled to their own opinion." Often, reflecting back on what was just said can also be a helpful strategy. For example, if she says, "What a bad picture of you!" respond by saying, "You think I don't look so good in that picture?" which puts the ball back in her court. Who knows? She may say, "Yes, you're much more attractive in real life."

3. Accept that some behaviors probably aren't going to change.

4. Walk away at times.

5. Try to understand that the behavior is about a context, not about you.

6. Refuse to be baited—silence can be a response!

Other In-Law Issues

The writer Paula Hall suggests that in general, some common areas of tension with in-laws include:

- Annoying habits, big and little
- Criticism
- Closeness, distance, or frequency of contact
- Privacy and boundaries
- Holidays and gatherings

I would add territoriality to that list, knowing that sometimes in laws can be such a tightly knit group before a newcomer arrives that even the most engaging person won't be admitted. Then, too, there are those families where in-laws are viewed as a threat, "stealing" the son away. A mother of two daughters and one son told me that "she took my son from me," when I asked her about her relationship with her daughter-in-law.

Dr. Forward warns that failing to address toxic in-law issues will not only cause them to increase in severity but may impact on your marriage and family of origin. She defines toxic in-laws as "people who, through various types of assaults on you and your marriage, create genuine chaos." Their "assaults," she believes, can be subtle or obvious.

On AskMaple.com: A Site about Relationships, the writer Siana Scatti offers suggestions for ways to have a positive relationship with in-laws. The following ideas can be applicable to both parents and siblings:

- Don't criticize them, especially not to your spouse. Even if there's a knock-down, drag-out fight, stay supportive but neutral.

- Be polite at all times. Small courtesies will go a long way in fostering a positive relationship.

- Don't compare families, either in negative or positive ways.

- Avoid being provoked, especially during holiday times when a "festive" spirit may lead your in-laws to overstep their boundaries.

■ Stay away from trouble. If you sense your relationship going downhill, take a break from the family.

Ex-RA

Now that my divorce is a quarter of a century behind me, I wish I had had the knowledge I gained through writing this book back when it all began. In addition to the wise words of experts and the stories of women shared in the chapters on relationships, developing a personal plan of action with concrete strategies for specific issues would have been a tremendous help. There were many hurtful years full of relational aggression, all of which affected deeply the children and adults involved.

Everyone's situation is unique, but perhaps some items on my wish list of things that could have been different will be relevant for others, too. So, if I had to go through all this again tomorrow, I would:

1. Go out of my way to develop a relationship with the new wife separate from my relationship with my ex-husband.

2. Find a way to communicate directly about mothering matters with my child's stepmother rather than through my ex-husband.

3. With the help of an outside facilitator, negotiate an agreement with my child's stepmother that addresses mothering concerns and expectations.

4. Not take on every battle that came my way. Feeling constantly attacked takes on a life of its own—when much of your energy is spent responding to comments and statements, it's natural to become supersensitive and to overreact to the next one.

5. Appreciate things the stepmother does well and be thankful for her caring efforts. Focusing on her kindnesses can provide a positive perspective and reframe a relationship.

6. Have more confidence in my own relationship with my child. This may be the biggest obstacle I confronted as he went off every other weekend to a different house.

7. Apologize, even when I didn't think I was wrong. It would have cost me little to say, "I'm sorry." Beverly Engel, a therapist and the author of *The Power of Apology: Healing Steps to Transform All Your Relationships*, describes many ways to apologize and many reasons for doing so. She says, "When someone apologizes, it makes it a lot easier for us to view him or her in a compassionate way." One of the adolescent girls I was working with was more practical during a discussion in Club Ophelia about alternatives to RA. She said, "Even if you aren't technically wrong, sometimes the easiest way to end RA is to just say, 'I'm sorry.'" When other girls objected to being dishonest, the first girl pointed out, "It isn't dishonest. You *are* truly sorry the conflict has occurred."

8. Put more effort into prayer than warfare. Looking beyond the immediate situation would have enabled me to distance myself from the emotion and to seek the grace to respond from a place of inner peace rather than anger.

9. Form a support group with other divorced women so that we might share our expertise to resolve challenges we all confronted. There's a fine line between expressing strong emotions around a subject and seeking solutions; I would have emphasized the latter.

10. Be able to look into the future and realize there will be an endpoint to the intense relationship, or at least a time of less intense contact.

Could I or any other woman do one or more of these things in the midst of an acrimonious separation and divorce? When emotions are heated and self-esteem threatened, it is certainly difficult, but the well-being of the family might be the one motivation that can help women set RA aside. Watching two mother figures engage in an ongoing word war has a profound effect on sons and daughters—even when the aggression has little to do with them. I hope that this list can provide incentive for mothers and stepmothers to shift from conflict to cooperation.

Relative RA: What a Therapist Has to Say

To explore the issue of female family feuds and what can be done to address them, I interviewed Dr. Pauline Wallin, a psychologist and the author of *Taming Your Inner Brat: A Guide for Transforming Self-Defeating Behavior*. Our conversation elaborated on many of the themes touched on throughout this book.

Cheryl: "Can family hurt us more than friends?"

Pauline: "We expect family to accept us, and we are more easily hurt by their criticism. The mother-in-law who comes in and cleans up while you are at work is an example. It wouldn't bother a man to think he is a bad housekeeper because that is not the role that he assumes that he should take, but a woman is interpreting it as 'I am not a very good housekeeper.' In fact, I've been asked: 'What you should do if your mother-in-law insinuates that you are a bad housekeeper?' I say, 'Agree with her.' Tell her, 'I know I am a slob. I appreciate your coming to clean up.'"

Cheryl: "What causes female family feuds?"

Pauline: "Family conflict is generated not so much from the other person's behavior but from *anticipation* about the other person's behavior. For many people with in-law conflicts, you are already rehearsing how hard and how terrible it's going to be before they set foot in your door. There is sometimes the assumption the in-laws are being hostile or critical or rejecting or jealous, so that you attribute certain characteristics or motivations that aren't necessarily there. They will ask a question: 'Well, why do you have your kitchen set up this way?' and then you think, 'Oh she doesn't like the way I have my kitchen set up,' because 'why' is a very confronting type of question."

Cheryl: "How can you handle situations like that?"

Pauline: "I have people kind of put it in perspective by asking themselves, 'Does that comment reveal more about me or about them?' and 'Is this what I would expect from her, is she just being herself?' If the answer is 'Well yes, she is always like that,' why are you surprised that this time is any different? If she asks why you set your kitchen up that way, does that mean it's set up terrible? If the answer is that she is always trying to rearrange it, does that mean your way is wrong? Of course not. So the interpretation is what can make *her* issues *your* problem."

Cheryl: "Any particular female family issues you hear about?"

Pauline: "Grandparents doting on the grandchildren and over-stepping their bounds. Women talk about this a lot. Men are more often bothered by their wife's close relationships with their mothers and sisters, and will complain that she's on the phone two hours a day with her mother . . . and that gets to him."

Cheryl: "How about women who have a sister-in-law they believe is always trying to 'one up' them—trying to make them look bad within the family? How would you advise a person to deal with a situation like that?"

Pauline: "I would ask them, 'Do you think she gets up in the morning and thinks, "How am I going to make her life miscrable?"'"

Cheryl: "What if she says yes? Like, I get along with my sisters but here is this person who is in my family because she's married to my brother, but I really don't like her even though I have to get along with her."

Pauline: "I would point out that maybe the sister-in-law feels uncomfortable in the family. Maybe the family is very close-knit and she has never been able to feel accepted so that is why she doesn't come that much, or when she is there, she isolates herself and sticks in the corner because you guys are always talking about stuff that only relates to the family and doesn't include her. Maybe there is something you are doing to contribute to the situation. Trying to put yourself in the other person's shoes and looking at it from their perspective helps. Also, if you can pinpoint a vulnerability in somebody that you are angry at or somebody that you resent, you don't resent them as much."

Cheryl: "How can a woman in a family differentiate between the normal conflict of family disagreements and aggressive behavior that's a problem?"

Pauline: "See how they treat other people and also consider, how often do you have to deal with them? Every problem has to be dealt with as you encounter it, whether it's just an isolated problem or it's an ongoing problem—to deal with each situation individually. If you only have to see your family once or twice a year and you have an irritating in-law, that's your duty; your gift to your spouse: you go and deal with it.

              "Also, people don't have to be perfect. If you know the Thanksgiving dinner is going to be a nightmare because your sister-in-law is going to be bragging about her new job, you just predict that's what is going to happen and you wait for the script. It's like you watch the movie of your family."

Cheryl: "How do you decide what is in line versus out of line with family?"

Pauline: "You could think about what would happen if somebody else in your family did the same behavior, like your husband or your kids, would that kind of situation still be out of line? That doesn't necessarily mean it's aggression. Your mother-in-law may feel very loving about an irritating behavior or action and actually think she is doing something helpful, or that you will appreciate it."

Cheryl: "When do women have a right to be angry?"

Pauline: "You have a right to be angry anytime, but what are you going to do about it? How much of a problem is it causing in your life? Measuring it by the degree of indignity on an objective scale isn't really as useful as how much it intrudes on you and how much it bothers you If it bothers you a lot, then you have to decide what you are going to do about it. Either talk to the person or move."

Cheryl: "So a mother might just be one of those women who is a bully and she uses that behavior with you, but if it doesn't bother you, that's okay, you can go on. It's only when the behavior becomes bothersome to you that you need to really be concerned about it?"

Pauline: "Yes. I am just thinking of somebody that comes to see me, and her mother-in-law is a bully and she tells her husband and he says, 'Look I have lived through this all my life. That's just how she is.'

"So look at reframing. A lot of times people don't talk about it, they let it sit inside them and dwell on it and blow it out of proportion. Then they will talk to everyone about it but the person who offended them. So the first thing is to just tell the person if they have done something you don't like and it doesn't have to be a hostile confrontation. It can be: 'I know you are probably trying to help but I am used to the furniture the way it is and I keep tripping over stuff so I am going to put it back and please don't rearrange it.'"

Cheryl: "Do you believe there is always an option to talk to someone? Sometimes she is your husband's mother, and in this case what if she is a little Italian matriarch and that is her way with the whole family?"

Pauline: "You have to weigh the options and see if it's worth it to you. If she is likely to react like she is really hurt and how can you do this to me, then it is probably not worth it."

Cheryl: "So then what do you do?"

Pauline: "Then you have your husband talk to her."

Cheryl: "What if he doesn't want to—it's *his* mom?"

Pauline: "If he won't, then you live with it, and on the scale of stuff that's wrong with your life and what other people in the world have to deal with, how bad is this?"

Cheryl: "Okay. But what if it gets worse, or is really bad, or you try to change things and it doesn't work and it's not something that you are going to be able to escape from?"

Pauline: "That's where the husband has to take charge and say, look, we've got our family here and we are still a part of this family but we're also raising our own family. That's the job of the biological child, the spouse, to intervene."

Cheryl: "What do you do if it's your sister who is very manipulative and hurtful? You can't have anybody else intervene."

Pauline: "You ask, 'How badly do I want this relationship?' If you do not want her to treat you like this for the rest of your life, you may need to have a confrontation and that is a risk. The other option is to continue to be treated that way and, again, so, it's weighing the options. When you make a decision to accept being treated that way, you don't mind it so much. When you decide that it's okay for somebody to treat you a certain way, then you feel empowered and you don't feel so victimized. It's an amazing transformation. Instead of 'I can't stand her and we are going to dinner,' it's 'I am going to go to dinner and I am going to sit there for an hour and I am going to listen to her yak away and an hour is an hour.' It's a completely different attitude. You're not so stressed.

"If your sister-in-law or daughter-in-law or whoever rejects you and confronts you and you get insulted, ask yourself: 'Is this about me, or is this about them?' 'Do they have a logical reason for being that way?' Maybe you did something you thought was helpful, but they didn't see it that way and are feeling a little put-upon.

"People who are the aggressors really usually don't recognize that in themselves. They wouldn't recognize that this was all about them; they would think it was all about the other person, or that the other person 'needs' them to be that way. So they go and rearrange your furniture or create crises. Like moms who call their sons in the middle of the night to come change a lightbulb.

"If you don't want the drama to be about you, and you are at a family gathering or you're on the phone with your in-law or family member, ask them a question about something else if you don't want the story to be about you. When they are talking about something else, show interest and say, 'Tell me more.' You are giving them permission to use you as an audience, and you don't really have to listen that intently. Showing interest gets you off the hook, lets them have their little drama, and then they are done."

Cheryl: "Thank you!"

Turning Relational Aggression into Relational Affection

As I completed an early draft of this book, a chance occurrence with someone to whom I am distantly related led to an amazing correspondence between myself and several women. The irony of this event was not lost to me as I alternated between tweaking a manuscript on female family connections and reading or writing long messages to a group of women I had never met but felt an instant electronic and emotional bond with. How can such a good thing happen without much effort at all? It happens because women who are family share an emotional bond that is deep, meaningful, and striving for positive expression.

At the same time, all that I've read and heard has sensitized me to the many little frictions that can easily cause feelings to intensify in the opposite direction, creating a no-holds-barred conflict between female family members. The smallest incident can lead to such hurt that it's hard to deny the special significance of these relationships for mothers, sisters, and others.

Cultivating the positive and working to transform the negative has been a theme in each of my books. It's my hope that the gathered wisdom in this book will help you appreciate the female family connections in your life. Perhaps there is a deep-seated conflict you need to let go of, or maybe a quiet tension that has simmered for years or even decades. Whichever the case, you now have the ability to enjoy kind, or at least cordial, relationships for years to come.

If your family has not experienced kitchen wars or other forms of relational aggression, you are role-modeling the "care and share" instinct inherent to women. Female family bonds have helped women survive emotionally and physically since the beginning of time, and they remain a vital source of support and sustenance for all of us—through better and worse.

References

Allinson, Bree. *How to Deal with Your Mother-in-Law.* Lincoln, NE: iUniverse, Inc., 2004.

Apter, Terri. "An Interview with Dr. Terri Apter." www.motherinlaw stories.com, 2005.

———. "Mothers-in-Law and Daughters-in-Law: Friendship at an Impasse." www.motherinlawstories.com, 2005.

Argosy University. "Ideas for Strengthening the Mother-Daughter Bond." Courtesy of ARA Content. www.pioneerthinking.com/ara-motherdaughter.html, May 4, 2004.

Atkins, Dale. Sisters: *A Practical Helpful Exploration of the Intimate and Complete Bond between Female Siblings.* New York: Arbor House, 1984.

Barash, David. *Revolutionary Biology: The New, Gene-Centered View of Life.* Somerset, NJ: Transaction Publishers, 2002.

Barash, Susan Shapiro. *Mothers-in-Law and Daughters-in-Law: Love, Hate, Rivalry, and Reconciliation.* Far Hills, NJ: New Horizon Press, 2001.

———. *Sisters: Devoted or Divided?* New York: Kensington, 1994.

Baron-Cohen, Simon. *The Essential Difference: Forget Mars and Venus and Discover the Essential Truth about the Opposite Sex.* London: Penguin Books, 2004.

Bengston, Vern, Alan Acock, Katherine Allen, Peggye Dilworth-Anderson, and David M. Klein, *Sourcebook of Family Theory and Research.* Thousand Oaks, CA: Sage Publications, 2004

Berscheid, Ellen, Mark Snyder, and Allen M. Omoto, "The Relationship Closeness Inventory: Assessing the Closeness of Interpersonal Relationships." *Journal of Personality and Social Psychology* 57, no. 5. (1989): 792–807.

Boncompagni, Tatiana. "A House Divided." *New York Times Magazine,* September 2, 2005.

Botton, Sara. "Take My Mother-in-Law, Please!" *New York Daily News,* www.nydailynews.com, May 5, 2005.

Brett, Jill Eggleton. "Mother-in-Law: Friend or Foe?" *Babies Today,* babiestoday.com/articles/245.php?wcat=39 (accessed March 23, 2006).

Brown, Roxanne. "Sister Love—Relationships between Sisters." *Ebony*, September 1989.

Burns, Linda Hammer, and Sharon N. Covington, eds. *Infertility Counseling: A Comprehensive Handbook for Clinicians.* New York: Parthenon Publishing Group, 2000.

Burton, Linda, and Peggye Dilworth-Anderson, "The Role of Extended Family Members in Minority Families." *Marriage and Family Reviews* 4/6, (1991): 311–330.

Byng-Hall, John. *Rewriting the Family Script: Becoming an Adult with Your Parents.* New York: Guilford Press, 1995.

Campbell, Anne. *A Mind of Her Own: The Evolutionary Psychology of Women.* New York: Oxford University Press, 2002.

Carey, Benedict. "In-Laws in the Age of the Outsider." *New York Times*, December 18, 2005, 1, 3.

Carson, Terry. "Summer Holidays with Family: A Recipe for Disaster?" www.theparentingcoach.ca/ask-the-parenting-coach.php?id=21 (accessed May 21, 2007).

Cicirelli, Victor G. *The Sibling Bond Revisited.* New York: Plenum Press, 1995.

———. *Sibling Relationships across the Life Span.* New York: Plenum Press: 1993.

Cloud, Henry, and John Townsend. *The Mom Factor: Dealing with the Mom You Had, Didn't Have, or Still Contend With.* Grand Rapids, MI: Zonderavan, 1996.

Caughran, Neema. "Fasts, Feasts, and the Slovenly Woman." *Asian Folklore Studies* 57 (1998): 257–274.

Coy, Peter. "Who Is Likely to Get Ahead at Your Company?" *Business Week*, August 21/28, 2006.

Crawford, Christina. *Mommy Dearest.* New York: William Morrow & Company, 1978.

Davis, Laura. *I Thought We'd Never Speak Again: The Road from Estrangement to Reconciliation.* New York: HarperCollins Publishers, 2002.

Davis, Karen. "What's in a Voice? Methods and Metaphors." *Feminism and Psychology* 4 (1994): 353–361.

Dickson, Rosaleen Leslie. *The Mother-in-Law Book.* Renfrew, ON: General Store Publishing House, 2005.

Douglas, Rebecca. *All in the Family: Dealing with Intergenerational Conflict.* University of Illinois Extension College of Agricultural, Consumer and Environmental Sciences, Springfield Extension Center.

Dudman, Martha Tod. *Augusta, Gone: A True Story.* New York: Simon & Schuster, 2001.

Duvall, E. M. *In-Laws: Pro and Con.* New York: Association Press, 1954.

Engel, Beverly. *The Power of Apology: Healing Steps to Transform All Your Relationships.* New York: John Wiley and Sons, 2001.

Evans, Dylan, and Oscar Zarate. *Introducing Evolutionary Psychology.* Blue Ridge Summit, PA: Totem Books, 1999.

Family Problem Solver, The. "Commitment: My Mother-in-Law Hates Me!" Family Problem Solver, www.committment.com/familyproblem.html (accessed May 21, 2007).

Felder, Leonard. *When Difficult Relatives Happen to Good People: Surviving Your Family and Keeping Your Sanity.* Emmaus, PA: Rodale, 2003.

Female Firsts.co.uk. "Anna Nicole Blasts Her 'So-Called' Sister." Female Firsts, www.femalefirst.co.uk/celebrity/34992004.htm (accessed June 28, 2006).

Fingerman, Karen. *Mothers and Their Adult Daughters: Mixed Emotions, Enduring Bonds.* New York: Springer Publishing, 2001.

• Forward, Susan. *Toxic In-Laws: Loving Strategies for Protecting Your Marriage.* New York: HarperCollins, 2002.

• Forward, Susan, and Craig Buck. *Toxic Parents: Overcoming Their Hurtful Legacy and Reclaiming Your Life.* New York: Bantam, 2002.

Gerlach, Peter K. "Some People Bond Better Than Others." Stepfamily in Formation, Stepfamily Association of America, sfhelp.org/Rx/kin/disinterest.htm (accessed May 21, 2007).

Gilligan, Carol. *In a Different Voice: Psychology Theory and Women's Development.* Cambridge, MA: Harvard University Press, 1982.

Ginsberg, Debra. *About My Sisters.* New York: Perennial, 2004.

Guttman, David. "Men, Women, and the Parental Imperative." *Commentary* 56, no. 6 (December 1973).

Ha, Jung-Hwa, and Deborah Carr. "The Effect of Parent-Child Geographic Proximity on Widowed Parents' Psychological Adjustment and Social Integration." *Research on Aging* 27, no. 5 (2005): 578–610.

Hall, Paula. "Getting On with the In-laws." bbc.co.uk Relationships, www.bbc.co.uk/relationships/couples/grumbles_inlaws.shtml, July 18, 2006 (accessed May 21, 2007).

Herst, Charney, and Lynette Padwa. *For Mothers of Difficult Daughters: How to Enrich and Repair the Relationship in Adulthood.* New York: Villard, 1999.

Hook, Misty. "Sister Acts: Examining Sister-to-Sister Connections." American Psychological Association, PsyCRITIQUES (2004).

Hyman, B. D. *My Mother's Keeper.* New York: William Morrow & Company, 1985.

Jayson, Sharon. "Marriage's Relative Discord." *USA Today*, www .usatoday.com/life/lifestyle/2005-05-16-mother-in-law-relation-ships_x.htm, May 16, 2005 (accessed May 21, 2007).

Jordan, Judith V., Alexander G. Kaplan. Jean Baker Miller, Irene P. Stiver, and Janet Surrey. *Women's Growth in Connection: Writings from the Stone Center.* New York: Guilford Press, 1991.

Keith, Pat, and Sook-Hyun Choi Lee. *In-Law Relationships, Coresidence, and Well Being of Adult Children in Korea.* Minneapolis: National Council on Family Relations, 1995.

Krasnow, Iris. *I Am My Mother's Daughter: Making Peace with Mom before It's Too Late.* Boston: Perseus Books, 2006.

Lara, Adair. *Hold Me Close, Let Me Go: A Mother, A Daughter, and an Adolescence Survived.* New York: Broadway, 2002.

Lawrence, D. H. *Sons and Lovers.* Edited by Helen Baron and Carl Baron. Cambridge: Cambridge University Press, 1992.

Linn, Ruth, and Sara Breslerman. "Women in Conflict: On Moral Knowledge of Daughters-In-Law and Mothers-In-Law." *Journal of Moral Education* 25, no. 3 (1996): 291–304.

Madhavan, Sangeetha. "Female Relationships and Demographic Outcomes in Sub-Saharan Africa." *Sociological Forum* 16, no. 3 (2001): 503–525.

Mall, E. Jane. *Caregiving: How to Care for Your Elderly Mother and Stay Sane.* New York: Ballantine/Epiphany Books, 1990.

Mandel, Debra. *Your Boss Is Not Your Mother: Eight Steps to Eliminating Office Drama and Creating Positive Relationships.* Chicago: Agate Press, 2006.

Maass, Vera Sonja. *Women's Group Therapy: Creative Challenges and Options.* New York: Springer Publishing 2002.

Mauthner, Melanie. *Sistering: Power and Change in Female Relationships.* New York: Palgrave Macmillan, 2002.

Merrell, Susan Scarf. *The Accidental Bond: The Power of Sibling Relationships.* New York: Crown Books, 1995.

Miller, Jean Baker, and Irene Pierce Stiver. *The Healing Connection: How Women Form Relationships in Therapy and in Life.* Boston: Beacon Press, 1998.

Millman, M. *The Perfect Sister: What Draws Us Together, What Drives Us Apart.* Orlando, FL: Harcourt Books, 2004.

Morris, Bob. "Home for the Hostages." *New York Times*, Dec. 18, 2005.

Nexhensil, Carol A., et al., eds. *Profiles in Caregiving: The Unexpected Career.* San Diego: Academic Press, 1995.

Putarlez, Martha, and Karen Bierman. *Aggression, Antisocial Behavior and Violence among Girls: A Developmental Perspective.* New York: New Guilford Press, 2004.

Pyke, Karen D., and Vern L. Bengtson. "Caring More or Less: Individualistic and Collectivist Systems of Family Eldercare." *Journal of Marriage and the Family,* 58, no. 2 (May 1996): 379–392.

Ranson-Polizzotti, Sadi. "The Family Myth." Blogcritics.org, blogcritics .org/archives/2005/01/03/123149.php, January 3, 2005 (accessed May 21, 2007).

Robbins, Martha. *Midlife Women and Death of a Mother: Study of Psychohistorical and Spiritual Transformation.* New York: Peter Lang, 1990.

Sandel, Todd. "Narrated Relationships: Mothers-in-Law and Daughters-in-Law Justifying Conflicts in Taiwan's Chhan-chng." *Research on Language and Social Interaction* 37, no. 3 (2004): 365–398.

Sanow, Arnold, and Sandra Strauss. *Get Along with Anyone, Anytime, Anywhere: 8 Keys to Creating Enduring Connections.* Vienna, VA: Nautilus Communications, 2004.

Scatti, Siana. "Surviving the 'In-Laws'" Web Wombat, www.webwombat .com.au/lifestyle/relationships/inlaws.htm (accessed May 21, 2007).

Secunda, Victoria. *When You and Your Mother Can't Be Friends: Resolving the Most Complicated Relationship of Your Life.* New York: Delta, 1991.

Sherman, Aurora M., Jennifer E. Lansford, and Brenda L. Volling. "Sibling relationships and best friendships in young adulthood: Warmth, conflict and well-being." *Personal Relationships* 13 (2006): 151–165.

Sichel, Mark. *Coping with a Family Rift.* New York Times Company, www.mentalhealth.about.com/cs/familyresources/a/sichelrifts.htm (accessed August 2, 2006).

Silverman, Ilena. *I Married My Mother-in-Law: And Other Tales of In-Laws We Can't Live with—and Can't Live Without.* New York: Riverhead Books, 2006.

Solomon, Dorothy Allred. *Predators, Prey, and Other Kinfolk: Growing Up in Polygamy.* New York: W. W. Norton, 2005.

Spungen, Deborah. *And I Don't Want to Live This Life.* New York: Ballantine Books, 1983.

Stocker, Clare M. "Brothers and Sisters: Beyond Childhood." American Psychological Association, PsyCRITIQUES (2004).

Straight, Susan. "We Are (Still) Family." "Lives," *New York Times Magazine,* December 18, 2005.

Sulloway, Frank. *Born to Rebel: Birth Order, Family Dynamics, and Creative Lives.* New York: Pantheon Books, 1996.

Tannen, Deborah. *You're Wearing That? Understanding Mothers and Daughters in Conversation.* New York: Random House, 2006.

Taylor, S. E., L. C. Klein, B. P. Lewis, T. L. Gruenewald, R. A. R. Gurung, and K. A. Updegraff. "Biobehavioral Responses to Stress in Females: Tend-and-Befriend, Not Fight-or-Flight." *Psychological Review* 107 (2000): 411–429.

Thurer, Shari L. *The End of Gender: A Psychological Autopsy*. New York: Routledge, Taylor and Francis Group, 2005.

Updegraff, Kimberly A., Susan M. McHale, and Ann C. Crouter, "Adolescents' Sex-Typed Friendship Experiences: Does Having a Sister versus a Brother Matter?" *Child Development* 71, no. 6 (Nov.–Dec. 2000): 1597–1610.

Updegraff, Kimberly A., Shawna M. Thayer, Shawn D. Whiteman, Donna J. Denning, and Susan M. McHale. "Relational Aggression in Adolescents' Sibling and Parent-Adolescent Relationship Quality." *Family Relations* 54, no. 3 (2005): 373–385.

Vera-Sanso, Penny. "Dominant Daughters-in-Law and Submissive Mothers-in-Law? Cooperation and Conflict in South India." *Journal of the Royal Anthropology Institute* 5 (1999): 577–593.

W2W Psychology Group. *Finding Your Voice: A Woman's Guide to Using Self-Talk for Fulfilling Relationships, Work, and Life*. Hoboken, NJ: John Wiley & Sons, 2004.

Widmer, Eric D., and Linda-Ann La Farga. "Boundedness and Connectivity of Contemporary Families: A Case Study." *Connections* 22, no. 2 (1999): 30–36.

Wilson, Andrea E., Kim M. Shuey, and Glen H. Elder, Jr. "Ambivalence in the Relationship of Adult Children to Aging Parents and In-Laws." *Journal of Marriage and Family* 65 (Nov. 2003): 1055–1072.

Wilson, Lee. "The In's and Out's of Life with In-Laws." Ministry Consultant Family Dynamics Institute, www.marriagemissions.com/family_issues/ins_and_outs.php (accessed May 21, 2007).

Women's Hour Radio Show, The. "Mother/Daughter Rivalry." bbc.co.uk, November 24, 2003. www.bbc.co.uk/radio4/womanshour/2003_47_mon_05.shtml (accessed May 21, 2007).

Women's Sports Foundation. "Athletics and Physical Activity: Women's Health Issues and Educational Fact Sheet." www.womenssports foundation.org, February 7, 2000.

Yount, Kathryn. "The Patriarchal Bargain and Intergenerational Coresidence in Egypt." *Sociological Quarterly* 46 (2005): 137–164.

Index